ORIGEN

Homilies 1–14 on Ezekiel

Ancient Christian Writers

THE WORKS OF THE FATHERS IN TRANSLATION

No. 62

ORIGEN:
HOMILIES 1–14 ON EZEKIEL

TRANSLATION AND INTRODUCTION

BY

THOMAS P. SCHECK

THE NEWMAN PRESS
New York/Mahwah, NJ

Library of Congress Cataloging-in-Publication Data

Origen.
[Homilies 1–14 on Ezekiel. English]
Origen : homilies 1–14 on Ezekiel / translation and introduction by Thomas P. Scheck.
p. cm. — (Ancient Christian writers, the works of the Fathers in translation ; no. 62)
This is the first English translation of Origen's 14 Homilies on Ezekiel, made from the Latin translation of St. Jerome.
Includes bibliographical references and indexes.
ISBN 978-0-8091-0567-0 (alk. paper)
1. Bible. O.T. Ezekiel—Sermons—Early works to 1800. 2. Sermons, Latin—Translations into English. I. Scheck, Thomas P., 1964– II. Jerome, Saint, d. 419 or 20. III. Title.
BS1545.54.O7513 2010
224′.406—dc22

2009023465

Published by The Newman Press
an imprint of Paulist Press
997 Macarthur Boulevard
Mahwah, New Jersey 07430

www.paulistpress.com

Printed and bound in the United States of America

CONTENTS

General Introduction 1

Preface of Jerome 23

Homily 1. The Vision of the Prophet (Ezekiel 1:1–6; 2:1ff.) 25

Homily 2. Against the False Prophets (Ezekiel 13:1–19) 46

Homily 3. Against the False Prophets and Elders (Ezekiel 13:1, 17–22; 14:1–8) 54

Homily 4. The Famine and the Ferocious Beasts (Ezekiel 14:12–22) 64

Homily 5. Sword, Death, Vine (Ezekiel 14:13–21; 15:1–4) 78

Homily 6. Iniquities of Jerusalem (Ezekiel 16:2–16) 86

Homily 7. The Beneficial Effects of God's Turning Away (Ezekiel 16:16–30) 99

Homily 8. Brothels, Head and Base of Streets, Gifts (Ezekiel 16:30–33) 110

Homily 9. Iniquities, Pride, Relative Justification (Ezekiel 16:45–52) 116

Homily 10. Shame, Return, Restoration (Ezekiel 16:52–63) 128

Homily 11. The Two Eagles, the Cedar, the Flourishing Vine (Ezekiel 17:1–7) 137

Homily 12. Interpretation (Ezekiel 17:12–24) 147

Homily 13. The Prince of Tyre, Pharaoh (Ezekiel 28:12–23) 154

Homily 14. The Closed Gate (Ezekiel 44:1–3) 166

Notes 171

Bibliography 191

Scripture Index 195

General Index 206

Index of Origen's Works 209

ABOUT THE TEXT

The present translation is based on the Latin text printed in Sources chrétiennes (SC) 352, which is a reproduction of the critical text established by W. A. Baehrens, *Origenes Werke VIII: Homiliae in Regn., Ez., et al.*, Die griechischen christlichen Schriftsteller (GCS) 33 (Leipzig: Berlin-Brandenburgische Akademie der Wissenschaften, 1925), 318–454. Unless otherwise indicated, I have followed the textual corrections listed in SC 352, p. 23. Marcel Borret's French translation was a source of immeasurable help to me. The subheadings are from this edition. I have aimed to conform the Scripture citations to the RSV as far as possible.

ACKNOWLEDGMENTS AND DEDICATION

I wish to express my gratitude to Dr. Ralph McInerny, director of the Jacques Maritain Center at the University of Notre Dame, who graciously awarded me a postdoctoral fellowship for the 2004–5 academic year, which enabled me to complete this project. I also wish to acknowledge my indebtedness to Erasmus of Rotterdam (1466–1536), to whose writings and theological work I attribute my return to the Catholic Church. May the Church that he endeavored to serve and purify one day recognize the greatness and sanctity of this remarkable priest-scholar.

This translation is dedicated to my two youngest children, Anne and Matthew.

GENERAL INTRODUCTION

Origen of Alexandria (185–254) was the son of a martyr, St. Leonides of Alexandria (d. 202), to whom he refers in the present work in Homily 4.8.1 in these words: "Having a father who was a martyr does me no good, if I do not live well myself and adorn the nobility of my descent." This admission well captures the humility and religious seriousness of the priest whose *Homilies on Ezekiel* are being published in the present volume for the first time in English translation. In spite of his humble demurs, Origen in fact so "adorned the nobility of his descent" from Leonides, through his own good life and holy death, that his heroic virtue was all but universally acknowledged. Origen died in his sixty-ninth year after he had experienced imprisonment and severe torture. This is described in gruesome detail in Eusebius, *HE* 6.39. Although Origen has never been canonized and is not formally considered a father of the church, since the church has never revoked the anathemas placed on his errors, he is listed as an ecclesiastical writer and hence as a "partial witness of the Tradition."[1] The esteem in which he is still held in the Catholic Church is shown by the fact that his writings are cited at least nine times in the recent *Catechism of the Catholic Church.*

Origen was probably the most learned and influential theologian of the third century. Among his many scholarly productions, he wrote the most important Christian apologetic treatise of antiquity, *Contra Celsum,* a work that has lost little of its relevance, even in the present day. There is a fresh vitality in this work that still bears pondering, and many of its doctrinal defenses are still valid.[2] From Origen's pen also came important Scripture commentaries and theological treatises, many of which were either translated into Latin (by St. Jerome and Rufinus of Aquileia) or assimilated into the Greek and Latin theological tradition by subsequent Christian theologians who infused Origen's insights into their own works.[3] Three very significant examples are St. Jerome's commentaries on Galatians, Ephesians, and Matthew.[4] Henri de Lubac wrote of Origen's legacy to the Middle Ages: "More than any other figure in the fields of hermeneutics, exegesis, and spirituality, he would be the grand master."[5]

Origen's homilies constitute the oldest body of Christian sermons in existence. In their Latin garb, they were a rich source of spiritual inspiration to Christians throughout the Middle Ages and Renaissance. Saints and mystics felt an irresistible attraction to Origen's writings, as did exegetes and theologians. Though Origen's theological reputation remained tainted because of the condemnation of "Origenism" at the Second Council of Constantinople (553), this did not prevent him from being studied, revered, and even loved. His fate in the West was similar to that of the layman Tertullian, who, however, unlike Origen, died outside the bosom of the church, having joined the Montanist sect. In contrast, the priest Origen died in the church, and some of his views were condemned some three centuries after his death. In any case, what was sought in Origen was not so much his doctrine as his mentality and spirit, and most of all, his way of interpreting Holy Scripture.[6] Origen's fiery soul, which is revealed in his writings, and his Spirit-filled exegesis ignited a spark of divine love in the hearts of countless Christians.[7] The source of this fire was sympathy for the central feature of Origen's spirituality, namely, his "absolute and passionate love for the Logos, which has taken on personal lineaments for us in Jesus Christ, suffusing the total cosmos of men and angels."[8]

Provenance of Origen's Homilies and of Jerome's Latin Translation

According to Eusebius *HE* 6.36, Origen did not permit his homilies to be transcribed until he was over sixty years of age. This would place the original delivery of Origen's homilies, including these on Ezekiel, in the year 245 at the earliest. The Eusebian tradition has been set aside in modern times, first by Jean Scherer and more radically by Pierre Nautin, who dates the delivery of Origen's *Homilies on Ezekiel* at the church of Caesarea in Palestine around 240.[9] Nautin has been followed by Joseph Wilson Trigg.[10] After making a detailed comparison between these and Origen's other homilies, Marcel Borret gives a date between 239 and 242, to which we give our tentative support.[11]

The Latin translation of Origen's Greek sermons was made by St. Jerome (347–420), ca. 379–381, after he came to Constantinople to study under Gregory Nazianzen.[12] Jerome was undoubtedly one of the most learned of the Latin fathers; his Scripture scholarship was warmly commended at the Council of Trent and in the twentieth century by Popes Benedict XV and Pius XII.[13] Francis X. Murphy has correctly observed that Jerome is still "an indispensable witness to the mind of the Church in dealing with the Word of God."[14] During his early career, Jerome was one of Origen's most vocal defenders; he described Origen as the "greatest teacher of the Church after the apostles,"[15] a man endowed with "immortal genius,"[16] who was of "incomparable eloquence and knowledge."[17] Origen "surpassed all previous writers, Latin or Greek."[18] Later, during the Origenist controversies, Jerome reversed his public standpoint concerning Origen without really altering his fundamental endorsement of Origen's exegetical genius. This matter cannot be discussed in detail here.[19]

Jerome's dedicatee is the priest Vincentius of Constantinople, with whom he had become acquainted in Constantinople. In 382 Jerome also dedicated to Vincentius his translation of Eusebius's *Chronicle*.[20] Jerome reports that he has just completed a translation of Origen's fourteen homilies on Jeremiah.[21] In the preface to the translation of the sermons on Ezekiel, he says he has striven for simplicity of language and has renounced every form of rhetorical splendor, for he wants the content to be praised, not the style of the words. He further assures Vincentius that he plans to translate many of Origen's works, a promise he never fulfilled. This task was largely taken over by Rufinus of Aquileia.[22]

Origen's Exegetical Method

Origen's method of expounding Ezekiel's text can best be described by saying that Origen strives with all his might to imitate St. Paul's method of interpretation of the Old Testament Scriptures. In Romans 15:4 Paul says: "For whatever was written in former days was written *for our instruction*, that by steadfastness and by the encouragement of the scriptures we might have hope." Paul repeats this idea in

1 Corinthians 10:11: "All these things happened to them figuratively,[23] *but they were written down for us,*[24] upon whom the end of the ages has arrived." Along similar lines Hebrews 8:5 and 10:1 speak of the Old Testament as a copy and shadow of the good things to come (cf. Col 2:16–17). Origen builds upon these apostolic principles. He presupposes that the Holy Spirit inspired the Old and New Scripture to benefit the souls of Christians.[25] The goal of Origen's exegesis is to explicate, or unfold, christologically and ecclesiologically, the fullness and reality foreshadowed in the Old Testament. This exposition takes place during the daily liturgies.

For Origen, Paul's practice of exegesis, as well as that found in the Letter to the Hebrews, is programmatic for Christians. Paul's method can be observed, for example, in 1 Corinthians 10:1–11; Galatians 4.21–31; 1 Corinthians 9.9; and so on. Thus, the New Testament itself provides Origen with a basic model for how to do exegesis and how to conduct homiletical exhortation. He wants to perpetuate the form of exegesis that the New Testament itself had inaugurated. As he says in *Peri Archon* 4.2.4: "We believe that the correct way to understand the Scriptures and to investigate the ideas they contain is that which Scripture itself teaches us to employ."

Modern scholars increasingly recognize Origen's fidelity to the New Testament patterns of interpretation. In his classic work *Medieval Exegesis,* Henri de Lubac says that some of the modern attacks on patristic exegesis are in fact veiled criticisms of the New Testament itself. For example, what is called "Philonism" in the work of Origen and others is often in reality fidelity to the teaching of the Letter to the Hebrews.[26] Along similar lines, John A. McGuckin writes: "Time after time the source of Origen's particularly nuanced biblical interpretations of the Old Testament text can be explained on the basis of the Pauline or Johannine text through which he is reading the old narratives."[27] However distasteful these methods have become to modern scholars, it is difficult for anyone to deny Origen's fidelity to the New Testament patterns of interpretation. Doubtless Origen would have been puzzled by the arbitrariness of Richard N. Longenecker's judgment, to the effect that modern Christians need not feel obligated to emulate the apostles' practice of scriptural exegesis: "Our commitment as Christians is to the reproduction of the apostolic faith and doctrine, and not necessarily to the specific apostolic exegetical practices....we cannot assume that the explication of their methods is necessarily the norm for our exegesis today."[28] For Origen, the apostolic faith, doctrine, and exegetical practice go together; to adopt only two of these three inheritances he would have deemed arbitrary and sub-Christian. This is not to dispute the right of modern exegetes to adopt other methods of interpretation, but to show that Origen's method is conscious imitation of the New Testament writers and that any global attack on Origen's method is an implicit critique of the New Testament.

In practice Origen uses a two-level approach to interpreting the text of the Old Testament: the literal/historical meaning and the deeper allegorical/mystical meaning. With very few insignificant exceptions, what moderns call the "literal meaning" of the Bible (in this case the text of Ezekiel) is always assumed to be factually true. A good sample of Origen's exposition of the literal/historical level of interpretation is seen in 11.2.5–6, where he explains the details of Ezekiel 17.1–7 by identifying their historical referents. But in Origen's judgment, these Old Testament texts were not preserved for the church primarily to satisfy the Christian's curiosity about history. Rather, there is need for a deeper level of interpretation that addresses the devotional, practical, and ecclesiastical needs of the readers. Whereas the literal explanation is precise and does not permit arbitrary deviations, the allegorical interpretation is freer and subject only to the one law that it must have a pious meaning in view.

In accordance with these principles, Origen interprets these same historical details as containing symbolic meaning for the Christian. Thus, Nebuchadnezzar represents the devil (11.5.2). Ezekiel's experiences foreshadow Christ and the church: Ezekiel's captivity really happened in accordance with the reliable testimony of history (1.3.6); but it happened as a sign pointing to Christian mysteries. Ezekiel's title "son of man" prefigures the name Christ took to himself, as does Ezekiel's age (thirty) and the opening of the heavens (1.4.1–3; 1.7.1). Indeed, for Origen every detail of Ezekiel's text has some sort of mystical application to Christ and the church. Origen's aim in unfolding this application is principally homiletical exhortation, which accords with the genre of this work.

Origen's method of interpretation was maligned during his own lifetime and continues to be much misunderstood today. He himself reports in 6.8.3:

> It is said to me: Do not allegorize, do not explain things figuratively. Let them answer: Jerusalem has breasts, and there is a time when they are bound up, there is a time when they are set, and she has an umbilical cord, and she is convicted because 'it was not cut.' How, pray, can these things be understood without an allegorical exposition?

He then fully expounds the symbolism of these details.

At the beginning of the fourth century, Methodius of Olympus attacked Origen for his method.[29] The German Reformers also dismissed him in the sixteenth century, but for different reasons.[30] These criticisms have been perpetuated in the modern period by the influential scholarship of R. P. C. Hanson, who accuses Origen of not taking history seriously.[31] Henri Crouzel responds to this critique by reminding us: "In spite of the spontaneous reactions of many modern scholars it must not be concluded from the fact that Origen allegorizes a story that he does not believe in the historicity of the literal account, which is perfectly compatible with the quest for a spiritual meaning."[32] The recent appearance in English of de Lubac's classic study *History and Spirit: The Understanding of Scripture according to Origen* is most welcome and will, one hopes, contribute to the further clarification of Origen's method of biblical interpretation. De Lubac shows, among other things, that in Origen's hermeneutics, the scholarly interpretation of Scripture is a specifically Christian exercise. Origen defines many hermeneutical terms differently from modern theorists. For example (as the above citation about Jerusalem's "breasts" shows), Origen's understanding of "allegory" is far more extensive than that of modern scholars; it is virtually the equivalent of "figurative." Moreover, Origen's notion of "literal" was diminutive in comparison with ours. This creates a barrier between Origen and modern scholars at the level of linguistic definitions. In response to Hanson's criticism that Origen was interested in history only as parable, one might ask whether it really follows that restricting a passage's meaning to its historical referent is the equivalent of taking history seriously. Since Origen aims to take the full symbolic potential of Old Testament events into consideration, and not to restrict the meaning of passages to what their human author intended for their audience at that time, it seems that he took history extremely seriously. Indeed, for Origen history is taken seriously only when the Christian exegete grapples with the symbolic and christological meaning of the Old Testament.

On the other hand, even scholars who are largely sympathetic to Origen's exegetical endeavors have criticized his system of interpretation on two points:[33] (1) Although reacting against Gnosticism, he remained under its influence, as seen by the way he invests meaning in biblical expressions that is foreign to the authentic sense. (2) He was too much under the influence of the allegorism of Philo, which led him to propose the idea that all passages of the Old Testament have a symbolic sense. These criticisms seem to me to be largely valid. In my opinion, however, they do not diminish the overall achievement of Origen's Old Testament exegesis. Origen compensates for these faults by what J. Lienhard has identified as the principal achievement of his homiletical endeavor: by working his way through the entire Old Testament, book by book, sentence by sentence, and word by word, Origen would guarantee "the proper and rightful place of the Old Testament in the Christian canon."[34] This is no small feat and helps account for Origen's popularity in the later tradition. In contrast to Origen's approach, much modern exegesis and theology denigrate the Old Testament.[35]

Survey of the Theological Themes of Origen's Homilies on Ezekiel

Polemic against the Heretics: Marcion and Valentinus

As Jean Daniélou has noted, Origen never aimed at anything but defending the faith against heretics, particularly against the teaching of Marcion and the Gnostic Heracleon, whom he engages in his *Commentary on John.* "Some of his [Origen's] opinions were afterwards rejected by the teaching authority, but he had always acknowledged the Church's right to condemn them and had brought them forward only as tentative suggestions."[36] In this present group of homilies, Marcion and Valentinus are prominent among the heretics who are refuted.

Marcion of Sinope in Pontus founded a heretical sect in Rome in the 140s. His doctrinal system was based on his conviction that justice and grace are irreconcilable, as are law and gospel, Judaism and

Christianity, the God of the Old Testament and the Father of Jesus. Marcion, like Valentinus, was a docetist.[37] He denied that Jesus was a real human being born of the Virgin Mary. Rather, he only appeared to be human. Marcion posited two supra-temporal and uncreated principles: an aloof and improvident "good" God (the Father that Jesus speaks of), who, before the advent of Jesus, in the manner of the god of Epicurus, had nothing to do with matter or with the governance of the world; and a just but wicked god, who, as a product of a defective emanation from the highest god, created the material universe and became the god of the Jews. Marcion repudiated the Old Testament in its entirety and denied that it predicted the coming of Jesus. He also taught his followers that the received form of the New Testament had been corrupted by Judaizing Christians, whom he identified as the Catholics of his day. Thus, he "edited," that is, mutilated and disfigured, the Gospel of Luke and ten of Paul's letters and made these documents the canon of his new church. By removing Luke's name from the Gospel material, and by cutting away texts even within these writings that he found incompatible with his antecedent theology, he attempted to sever the link between his new, allegedly "Pauline" religion and the religion of the Creator God, that is, Old Testament Judaism and traditional Catholic Christianity.

Valentinus was an Egyptian heretic of the second century who spread Alexandrian Gnosticism in Rome between 135 and 160. He exerted a considerable influence and was refuted in turn by Justin, Irenaeus, Hippolytus, Tertullian, and Origen. In addition to his basic Gnostic teaching, which rejected the identity between the Creator God of the Old Testament and the Father of Jesus, Valentinus taught a sort of natural predestination, which divided human beings into three categories based on the inborn natures of their souls. The redeemer, Jesus, saves humans from the world by giving them saving knowledge, or *gnōsis* (from which Gnosticism derives its name). The *gnōsis* is available only to the spiritual (*pneumatikoi*). The second kind of nature is that of the "soulish" ones (*psychikoi*), ordinary members of the Catholic Church, who can achieve some kind of salvation by faith and good works. The third group is the rest of humankind, or the "natural" (*hylikoi*), who have no chance at redemption.

For Origen, the common denominator of all Gnostic systems, including Marcion's special form, is their polytheistic or dualistic tendency. They all deny the one God as unique source of all creation, revelation, and grace. They all accept Christ but introduce plurality into the divinity. In contrast to the heretical approach to the Scriptures, the basic principle of Origen's exegesis is the unity of the Godhead and of the Scriptures. In 1.3.8 Origen speaks of the "consonance" between the words of the prophets and the words of the Gospel. This term has been shown to be an important one in patristic theology, particularly that of St. Irenaeus.[38] Origen's whole theology also reflects the prominence of this central patristic idea.

Origen engages Marcion's religious system throughout these homilies, descending into mockery only in 8.2.3, where he says: "Heretics build a brothel on every way, as for example the teacher of Valentinus's training school, the teacher of Basilides' band, the teacher of Marcion's tavern, and of the other heretics." Origen tends to group the trilogy of Marcion, Valentinus, and Basilides together (see 3.4.2; 7.4.2; 8.2.3). Crouzel observed that the objections Origen makes to this trio and the ideas that he attributes to them are "somewhat stereotyped and do not reflect a very deep first-hand knowledge of them."[39] On the other hand, Origen's principal concern is with the contemporary forms of heretical religion, which were extremely diverse, and not necessarily with the original forms, which are, in any case, not easily recoverable.[40]

According to Origen, Marcion misunderstands the nature of God's wrath when he accuses it of being limitless (1.1.2). Origen states that Marcion completely invalidated the incarnation (1.4.2), corrupted the Scripture in order to dissociate Jesus from the Creator (1.6.2), and aspersed both the Creator God and his prophets (1.11.2). Origen notes the polytheistic tendency of Marcion in 1.9.1. In 2.5.3 Origen observes that Marcion's followers accept his authority as a teacher. Origen allows that some of Marcion's followers are chaste and meek (7.3.1). In a very effective passage that is based on a careful reading of the biblical text (1.9.1), Origen notes that those like Marcion who accuse the God of the Old Testament of being inhumane fail to observe that some Old Testament passages actually show greater humanity than their counterpart texts in the New Testament. The genius of Origen's refutation of Marcion is found in the way he exposes the inconsistency and duplicity of Marcion's attacks on the Old Testament and the Creator. That is to say, Origen argues that if Marcion were consistent in the application of his critical principles, his program would necessarily condemn Jesus and Paul as well.

With respect to Valentinus, Origen explicitly notes that his followers are often dissolute in morals (3.4.2), though some are admittedly chaste (7.3.1). Valentinus's principal error is his predestinarian-type belief that some men have been created for destruction (13.2.1). Origen regarded this doctrine as fatal, since it amounts to a denial of the goodness of God and of the scriptural teaching on the free choice of the will. Origen's words in 1.3.8 make clear that the denial of freedom of will leads to laziness and negligence.

> But you, O man, why do you wish to be deprived of your choice? Why do you resent striving, working, struggling, and by good works becoming yourself the cause of your salvation? Or will it please you more to rest in eternal happiness in a state of slumber and idleness? "My Father," he says, "is working until now, and I am working" [John 5:17]. And you who were created to work [cf. Gen 2:15] do not like to work? Do you not want your work to become justice, wisdom, and chastity? Do you not want your work to be fortitude and the other virtues?

Origen's religious ideals were the reverse of Gnostic determinism. They even proved to be quite disturbing to Martin Luther, who made the total satanic enslavement of the human will the central tenet of his theology.[41] In fact, Luther formulated his theology explicitly against the theology of freedom represented by Origen and St. Jerome.[42] In *De servo arbitrio,* Luther says with reference to their interpretation of Romans 9 (the hardening of Pharaoh's heart) that "no writers have handled the Divine Scripture more ineptly and absurdly than Origen and Jerome."[43] Erasmus of Rotterdam (d. 1536) wrote a lengthy defense of the Catholic doctrine of free will against Luther's attacks.[44]

In contrast to such ideas, Origen sees human beings as actively cooperating in the process of their own salvation. Human sanctification is the outcome of union with God, and holiness is an ascent to God that is accomplished by steps or degrees. Origen stresses that the Christian's heavenly rewards depend not on an inborn nature but on earthly merit, on a good and responsible use of one's free will, and on achieving a spiritual victory over the devil. It is no wonder that Origen became a patron theologian for monasticism and its ideal of ascetic, that is, disciplined, spirituality, which advocates that Christians maintain an appropriate measure of voluntary self-denial.

Purification

A central theme of Homily 1 is that God's punishments in the Old Testament as well as the New are "disciplinary rather than punitive and are invariably mixed with mercy."[45] It might be more accurate to say that, for Origen, God's punishments are both disciplinary and punitive.[46] Origen teaches that when Christians sin, they store up dishonor and shame for themselves in the future (10.5.3). We should therefore embrace the opportunity given in this earthly life to obtain disciplinary purification from the hand of God. Otherwise, we may need to undergo a much more painful purification in the afterlife. In brief, Origen is a key ancient witness to the church's belief that most Christians will stand in need of purgatorial fire before final salvation can be attained. In 1.3.3 Origen interprets this fire in a nonliteral fashion and stresses that after death one cannot enter the sanctuary (heaven) with the works of sin, since this would contaminate God's kingdom. Sinful works must therefore be atoned for by the fire of God's remedial judgment.

It is worth noting that Origen stresses in 10.2.3 that priests and church leaders who sin have the most to fear from these punishments: "For the nearer we have been to God and the closer we have been to beatitude, the farther we put ourselves from it when we sin, and the closer we put ourselves to terrible and very great punishments. For God's judgment is just, and 'the powerful suffer powerful torments.'" But the warnings apply to all Christians who sin in a state of belief, as he says in 12.1.2:

> And indeed, as for us who are saying these things and who have once believed in God, if we sin, we are said to exasperate his words; but the one who has completely fallen away from faith in him and those who have not entered the Church, they do not make the words of God bitter. For how can they exasperate the sweetness of words in which they have not yet believed? And therefore the torments that are reserved for us who seem to believe and who sin in that state of belief are different from the penalty that will come to those who did not even have a commencement in the state of belief.

In the development of Catholic theology, the Western church, at least, largely endorsed Origen's purgatorial understanding of the afterlife, but the church rejected certain aspects of it, such as Origen's openness to the possibility of remission of mortal sins in the future life. Origen's optimism, which seems to have embraced the possibility of restoration of impious men and of fallen angels, was condemned at the Fifth General Council in 553.[47] St. Thomas Aquinas identified as Origen's principal eschatological error not his purgatorial conception of the afterlife but his misapprehension of the volitional powers of the damned.[48] In his work *De haeresibus,* St. Augustine makes clear what he believes to be the errors in Origen that no Catholic can deny:

> But there are other teachings of this Origen which the Catholic Church does not accept at all. On these matters, she does not accuse him unwarrantably, and cannot herself be deceived by his defenders. Specifically, they are his teachings on purgation, liberation, and the return of all rational creation to the same trials after a long interval. Now what Catholic Christian, learned or otherwise, would not shrink in horror from what Origen calls the purgation of evils? According to him, even they who die in infamy, crime, sacrilege and the greatest possible impiety, and at last even the devil himself and his angels, though after very long periods of time, will be purged, liberated and restored to the kingdom of God and of light.[49]

Augustine refers to his recently written *City of God,* where he says he has discussed these matters thoroughly, as well as Origen's error about the preexistence of souls (City of God 21.17).

In Origen's defense, one might insist against Augustine's assertions that it appears that with the exception of his doctrine of preexistence of souls, Origen did not dogmatically *assert* any other of these defective views, but instead he tentatively put them forward for the sake of discussion as interpretive possibilities in his attempt to refute the arguments of his Gnostic opponents. Origen surely does not seem to have had any intention of consciously violating the church's rule of faith, and there was no obstinacy in his erroneous views. There are even scholars who deny that Origen held these views in the form in which Augustine lists them.[50] It would seem more accurate to say that

Origen affirmed the logical possibility of restoration of all rational creatures and also the possibility of failure of such a hope, but he did not assert its inevitability. Daniélou shows the difference between Origen's thought and Gregory of Nyssa's in the following passage:

> Origen saw clearly enough, then, that there were two things involved—God's love and man's freedom. But his attempts to reconcile them led him to put forward two theses, one of which—the metaphysical necessity of the ultimate elimination of evil—safeguards God's love but destroys man's freedom, while the other—the perpetual instability of the free—safeguards man's freedom but destroys God's love. Gregory of Nyssa was humbler in the face of the mystery of the *apocatastasis*; he was content with admiring it as the supreme work of love that would do no violence to freewill. To him it stood for the certitude that in Christ salvation had been acquired for man's nature without any possibility of loss, but that the individual still had the power of dissociating himself from it by his own free choice.[51]

Daniélou's apparent endorsement of Gregory of Nyssa's form of universalism strikes me as a questionable theological conclusion in light of the church's repudiation of such a view.

The Suffering of God

One of the axioms of Greek philosophy was that the supreme divinity is immutable and not capable of suffering. Plato said that it is impossible for the god to desire to alter himself, because every god abides forever in his own form (Republic 381c). According to Aristotle, one must posit as the first origin of all things an unmoved mover that stands above all change and remains forever pure actuality without any potentiality (*Metaphysics* 1072a25; 1073a27; 1072b25).[52] After Aristotle, the metaphysical principle prevailed that the divine being does not suffer and does not change. In light of the alleged influence of Greek philosophy upon Origen, one would expect that the doctrine of divine impassibility would ring forth clearly in his theological writings. What we in fact find in Homily 6.6.3 is a most remarkable passage where Origen speaks eloquently of the suffering of God and the suffering of the preexistent Savior, who in his pity for the human race suffered in heaven. Moreover, Origen says, God the Father is not impassible. De Lubac described this as "no doubt one of his most beautiful pages, both his most human and his most Christian."[53]

At first glance Origen's words appear to be giving leeway to the suffering of God, a view that would seem to undermine the traditional patristic notion that God is impassible. Such views have become attractive to theologians in the modern era, who prefer to view God as being within the process of this universe and not above it. However, a study of the totality of Origen's writings shows that Origen does not really support the contemporary theological consensus that judges God to be passible, that is, capable of suffering in his essential nature. For Origen makes clear in *Peri Archon* 1.1.6 that, strictly speaking, God does not partake of movement, change, or even in being. For this reason, Origen says, one must not take literally those scriptural passages that speak of God having passions and emotions. Moreover, in *Contra Celsum* 4.72 Origen writes: "We do not attribute human passions to God, nor do we hold impious opinions about him."

Thomas G. Weinandy has shown that when Origen asserts that the Son of God suffers as man, and also that the Father also suffers, his words need to be harmonized with his previously articulated theological principles. Weinandy summarizes Origen's position by making a very important distinction in the way that Origen upholds both the impassibility of God and the passion of God, namely, that when Origen says that God is impassible, he is denying emotional change of states within God. It is a negative way of upholding the absolute otherness of God and of his radical perfection. However, although God does not undergo any passible change of emotional states, precisely because of his immutable perfection, he is perfect in his passionate love for the human race. For the impassible perfection of God's love demands that he love with perfect passion.

> For Origen, if the Son had not suffered over our fallen condition prior to the Incarnation, he would not have become incarnate....Thus Origen is neither supporting the contemporary understanding of a passible and so suffering God, nor is he contradicting himself when he argues that God is both impassible and passionate.[54]

In other words, in this beautiful text in the *Homilies on Ezekiel*, Origen is essentially repeating the scriptural truth that God is unchanging and impassible in his perfect love. Paradoxically, precisely for this reason, God is supremely passionate in his love. Although God remains immutable in his essence, nevertheless, because of his providence and concern for human salvation, he descends to human affairs.[55] The upshot of this analysis is that the modern theological consensus that God is passible, and so suffers in himself, finds no support in Origen.

Human Justification

Because Origen accepts at face value the words of Ezekiel that speak of degrees of human sinfulness and degrees of righteousness, and of obedience to God as the means of becoming righteous, Origen's understanding of justification has been accused of "diluting the Pauline vision of universal sinfulness."[56] In a lengthy online discussion of Melanchthon's banal critique of Origen entitled "Melanchthon against Origen on Justification," J. O'Leary claims that the "Reformation challenge" to the Catholic understanding of justification as an intrinsic sanctifying renewal "remains central in any contemporary attempt at the critical retrieval of Patristic theology."[57] In Melanchthon's footsteps, O'Leary virtually identifies Luther's doctrine with that of St. Paul and consequently accuses Origen of "conflating justification and sanctification" (as if Paul separated them). O'Leary omits mentioning any texts in St. Paul that speak of a coming judgment according to works (Rom 2:6; 14:12; 2 Cor 5:10). He then endorses Melanchthon's criticism of the Catholic theological tradition and identifies Origen as the "root of medieval Pelagianism that Luther saw as enslaving consciences and making the Gospel opaque" (p. 69). In reality, it is O'Leary and Luther who "makes the Gospel opaque" by excluding from their doctrine the pervasive Pauline doctrine of judgment according to works.[58]

In this connection Ezekiel 16 and 18 are important passages in the Old Testament. The verb δικαιόω ("justify") is used three times in Ezekiel 16:51–52: "But you [sc. Jerusalem] have multiplied your iniquities beyond them [sc. Samaria], and you have justified your sisters in all your iniquities which you have committed. Therefore bear your punishment, because you have corrupted your sisters by your sins which you have committed beyond them; and you have justified them beyond thyself." Moreover, the cognates δίκαιος and δικαιοσύνη are used repeatedly in Ezekiel 18:21–28. For Origen, as for Ezekiel, we obey *in order to become* righteous. We *become* unrighteous by disobedience and sin. Δίκαιος (*dikaios*, "just," "righteous") describes the person who obeys God and who does δικαιοσύνη (*dikaiosynē*, "justice," "righteousness"). Objective righteousness is thus the criterion of judgment. *Dikaios* is not reduced to the idea of "pardoned" or "forgiven."[59]

Based on Ezekiel 16:51–52, Origen's Homily 9.2–4 contains his explanation of the biblical term *justification* as well as a detailed discussion of the sin of pride. It is evident that Origen conceives of justice as that which is inherent in both God and humans owing to the good they have done. Justification is understood as an intrinsic condition that is relative and comparative. In 9.2.4 Origen says:

> It is one thing to be justified, something else to be justified by another. That the tax collector was justified by the Pharisee is similar to the way Sodom and Samaria were justified in comparison with a sinful Jerusalem. For we must know that each one of us, on the Day of Judgment, will be justified by one and condemned by another. Even when we are justified by another, that justice is less an object of praise than of blame. If, for example, I am found guilty of Sodomitic sins and someone else is brought forward who has committed twice as many serious sins, I am justified, to be sure; but I am justified not as a just man, but as it were in comparison with one who has committed more. I am judged to be just, although I am a long way from justice. Woe to that man who is justified by many sinners. Conversely, blessed by far is he who is shown to be just in comparison with the just....Would that I might be found to be wise when I am compared with the wise, and that I might be judged to be just by the just. For I do not wish to be justified by the unjust, because such justice is blameworthy.

Origen rightly recognizes the complex range of meaning of "justification" in the Scriptures. Far from "diluting" Paul (who in any case can hardly be interpreted in complete isolation from Ezekiel), Origen's broader understanding of the term actually agrees with Paul's usage (cf. Rom 2:13; 4:25; 6:7, 16, 19; 1 Cor 1:30; 4:4; 6:11), as well as that of Jesus (see Matt 10:37; 11:21–24).[60] For Origen, justification cannot be reduced to a purely external imputed status or label that results from the forgiveness of one's past sins in baptism. Rather, it embraces the sanctifying renewal in virtue as well as the intrinsic justice achieved through divine grace by the human being's doing of just deeds. Thus, it is an interior process that can be increased, decreased, or repudiated.

C. Verfaillie argued that in fundamental respects, Origen's understanding of justification anticipates the definitions of the Council of Trent.[61] This makes Origen's discussions of this theme all the more relevant to modern theology. The fact that Origen's interpretations generated such intense hostility from the German Reformers only makes this theme all the more interesting.[62]

Church Unity

A remarkable feature of Homilies 10 and 11 is Origen's strong vision for the unity of the church. He challenges "the vine who is listening to me, if you want to be great, do not leave the boundaries of the Church. Remain in the holy land, Jerusalem" (11.4.2). Daniélou observed that Origen's feeling for the church grew stronger as his life went on and that his finest discussion is found in one of his latest works, the *Homilies on Joshua.*[63] In *Hom. in Jos.* 7.6 Origen said: "I bear the title of priest and, as you see, I preach the word of God. But if I do anything contrary to the discipline of the Church or the rule laid down in the Gospels—if I give offence to you and to the Church—then I hope the whole Church will unite with one consent and cast me off." The converse of such an ecclesiology is seen in Homily on Ezekiel 10.1.4–6, where Origen declares his abhorrence of schism and his insistence on clerical submission to ecclesiastical judgments:

> It is an infamy to be separated from the people of God and from the church. It is a disgrace in the church to leave the congress of the priesthood or be expelled from the rank of deacon. And indeed, of those who are thrown out, some cause dissensions, but others accept with all humility the judgment made against them. Those, then, who out of indignation over their deposition, are incited to gather people together in order to make a schism, and who stir up a multitude of evils are not "bearing their disgrace" [cf. Ezek 16:52] in the present. On the contrary they are "stor-

> ing up for themselves a treasure of wrath" [cf. Rom 2:5]. But those will gain mercy from God who with all humility leave the judgment to God and patiently bear the judgment made about them, whether they have been rightly or wrongly deposed. And frequently men even call them back to their earlier office and to the honor they had lost.

Such a text recalls the teaching of Origen's great contemporary St. Cyprian, who had also manifested a deep concern for the church and its unity. Origen's conviction dates from his youth and remained a feature of his life to the end. For Origen, it is necessary for a priest or deacon who has been deposed humbly to accept his being deposed, even if the action taken against him was unjust. For to create a schism in the church out of indignation in response to an unjust deposition will only result in accumulating God's greater wrath against the schismatic. It is perhaps relevant to recall that in 213, when Origen was in his late twenties, the African theologian Tertullian left the Catholic Church and adhered to the Montanist sect. St. Jerome (*De viris illustribus* 53) suggests that it was the envy and false accusations of the Roman clergy that pushed Tertullian into this sect. In any case, Origen would have clearly condemned Tertullian's action.

Martyrdom

Finally, we should mention the recurring presence of a basic theme of Origen's theology and spirituality, namely, the prime importance of martyrdom. For Origen, martyrdom is the highest form of faithfulness to Christ in all circumstances. It involves uniting oneself with the passion of Christ in the present life, and it issues in one's gaining access to the presence of Christ after death. By means of martyrdom the believer participates in Christ's work of redemption through the routing of the devil's power. And since the martyr shows himself impervious to suffering in particular, he experiences by the grace of God a sort of foretaste of the resurrection in this life and thus continues the work of redemption in this world. Crouzel observed: "Origen always desired martyrdom and constantly made clear, in his *Exhortation to Martyrdom* as well as in his homilies, the esteem in which he held this crowning testimony to our belonging to Christ."[64]

In the present homilies there are some remarkable passages on martyrdom. In 3.4.2, Ezekiel's mention of "pillows" reminds Origen of the soft way of life followed by some heretics, who aim for nothing strong and manly, but only for what is luxuriant and soft. Indeed, Origen says, the heretic Basilides goes so far as to deny the command pertaining to martyrdom. The heretics do not truly take up the cross of discipleship but implant luxury into the souls of their adherents. Homily 4.7.2 contains Origen's eyewitness testimony to martyrdom, which probably reflects his earlier experience in Alexandria:

> I have known just men who persevered in the faith who were handed over to wild beasts and were torn to pieces by them. They consummated martyrdom, and yet they did not cease to be blessed. For they were not handed over to the spiritual and invisible beasts that tear apart the souls of sinners and fasten their teeth into the hearts of the impious.

The experience of martyrdom does not terminate God's blessing for the saint, but causes it to reach consummation. This is the precise point that Paul makes in Romans 8.31–39.

Probably Origen's most memorable reflection on martyrdom in these homilies is his reference to his own martyred father, Leonides, in 4.8.1. The context shows Origen to be defending the doctrine that salvation depends both on our faith and on our living a good life. We must not place our hope of salvation in the intercession of saints or in our physical relationship to holy persons. Origen rebukes silly persons who think that they can be saved merely by the prayers of others, or by their physical descent, without possessing justice and holiness personally.

> They frequently say: "It will happen that each of us by his own prayers will snatch anyone he wants from Gehenna," and they introduce iniquity to the Lord, for they do not see that "the justice of the just man will be upon him and the iniquity of the unjust will be upon him," and each one "will die in his own sin and will live by his own justice" [Ezek 18:20, 22, 24]. Having a father who was a martyr does me no good, if I do not live well myself and adorn the nobility of my descent. That is, I must adorn his testimony and confession by which he was illustrious in Christ.

In Origen's reckoning, there can be a reprehensibly excessive reliance on the prayers of the saints. Since God has no spiritual grandchildren, each Christian is personally responsible for one's own life before God. Origen goes on to say that, if it is to no advantage for him to be physically related to his martyr-father, neither does it profit the Jews to claim Abraham as their father (see John 8:39). No one will be saved simply because of physical descent. Just as Origen must adorn his noble descent from a martyr with good works, so the Jews must adorn their descent from Abraham's line with Abraham's faith.

> Let none of us put trust in a just father, in a holy mother, in chaste brothers. "Blessed is the man who has hope in himself" [cf. Ps 34:8] and in an upright life. But to those who have confidence in the saints, it is not unfitting for us to bring forward a citation: "Cursed is the man who has hope in man" [Jer 17:5] and the following: "Do not trust in men" [Ps 146:3] and even another: "It is better to trust in the Lord than to trust in princes" [Ps 118:8–9]. But if it is necessary to hope in anyone, when all others have been forsaken, let us hope in the Lord, saying: "Though they set up encampments against me, my heart will not fear" [Ps 27.3].

A fundamental theme of Origen's theology is present in this text, namely, the necessity of free and personal cooperation in order to achieve salvation, a cooperation that extends to all that pertains to salvation: election, interior transformation, and perseverance.[65] In Origen's outlook, for Christians to place their hope of salvation in the saints is illusory apart from personal holiness. For God demands a good life of each of us and threatens to exclude those who lack it. To hope in the Lord is, for Origen, not exclusive of hoping for salvation in one's own good life.[66]

This, of course, has nothing to do with Pelagianism, in spite of repeated anachronistic accusations to this effect that have persisted until the present day.[67] For Origen nowhere denies that human beings are born into a fallen condition. He says repeatedly that no one is free from sin, not even one whose life lasts but one day.[68] Moreover, to Origen the good life is really God's gift to us. In fact, in 9.5.6 Origen makes this point explicit when he argues that, while it is true that the Christian doctrine of salvation entirely excludes religious boasting, it nevertheless requires flight from sin and genuine human merit or service to God through voluntary goodness and justice. The proud and boastful will be excluded from salvation, but so will those who lack justice and goodness.

> If then someone is conscious of his own purity and boasts in himself, forgetful of the statement: "But what do you have that you have not received? But if you received it, why do you boast as though you had not received it?" [1 Cor 4:7], he is deserted. And once abandoned, he learns by experience that in these goods in himself of which he was conscious, it was not so much he himself who stood forth as the cause, but God who is the font of all virtues. From this it appears that both the sufficiency of bread and the spiritual gifts generate pride in him who is not able to sustain these things. Therefore let us flee from Sodom and its sins. Let us flee from Samaria and the charges for which wretched Jerusalem is rebuked, so that in all things, as God supplies the strength to us, we might attain to humility and justice in Christ Jesus, "to whom is the glory and power for ages of ages. Amen" [1 Pet 4:11].

Origen's optimistic conviction that we can help ourselves to attain our heart's desire, whether God, salvation, or sanctification, has for a corollary our responsibility to do so. It also presupposes that the effectual achievement of these aims is possible through the strength that God supplies.

ORIGEN'S HOMILIES 1–14 ON EZEKIEL, TRANSLATED BY JEROME

Preface of Jerome

It is indeed a great thing that you are asking, my friend,[1] that I make Origen a Latin and give to Roman ears[2] the man who in the opinion of Didymus the Seer[3] was the second teacher of the churches after the Apostle.[4] But I am afflicted with pain in my eyes, as you know, a problem I contracted from my inability to resist reading too much.[5] Moreover, I have no secretary, for poverty has stripped this form of assistance too. Thus, I am not able to fulfill what you rightly desire with the same eagerness with which you so ardently desire this. And so, after the fourteen homilies on Jeremiah that I have already translated in no particular order, I have also dictated at intervals these fourteen on Ezekiel. I have taken care in particular that the translation preserves the idiom and simplicity of language of the above-mentioned man.[6] For these things alone are helpful to the churches. I have also renounced every form of rhetorical and artistic splendor. For we want the content to be praised, not the words.

(2) Now let me briefly remind you of the following. Origen's works on the whole of Scripture are of three sorts.[7] The first are his *Selections*,[8] which in Greek are called σχόλια. In these in a brief and summary fashion, he lightly touched on things that seemed obscure or that contained some difficulty. The works of the second kind are homiletical in nature. The present translation belongs to this genre. The third kind are those that he inscribed as τόμοι. We can call them commentaries.[9] Here he raised all the sails of his genius to the blowing winds, withdrawing from the land and going out to the middle of the ocean.[10] I know that you want me to translate every kind of his writ-

ing. I have already told you why I can't do this. But I do promise this, that if Jesus gives me health in answer to your prayers, I will dictate a translation, not of all his works, which would be a rash promise, but of very many of them. My only condition is the one that I have often set, that you supply the secretary, I will supply the words.

ORIGEN'S HOMILIES ON EZEKIEL
HOMILY 1

The Vision of the Prophet
(Ezekiel 1:1–6; 2:1ff.)

Two Reasons for Captivity

1. Not everyone who is a captive endures captivity on account of his sins.[1] For though a multitude was forsaken by God because of their sin, and was seized by Nebuchadnezzar to endure captivity, and was cast out of the holy land and "was led to Babylon" [cf. Jer 24:1], yet there were a few among the people who were just. They endured the captivity not because it was their own fault, but so that the sinners who were oppressed by the yoke of captivity would not be entirely deprived of support. For let us imagine that the just had remained in the old territories when the sinners were led away to Babylon. The result would have been that the sinners would never have attained a remedy. Therefore, God, who is clement and kind and a lover of human beings, arranged it so that along with the punishments by which he punishes sinners, he intermingles the goodness[2] of his visitation as well. He does not overwhelm the poor sufferers with punishment without limit. God is always like this, he torments those who do harm, but as a good father he joins clemency in with the torments.

(2) Now if you want to know that what we are saying is true, notice what happened in Egypt during the famine. If God had solely wanted to kill and punish the Egyptians by tormenting them with a seven-year famine, surely he would have done what he wanted; and Joseph would not have "gone down to Egypt" [cf. Gen 39:1ff.], nor

would Pharaoh have "had the dream" [Gen 41:1ff.] about what would happen in Egypt, nor would the chief cook have made known to the ruler that there was someone locked up in prison who could interpret the dream for the king. But now, as you see, God scourges like a father, but on account of his special gentleness, he spares not only Israel but also the Egyptians, though they are foreign to him [cf. Gen 45:5, 7]. And it is obvious that the work of the good God is exercised upon them, when Joseph goes down to Egypt, when the Pharaoh is warned in dreams, when the chief steward[3] points out the interpreter, when the interpreter explains the vision [cf. Gen 41:25ff.]. And thus by the crops gathered in the period of fertility, the scarcity that occurred during the later famine is overcome when the crop is gathered in. From all of this it is clear that the wrath, which heretics turn into a charge against the Creator, is not without limit.[4] We could recount many stories to prove what I have said, but lest I seem to digress from my theme, I will keep my words few. For my purpose is to explain the reason why the people of Israel were taken captive on account of their sins.

Providence and Mercy

2. And lest perhaps someone should think that the sinners who have been handed over by God are no longer governed by him and that once they are led off into captivity they do not merit his further providential care and mercy, let us consider the present passage more diligently. Daniel did not sin; Ananias, Azarias, Mishael were free from sin, and yet they became captives [cf. Dan 1:6, 19],[5] so that while placed there they could console the captive people and by the encouragement of their voice restore the penitents to Jerusalem, after they had been chastised long enough. For they suffered the punishments of servitude for seventy years [cf. Dan 9:2]. And so then, they returned to their own homes. For the holy words of the prophets had lifted up their dejected hearts. But there were not only these four prophets in the captivity; Ezekiel was also one of them and Zachariah son of Barachiah also prophesied[6] during the time of captivity under Darius the king [cf. Zech 1:1]. We have also found that Haggai [cf. Hag 1:1] and many other prophets prophesied during these same times. From

this it is shown that God not only punishes those who sin, but that he intermingles mercy along with the punishments.

(2) But if you are in doubt, hear the voices of those enduring the torments. For in a holy way they express the kindness of God even in the midst of their tortures: "You will feed us with the bread of tears, and you will cause us to drink in tears by measure" [Ps 80:5]. He does not say "tears" without qualification, but "tears by measure." For the mercy of God is in balance.[7] If it were not beneficial for the conversion of sinners to administer torments to those who sin, the merciful and kind God would never punish wicked acts with punishments. But it is in the same way that a very indulgent father chastens his son in order to shame him, and as a most caring teacher chastises the undisciplined student with a look of severity, lest the student perish while thinking that he is in good standing.[8] Look at what Solomon, the wisest man of all [cf. 1 Kgs 4:29–34], thinks about being chastened by God: "Son, do not be faint-hearted about God's discipline, do not faint when you are chastened by him. For whom the Lord loves, he chastens; he scourges every son whom he receives" [Prov 3:11–12; Heb 12:5–6]. The apostle says: "For there is no son who is not scourged by his father" when he sins. And to this, he has added marvelously when he says: "Persevere in discipline; God is treating you as sons; for what son is there whom his father does not chasten? But if you are without the discipline in which all have come to share, then you are illegitimate children[9] and not sons" [Heb 12:7–8].

(3) But there may perhaps be someone who takes offense even at the term "wrath" and objects to it with reference to God. We will respond to him that God's wrath is not so much wrath as necessary governance. Hear what the action of God's wrath is for: to rebuke, to chasten, to improve: "Lord, rebuke me not in your wrath, nor chasten me in your fury" [Ps 6:1]. The one who says these things knows that God's fury is not without usefulness for healing. On the contrary, the reason it is administered is to cure the sick, to improve those who have despised listening to his words. And that is why he is now praying that he not be chastened by such remedies: he does not want to receive back his original health by means of a penal cure. It is as if a slave who had already been exposed to the lash were to beg his master and promise him that in the future he will keep his commands. He says: "Lord, rebuke me not in your wrath, nor chasten me in your fury." Everything that comes from God is good, and we deserve to be chas-

tened. Pay attention to what he says: "I will rebuke them in the hearing of their anguish" [Hos 7:12]. Therefore we hear things that pertain to tribulation in order that we may be chastened. Also, among the curses of Leviticus it is written: "If after those things they do not obey nor become converted to me, I will add seven plagues to them for their sins. But if after these they are not converted, I will chasten them" [Lev 26:27–28]. Everything that comes from God that seems to be bitter is advanced for instruction and healing. God is a physician, God is a Father, he is a Master, and he is not a harsh but a mild Master.

(4) When you come to the passages of Scripture that speak of those who have been punished, "compare Scripture with Scripture" [cf. 1 Cor 2:13], as the Apostle also teaches you, and you will see that there, where things are thought most bitter, they are most sweet. It is written in the prophet: "In judgment he does not punish twice for the same thing" [Nah 1:9]. He punished once in judgment by the flood [cf. Gen 7–8]. He punished once in judgment against Sodom and Gomorrah [cf. Gen 18:20—19:28]. He punished once in judgment against Egypt and the six hundred thousand Israelites [cf. Exod 12:37]. Do not think that this vengeance was a punishment solely for the sinners, as if after death and punishments, they will again be subjected to punishment. They are punished in the present so that they do not have to be perpetually punished in the future.[10] Consider the poor man in the Gospel: he is oppressed by squalor and poverty, and afterwards he rests "in Abraham's bosom" [Luke 16:22]. "He received his bad things in his own lifetime" [cf. Luke 16:25]. How do you know that those who were killed in the flood received their evils in their own lifetime? How do you know whether Sodom and Gomorrah suffered for their own evils in their lifetime? Listen to the testimony of the Scriptures. Do you want to hear a citation from the Old Testament? Do you want to be instructed out of the New? "Sodom will be restored to its ancient condition" [Ezek 16:55]. Do you still have doubts about whether the Lord is good when he punishes the Sodomites? "It shall be more tolerable on the day of judgment for the land of the Sodomites and Gomorreans" [Matt 10:15], says the Lord, as he shows mercy to the Sodomites. Therefore God is kind, God is clement. Truly, "he makes his sun rise on the good and on the evil"; truly "he rains on the just and the unjust" [Matt 5:45]. This refers not merely to this sun that we see with our eyes, but also to that sun that is seen with the eyes of our mind. I was evil, and "the Sun of justice"

[cf. Mal 4:2] has risen for me;[11] I was evil, and the rains of justice came upon me.[12] The goodness of God is even in these things that are reckoned as bitter.

The Heavenly Vision and Fire

3. So then, the prophet "was found in captivity" [Ezek 1:1]. Observe what "he sees," that he might not feel the pains of the captivity. Below he sees troubles, but above, when he lifts up his eyes, he takes in "the heavens opened" [Ezek 1:1]. He sees the heavenly things unlocked for him, he sees the "likeness of the glory of God" [Ezek 2:1]; he also sees "four living creatures" [Ezek 1:5]. There is much to say about these things, and the interpretation is difficult. He sees the "charioteer of the four living creatures" [Ezek 1:5]; he sees the "wheels containing themselves mutually" [Ezek 1:16].

(2) The charioteer of the four living creatures is not completely fiery,[13] but only from the feet up to the loins, and from there to the top it glows red with the gleam of amber [cf. Ezek 1:27]. For God does not have only torments; in him there is also refreshment. He punishes sinners, but through the services that are below; for the prophet sees no fire on the head, or in the limbs that rise from the confines of the loins to the top. God is "fire," but "from the kidneys to" the feet. By this he shows that those who are involved in reproduction have need of fire. For "kidney" signifies coitus.[14] Abraham "was still in the loins of his father" Levi, "when Melchizedek met him" [Heb 7:10]. And in the Psalm it says: "From the fruit of your loins I will set [one] upon my throne" [Ps 132:11]. God is "fire from the kidneys on down." For the deeds of reproduction and lust need to be corrected by the punishments of Gehenna. God is fire, but he is not completely fire. His upper parts are amber. Amber is more precious not only than silver, but even than gold. But the Scripture has recorded amber as an illustration of brilliance; it is not that God is truly composed of amber. And just as God was not like the amber such as it was seen, so he is not like the fire such as it appeared from the kidneys to the end of the feet. That fire consumes, but he does not tell us what it consumes, so that you, by seeking, may discover what it is that is consumed by the fire of God.

(3) "Our God is a consuming fire" [Heb 12:29].[15] What does this fire consume? Not the wood that we see, not sensible hay, not straw

that is seen; but "if you build on the foundation of Christ Jesus" with "wood"—that is, the works of sin—with "hay"—that is, the works of sin—with "straw"—that is, the lesser works of sin [cf. 1 Cor 3:2], this fire comes and "examines" all that.[16] What is this fire that the law proclaims and that the gospel is not silent about? "The fire will test the quality of each one's work" [1 Cor 3:13]. What is this fire, O Apostle, that tests our works? What is this fire that is so wise[17] that it guards my "gold" and shows forth my "silver" more brilliantly, that it leaves undamaged that "precious stone" that is in me, so that it consumes only the evil I have done, the wood, hay, and straw that I have built up? [cf. 1 Cor 3:12–15]. What is this fire? "I came to cast fire upon the earth; and how I wish that it were kindled!" [Luke 12:49]. Jesus Christ says: "How I wish that it were already kindled!" For he is good, and he knows that if this fire were kindled, wickedness will be consumed.

(4) It is written in the prophets: "He sanctified him in burning fire, and devoured the forest like straw" [Isa 10:7]; and again: "The Lord of Hosts will send forth contumely in your honor, and a burning fire will be kindled for your glory" [Isa 10:16]. This means that fire is sent forth against the works of your sins so that you will be glorified. Do you still want to learn from the prophets that the torments of the good God are appointed for the benefit of those who endure them? Hear the same prophet speaking: "You have coals of fire, you will sit upon them, they will be a help to you" [Isa 47:14–15].

(5) It was necessary to conceal these things and not bring them out into the open—but the heretics force us to bring out in public things that should remain hidden—, for these things are kept covered as a benefit to those who are still "little children" [cf. 1 Cor 3:1] according to the age of their soul and who need the fear of teachers. They need to be chastised by threats and terrors in order to be able to attain healing. Thus by means of bitter remedies they may one day desist from the wounds of sins. For the mysteries of God are always covered by veils on account of the hearers who are children. "How great is the abundance of your sweetness, O Lord, which you have hidden from those who fear you!" [Ps 31:19].[18] The God of the law and the prophets hides the multitude of his goodness not from those who love him but from those who fear him. For the latter are little children. They are incapable of learning to their own profit that they are loved by the Father, lest they be set loose and despise the goodness of God [cf. Rom 2:4].

(6) Therefore, when you hear about the captivity of the people, to be sure you should believe that the captivity really happened in accordance with the reliable testimony of history. Yet it came first as a sign of something else, and it pointed to a subsequent mystery. For even you who are called faithful sojourn in Jerusalem, you who see peace[19]—for Christ is our peace [cf. Eph 2:14]. But if you sin, God's visitation will abandon you, and you will be handed over as a captive to Nebuchadnezzar,[20] and having been handed over, you will be led to Babylon. For since your soul has been thrown into confusion by vice and disturbances, you will be led off into Babylon. For Babylon means "confusion."[21] But if you again do penance and procure mercy from God through the conversion of a true heart, an Ezra is sent to you, who leads you back and makes you build Jerusalem [cf. Ezra 7:1–10]. For Ezra means "helper." And he is sent to you as a helping word, that you may return to your homeland.

(7) And what is said by Daniel enigmatically is also a mystery. And it is narrated by the Apostle as one who is hiding and revealing at the same time: "In Adam we all die, and in Christ we are all made alive" [1 Cor 15:22]. For Adam was in paradise, but the serpent arose as the cause of his captivity. It was he who caused him to be expelled, whether from Jerusalem or from paradise [Gen 3:1–2],[22] and he went to this "place of tears" [cf. Judg 2:5; Pss 43:20, 26; 83:7]. The serpent is an enemy who is hostile to the truth. But he was not created hostile from the beginning, nor did he at first go on his chest and belly [cf. Gen 3:14], nor was he accursed from the beginning [cf. Gen 3:14]. In the same way that Adam and Eve did not sin at once when they were made, so also at one time the serpent was not a serpent, when he was living in the "paradise of delights" [cf. Gen 2:8]. This is why, after he fell on account of his sins, he deserved to hear: "You are a seal of the likeness" [Ezek 28:12]; "you were born as a crown of beauty in the paradise of God" [Ezek 28:13]; "until iniquity was found in you, you went immaculate along your ways" [Ezek 28:15]. Job too makes mention of him and says that he was haughty in the presence of Almighty God [Job 1:6]. "For Lucifer fell from heaven, who rose at dawn, he is crushed upon the earth" [Isa 14:12].

(8) Notice the consonance between the prophetic words and the words of the Gospel. The prophet says: "Lucifer fell from heaven, who rose in the morning, he is crushed upon the earth" [Isa 14:12]. Jesus says: "I saw Satan fall like lightning from heaven" [Luke 10:18].

What difference is there in speaking of "lightning" and of "Lucifer" "falling from heaven"? The important thing is that there is complete consonance concerning the one who falls. "For God did not make death" [Wis 1:13]. Nor did he work evil.[23] To man and angel he conceded free choice in all things. What needs to be understood in this is how, through freedom of choice, some climbed to the summit of good things, but others fell into the abyss of evil.[24] But you, O man, why do you wish to be deprived of your choice? Why do you resent striving, working, struggling, and by good works becoming yourself the cause of your salvation? [cf. Phil 2:12]. Or will it please you more to rest in eternal happiness in a state of slumber and idleness? "My Father," he says, "is working until now, and I am working" [John 5:17]. And you who were created to work [cf. Gen 2:15] do not like to work? Do you not want your work to become justice, wisdom, and chastity? Do you not want your work to be fortitude and the other virtues?

(9) Therefore, those who have earned the punishment of captivity on account of their sins are led into captivity. And Jesus Christ came "to proclaim remission to the captives and sight to the blind" [cf. Isa 61:1–2; Luke 4:18]. He cries out to those who are in chains: "Come forth!" [cf. John 11:43–44] and to those who live in darkness: "See!" [Isa 49:9; Luke 8:29; 1:79; Matt 9:30]. Now we were in the chains of sins, and at one time we were living in darkness, struggling "against the rulers of darkness of this world" [Eph 6:12]. Jesus came, who had been predicted by the voices of all the prophets, and said to those who were bound up: "Come forth!" [cf. John 11:43–44] and to those who were in darkness: "See!" [cf. Matt 9:30].

Ezekiel Prefigures Jesus Christ

4. Now if you are willing to hear Ezekiel, the "son of man" [Ezek 2:1], preaching in the captivity, he too was a type of Christ.[25] "And it came about," it says, "in the thirtieth year, in the fourth month, on the fifth day of the month, and I was in the midst of the captivity by the river Chebar, and the heavens were opened" [Ezek 1:1]. So then, by the river Chebar, Ezekiel saw the heavens opened when he was thirty years old. And the Lord Jesus Christ, "when he began he was about thirty years old" [Luke 3:23], by the Jordan River [cf. Matt 3:13], and

"the heavens were opened" [Luke 3:21]. And throughout the entire prophecy of Ezekiel, he is called: "son of man."[26]

Son of Man

(2) But who is such a "son of man" as my Lord Jesus Christ? Let the heretics[27] answer me, who trick his birth out in unreality: Why is Christ called "Son of man"? I affirm that he was a "Son of man." For the one who took on human sufferings[28] must first before suffering have undertaken birth. For he would not have been capable of human feelings, words, behavior, the cross and death if he had not received a human beginning. And it was consistent for those who denied his birth to deny also his passion and simply to say: Jesus was not crucified. But now you confess the cross and you are not ashamed of preaching that he was crucified, "a stumbling block[29] to the Jews and foolishness to the Gentiles" [1 Cor 1:23]. And are you ashamed to confess his birth, which is a lesser scandal than his suffering or death? No doubt it is more of a scandal that Jesus was born than that he died! Or, if the Christian religion[30] does not fear scandal, why are you afraid to say lesser things, you who have confessed greater things? This is especially the case since his birth is not believed to be "from the seed of a man and a woman coming together in sleep" [Wis 7:2], but in accordance with the declaration of the prophet who said: "Behold a virgin will conceive in her womb and she will give birth to a son, and you will call his name Emmanuel" [Isa 7:14]. To say "Emmanuel" is not to pronounce an empty name, but it signifies a reality. For when Jesus comes, we say: "God is with us" [cf. Matt 1:23].

Names, Ages, and Dates

(3) Not in vain, then, does Ezekiel prophesy "in the thirtieth year" [Ezek 1:1]. For even his name is a figure of Christ. For Ezekiel means "power of God." But the power of God is none other than Christ the Lord [cf. 1 Cor 1:24]. It is also written: "son of Buzi" [Ezek 1:3], which means "despised." If you come to the heretics and hear them spurning the Creator and regarding him as nothing, and over and above this, even raising charges [against him], you will see that according to them, Jesus Christ our Lord is the Son of the most despised Creator. But if someone resists this interpretation and does not want to receive as prophecy these things that we have explained,

I will ask him why it is written that the heavens were opened in the thirtieth year of Ezekiel's life, and that he saw these visions that are contained in his book. How does the number of years help me[31] if not in this way, that when I learn that the heavens were unbolted in the thirtieth year, both for the Savior and for the prophet, by "comparing spiritual things with spiritual things" [1 Cor 2:13], I will recognize that everything that is written are the words of the same God. For "the words of the wise are like goads, and like nails deeply fixed, which are given by those who arrange [them] by one shepherd" [Eccl 12:11].

(4) When, in accordance with the capacity of my understanding, I investigate what is also said: "In the fourth month, on the fifth day of the month" [Ezek 1:1], I pray to God that I may be able to understand what is in agreement with the intention of the Scriptures. A new year is now imminent for the Jews, and among them the first month is numbered from the commencement of the new year [cf. Num 28:16]. (But another new year is counted from Passover: "Among the months of the year, it will be to you as the beginning of the months" [Exod 12:2].) From this year count with me the fourth month and understand that Jesus was baptized in the fourth month of the new year. For in that month, which is called January among the Romans, we know that the baptism of the Lord was carried out.[32] It is the fourth month from the new year according to the reckoning of the Hebrews. And since he had assumed a body subsisting of the four elements of the world and likewise received [the five] human senses, perhaps that is the reason he saw the vision in the fourth month and on the fifth day of the month.

Presence of Christ

5. "And I was *in the midst of* the captivity" [Ezek 1:1]. It seems to me that this was said ironically: "I was in the midst of the captivity." "And I," as if it is indeed the prophet who is saying this according to history: And I, who was not included *in* the sins of the people,[33] was *in the midst of* the captivity; but according to allegory, it is Christ speaking: And I came to the place of captivity, I came to those regions where there was slavery, where captives were being held. You have words of this sort from our Savior in the prophets when he is angry that we men are not acting in a manner that is worthy of his providential care, and

especially since we supposedly believe in him. For he says to his Father: "What profit is there in my blood, when I go down to corruption? Shall the dust give praise to you, or will it declare your truth?" [Ps 30:9]. I find another word too like this, which is spoken under the persona of our Savior through the prophet. He is seeking souls filled with justice, filled with divine thoughts, filled with holy fruits, and he seeks true grapes from the true vine [cf. John 15:1],[34] but he finds very many sinners who are unproductive of good. On that account he says: "Woe to me, for I have become as one gathering straw in the harvest and as one gathering clusters in the vintage, when no grape remains to eat as the first fruit" [Mic 7:1]. Woe to me! It is not the voice of divinity of the firstborn of all creation [Col 1:15] that says: "Woe to me!" but that of the human soul he assumed. This is why he adds: "Woe to me, soul, for the reverent has perished from the earth, and there does not exist anyone among men who chastens. All are judged for blood, each one afflicts his neighbor with affliction" [Mic 7:2].

The River Chebar

(2) These things have been recorded because the prophet says: "And I was in the midst of the captivity by the river Chebar" [Ezek 1:1], which means "heaviness." For the river of this world is heavy, as is said elsewhere in a mystery (and for the simple and for those for whom it unfolds history; but for those who hear the Scriptures spiritually, it signifies the soul, which has fallen into the eddies of this life). "By the rivers of Babylon, there we sat down and wept, when we remembered Zion. We hung our instruments on the willows in the midst of it. For there those who had led us as captives asked us for the words of songs" [Ps 137:1–3]. These are the rivers of Babylon next to which they sit and reminisce for the heavenly fatherland. They mourn and weep when they hang their instruments on the willows, namely, on the willows of the law and of the mysteries of God. For it is written in a certain book that "all believers receive a willow crown."[35] And it is said in Isaiah: "They will spring up as grass between the water and as a willow on the flowing water" [Isa 44:4]. And in the solemn feast of God, when the tabernacles are arranged, they put willow branches at certain places on the tabernacles [cf. Lev 23:40].

The Heavens Open

6. "By the river Chebar" [Ezek 1:1]. This refers to that very heavy river of the world. "And the heavens were opened" [Ezek 1:1]. The heavens had been closed and they are opened for the advent of Christ, so that when they are unbolted the Holy Spirit may come upon him in the form of a dove [cf. Matt 3:16]. For he could not pass to us unless he first came down to one who shares in his own nature [cf. John 16:7]. Jesus "ascended on high, he led captivity captive, he received gifts among men. The one who descended is also the very one who ascended above all the heavens, that he might fulfill all things. And he gave some to be apostles, some to be prophets, some to be evangelists, some to be pastors and teachers, for the perfection of the saints" [Eph 4:8, 10–12].

7. "The heavens were opened" [Ezek 1:1]. It is not sufficient for one heaven to be opened, but many are opened, so that not from one but from all the heavens angels may come down to those who are being saved [cf. Heb 1:14]. These are the "angels who were ascending and descending upon the Son of man" [John 1:52]. And "they came to him and were attending him" [Matt 4:11]. Now the angels descended because Christ had first descended. They feared to descend before "the Lord of powers" [Ps 47:8–9] and [the Lord] of all things had ordered them to. But when they saw the ruler "of the heavenly host" [Luke 2:13] living in the earthly regions, then they went forth by the open road, following their Lord and obeying the will of him who distributed them as protectors of those who believe in his name [cf. Deut 32:8]. Yesterday, you were under a demon, today you are under an angel. The Lord says: "Do not despise one of these least ones" [Matt 18:10], who are in the church. "For Amen I say to you that their angels constantly see the face of my Father who is in heaven" [Matt 18:10]. Angels are employed for your salvation [cf. Heb 1:14]; they have pledged themselves for service to the Son of God, and they say among themselves: If he descended, and descended into a body, if he was clothed with mortal flesh [cf. John 1:14] and endured the cross [cf. Heb 12:2] and died for men, why are we resting? Why are we sparing ourselves? Let us go, all angels, let us descend from heaven! And that is the reason "there was a multitude of heavenly host praising and glorifying God" [Luke 2:13], when Christ was born.

(2) All things are full of angels. Come, angel, receive an old man who has converted from his former error, from the doctrine of demons [cf. 1 Tim 4:1], from "uttering iniquity on high" [Ps 73:8]. Receive him, and like a good physician take care and establish him; he is a child, today an old man is born, a recent old man is becoming a child again; and when you are received, give him the "baptism of the second birth" [Titus 3:5], and summon to yourself other companions of your ministry, that you may instruct in the faith everyone equally, who were once deceived. "For there is more joy in heaven over one sinner who does penance than over ninety-nine just men for whom there is no need of repentance" [Luke 15:7]. All creation exults, praises together, and applauds those who are being saved. For "the expectation of creation awaits the revelation of the sons of God" [Rom 8:19]. And although those who have corrupted[36] the apostolic Scriptures are unwilling that words of this sort be found in their books by means of which Jesus Christ can be proved to be the Creator, nevertheless in those very books[37] all creation awaits the sons of God, when they will be delivered from transgression, when they will be removed from the hand of Zebulon,[38] when they will be ruled by Christ. But it is now time for us to touch on a few things from the present passage. The prophet saw not a vision, but visions of God. Why did he not see one, but many visions? Listen to God as he promises and says: "I have multiplied visions" [Hos 12:10].

8. "On the fifth [day] of the month; this was the fifth year of the captivity of King Joachim" [Ezek 1:2]. In the thirtieth year of the life of Ezekiel and in the fifth year of the captivity of Joachim, the prophet is sent to the Jews. The most clement Father did not despise them, nor did he abandon the people for a long time without calling them to mind. It is the fifth year. How much time intervened? Five years intervened from the time when the captives were enslaved. At once the Holy Spirit descended; he opened the heavens, that those who were oppressed by the yoke of captivity would see the things that were seen by the prophet. For when he says: "And the heavens were opened" [Ezek 1:1], in a certain manner they too were beholding with the eyes of their heart [cf. Eph 1:18] the things that he likewise had seen with the eyes of his flesh.

The Word of the Lord

9. "And the word (*sermo*) of the Lord came to Ezekiel, son of Buzi, the priest" [Ezek 1:3]. This is the "word (*sermo*) of the Lord," who "in the beginning was God, the Word (*verbum*) with the Father" [John 1:1]. This is the word that makes believers into gods [cf. 2 Pet 2:4]. For "if he called them gods [cf. Ps 82:6],[39] to whom the word (*sermo*) of God came, and Scripture cannot be broken" [cf. John 10:35], and to whomever the word of God has come, they become gods, then Ezekiel too was a god, since the word of God came to him. "I have said: You are all gods and sons of the Most High; but you will die like men, and you will fall like one of the rulers" [cf. Ps 82:7].[40] Where in the New Testament do you have a promise of this sort? If one must distinguish the testaments[41] and say that the gods of the two testaments are divided between themselves[42]—even to suspect this is sacrilegious, but we are speaking "improperly"[43]—I shall speak really boldly and say that greater humanity by far is shown in the Old Testament[44] than in the New. "I have said: you are *all* gods and sons of the Most High" [Ps 82:6]. He did not say: *Some* of you are gods and some of you are not, but you are *all* gods.[45] But if you sin, listen to what follows: "But you will die like men" [Ps 82:7]. Here the fault does not lie with the one who is calling them to salvation; it is not he who is inviting them to divinity and to the adoption of a heavenly nature [cf. 2 Pet 1:4] who is the cause of death, but the fault lies in our sin and in our wickedness. For it says: "But you will die like men, and you will fall like one of the rulers" [Ps 82:7]. There were many rulers, and one of them fell. It is written about him in Genesis: "Behold, Adam has become" not as *us*, but "as *one* of us" [Gen 3:22]. Therefore, when Adam sinned, at that time he became as one who falls.

10. "And the word of the Lord came to Ezekiel, the son of Buzi" [Ezek 1:3]. Even if you want to understand these things as spoken of the Savior, do not fear. Even so the allegory has its meaning. The word of God who was born of the virgin came to him, that is, to the man, the Word ever abiding in the Father [cf. John 1:1, 18], so that the two [natures] might become one, and the man whom he had put on for the sake of the mystery [cf. 1 Tim 3:16] and the salvation of all humanity would be joined in a union with his deity and with the nature of the only begotten God [cf. John 1:18].

(2) "The word of the Lord came to Ezekiel, the son of Buzi, a priest in the land of the Chaldeans" [Ezek 1:3]. Chaldeans discuss

heavenly matters; Chaldeans calculate the timing of men's birth. "In the land of the Chaldeans," as if he is saying: [in the land] of those who teach fate, of those who claim that the causes of the universe lie in the course of the stars. Therefore, the "land of the Chaldeans" is a figurative signification of that present error and that perversity of mind.[46]

(3) "In the land of the Chaldeans, by the river Chebar. And there the hand of the Lord came upon me" [Ezek 1:2–3]. Both the *word* of the Lord came to the prophet, and the *hand*, so that he would be adorned with both actions and words. "And I saw visions" [Ezek 1:1]. I will touch on a few things here. Although in view of time constraints what I have said could suffice, yet I will touch on the core aspects from the whole substance of the vision.

Cohesion of the Vision

11. "And I looked, and behold, a rising spirit[47] was coming out of the north" [Ezek 1:4]. Consider carefully the number of themes that are mentioned. A "rising"—or "removing"—spirit was coming out of the north, behold one theme. "And there was a great cloud on it" [Ezek 1:4], behold two themes. "And brightness round about it" [Ezek 1:4], behold three themes. "And gleaming fire" [Ezek 1:4], four. "And in the midst of it, as it were, the appearance of amber in the midst of the fire" [Ezek 1:4], five. "And light in it" [Ezek 1:4], six. After these things, "the likeness of four living creatures" [Ezek 1:5], and "the appearance of them" [cf. Ezek 1:5ff.] and the description of their "appearance," seven. "And in the midst of the living creatures, as it were coals of fire" [Ezek 1:13], eight.

(2) Who can explain each of these details? Who is there who is so filled with the Spirit of God that he can elucidate these mysteries? It was necessary that the accusers of the Creator and of God's prophets first understand what the prophets have said, and then bring their charges. For the one who accuses truly should accuse things that he knows. But if the heretics do not even come near the divine understanding, how is it rational for them to accuse what we can prove they do not understand? Let them learn what is the meaning of this vision. First, the removing spirit appears; second, there is a great cloud in the removing spirit; third, there was brightness around the removing spirit; fourth, there was gleaming fire; fifth, in the midst of it there was

something like the appearance of amber, doubtless in the midst of the fire; sixth, there was brightness in the same amber.

There Is Danger in Speaking about God

(3) I freely confess the maxim spoken by a wise and faithful man, which I often invoke: "It is dangerous even to speak truly about God." For not only are the false things said about him dangerous, but likewise things that are true and that are brought forth at the wrong time give rise to danger to the one who speaks them.[48] It is a true "pearl," but if "it is cast before swine," a dangerous moment comes to the one who "subjects it to their feet" [cf. Matt 7:6]. For our part let us offer an example. Not only in Aelia,[49] not merely in Rome, not [solely] in Alexandria, but simultaneously in the entire world, people speak of gatherings by using the comparison with a net that takes every kind of fish [cf. Matt 13:47; John 21:11]. It is not possible that everything that falls into it is good. For the Savior says: "When they drew it out and sat by the shore, they will pick out the good in containers, but they will throw the bad outside" [Matt 13:48]. Therefore, in the net of the whole church it is necessary that there are both good and bad.[50] If everything is already pure, what are we leaving for the judgment of God?

(4) And according to another parable, both grain and chaff are contained on the threshing floor, though only the grain will be gathered into Christ's barns. The chaff will be separated from him. "His winnowing shovel is in his hand, and he will cleanse his threshing floor and will gather the grain into the barn, but he will consume the chaff with inextinguishable fire" [Luke 3:17]. Now I do not assert that the threshing floor is the whole world, but I do understand it to be the gathering of Christian people.[51] For just as each threshing floor is circumscribed and is full of grain or chaff, it is neither all grain nor all chaff, so in the churches on earth there is some grain, some chaff. But in the former case, the chaff is chaff, not because of itself, nor through its own will; nor does the grain choose to be grain; but in the latter case, whether you are chaff or grain has been put under your own control [cf. Sir 15:14–17].

(5) This should teach us that if someone at some time sees a sinner in our congregations, he should not be scandalized and say: "Behold there is a sinner in the assembly of the saints! If this is permitted, if this is granted, why should I too not sin?" While we are in

the present world, that is, on the threshing floor and in the net, both the good and the evil are contained in it. But when Christ comes, there will be a discrimination, and what is said by the apostle will be fulfilled: "We all must stand before the tribunal of Christ that each one will receive back for what he has done in the body, whether good or evil" [2 Cor 5:10].[52] My eager mind has spoken these things as a prelude to the interpretation of the visions. My mind hesitates about what it should be quiet about, what it should bring forth, what it should leave lightly touched upon, what things from these words should be explained more openly, what more obscurely. Would that we could only fulfill what we desire.

The Spirit

12. First, then, one sees the "removing spirit" [Ezek 1:4]. What we said a little earlier, that "our God is a consuming fire" [Heb 12:29], we now again repeat and say that this agrees with this citation. Why is "removing spirit" recorded? "God is spirit" [John 4:24] and the removing spirit is seen.[53] What does he remove from me and from my soul so that he is deservedly proclaimed "removing"? Surely evils; and then, I think, [he removes] his goodness, if he has removed all evils from me. But neither should one think that there is an end of blessedness, if we are delivered from evils: being free from sin is the beginning of happiness.

(2) And in Jeremiah it is written—for I lay claim to everything that is written in the prophets of the most gentle God—: "Behold, I have given my words in your mouth; behold, I have appointed you today over nations and kingdoms, to uproot and to undermine, to destroy, to build up and to plant" [Jer 1:9–10]. God is kind when he gives words to uproot. But what is it that needs to be uprooted and undermined? If there is some planting in the heart that is evil, if there is some evil sect, the prophetic words uproot this, they undermine this. Would that it come to pass that such words be given me that uproot the seeds of the heretics and the teaching springing out of the font of Zebulon,[54] which would remove the planting of idolatry from the soul of the one who now enters the church!

(3) "I have given my words in your mouth; behold, I have appointed you to uproot and to undermine" [Jer 1:10]. This means that if there is an evil building, it must be destroyed. And how I wish I could undermine what Marcion has built up in the ears of those

whom he has deceived. Would that I could uproot, undermine, and destroy it, as Jacob destroyed the idols [cf. Gen 35:4]. The work of destroying and building up goes on until the present day. The heretics only hear the words about destroying and undermining. They turn their deaf ears away from words that speak of building up and planting. For they do not want to see that grievous things are spoken first, but there are joyful things in the second place.[55] Why do we mention this now? Namely, that it would be clear that God's words undermine evils and build up what is best. They undermine vice, like a good farmer, so that when the field has been purged, a very abundant harvest of virtues might arise.[56] These things have been said about the "removing spirit."

The Cloud

(4) For he sees first a "removing spirit," then a "great cloud" in it [Ezek 1:4]. When you have been purified by the removing spirit to the extent that all evil is removed from you and everything that is involved in evil in your soul, then you will begin as well to enjoy the great cloud that consists in the removing spirit. This cloud is near to that cloud of which we read in the Gospel, from which the voice came: "This is my Son, in whom I am well pleased" [Matt 17:5]. So then, there is the removing spirit, then the great cloud in it, finally the very brilliant light round about it [Ezek 1:4]. Evil is removed from you; a great cloud is given to you, so that it may pour down rain upon your vineyard, according to what is said elsewhere: "I will command the clouds not to rain upon it" [Isa 5:6], that is, upon an evil vineyard. But if this is commanded of the evil one, it is scarcely to be doubted that conversely, if you become a good vineyard, the cloud will rain on you.[57]

The Fire

13. "And there was brightness round about it; then a gleaming fire, and in the midst of it there was something like a vision of amber" [Ezek 1:4]. God removes evil from us in two ways, by Spirit and by fire. If we are good and attentive to his precepts, and we learn his words, he removes our evils by the Spirit, according to what is written: "But if by the Spirit you put to death the works of the flesh, you will live" [Rom 8:13]. But if the Spirit has not removed evils from us, we stand in need of the purification of fire. That is the reason you must care-

fully observe each of the connections. The first connection is between spirit and cloud, the second between fire and light, the third between amber and brightness. Each detail, though it appears grievous, is counterbalanced by the proximity of joyful things. For if a spirit rises, at once a cloud follows; or if fire appears, light is joined to it; or if amber precedes, there is brightness round about it. For it is necessary that amber burn us with its most intense fire, "as gold in a furnace" [Wis 3:6]. And in this prophet whom we are now explaining, you have the Lord sitting "in the midst of Jerusalem and burning those who are mixed with silver and tin and brass and lead" [Ezek 22:18]. With a voice of complaint, he pleads against those who have a co-mixture of worthless material in themselves [cf. Ezek 22:19–23]. He says: "You have become mixed silver, and like the seed of a grape, you have become rejected silver." For when from our evils we cause vices and passions to come upon God's creation, which is good from the beginning, then we are mixing brass, tin, and lead with silver and gold. Fire then becomes necessary to purify it. And that is the reason one must take great care that, when we come to that fire, we may pass through it unscathed. Like gold, silver, and precious stone that are without a trace of adulteration, may we not so much burn in the conflagration as be tested [cf. 1 Cor 3:12].

The North

14. "Behold, a removing spirit was coming out of the north (*aquilo*)" [Ezek 1:4]. Even this removing spirit that was coming out of the north and later returns [cf. Ezek 43] has a rationale. For out of the north they burn the evils upon those who dwell on the earth. *Aquilo* is a very violent wind. We call it by another name, the right,[58] which is one of the four cardinal points of the sky from which the winds are said to blow. It is the colder and more violent one. Indeed, even what is written in Numbers concerning the arrangement of the camps in Israel offers a figurative representation of this matter.[59] For the camps of Dan are placed last, toward the north [cf. Num 2:25]. The camps of Judah are set up first, facing the east [cf. Num 2:3]; then they put the camp of Reuben, Ephraim along the sea [cf. Num 2:18]; and at the border, as we have said, they set Dan, toward the north (*aquilo*). And the "boiling cauldron" that is described is burning from the face of the north [cf. Jer 1:13]. For *aquilo* is said figuratively and means "contrary strength,"[60] that is, Zebulon, who is truly "a very hard

wind" [cf. Sir 43:20].[60] This removing spirit comes out of the north, then, which is why it is written: "The removing spirit was coming out of the north and there was a great cloud in it," as we have already explained. "And there was brightness round about it and a gleaming fire" [Ezek 1:4]. He could have said "burning fire," but the Scripture was reluctant to name a grief and to describe its activity. And therefore, in place of the penal vision, it added only "brightness" of the fire.

The Living Creatures and Their Symbolism

15. "And in the midst of the fire, there was something like the likeness of four living creatures; this was their appearance: the likeness of a man was in them; and there were four faces in [each] one, and there were four wings in [each] one, and their legs were straight, and their feet were wings" [Ezek 1:5–7]. You see what sort of things there are that are ruled by God, as there: "You who sit," it says, "upon the Cherubim, appear!" [Ps 80:1]. Cherubim means "fullness of knowledge,"[61] and whatever is full of knowledge becomes a cherubim that God rules.[62] But what do the four faces mean in themselves? Things that are to be saved bend the knee before the Lord Jesus. These are named by the apostle in three ways: "That at the name of Jesus every knee should bow, of heavenly things and of earthly things, and of things below (*infernorum*)" [Phil 2:10]. Things that bow the knee to the Lord Jesus are subjected to him. And things that are subjected say: "Is not my soul submitted to God? For my salvation is with him" [Ps 62:1], and: "He must reign until he puts all his enemies under his feet" [1 Cor 15:25]. What then is the fourth [face]? For heavenly, earthly, and infernal are only three. Is it not this: "Praise the Lord, heavens of heavens and the waters that are above the heavens, let them praise the name of the Lord" [Ps 148:4]?[63] All these things are ruled by God and are led by his majesty.

16. "Wherever the spirit went, the living creatures also went" [Ezek 1:12]. These living creatures have this "likeness over themselves of a man," though they are "of four faces" [Ezek 1:5]. It is not said at the beginning that they are of four faces, but since among the four faces a human face rises above and holds precedence, it is described. It is also called "a human face and the face of a lion on the right of the four parts, and a face of a calf to the left of the four, and a face of an eagle to the four parts" [Ezek 1:5, 10]. Let us see, then, whether it signifies the tripartite soul concerning which it has also been dis-

cussed in the doctrines of others. Let us see whether in the tripartite soul another part, the fourth, that is, force, presides. What is the tripartition of the soul?[64] By "man" its rational part is being indicated; by "lion" its irascible part; by "calf" its desirous part. But the "spirit" who presides to help is not "to the right," as the man and lion, he is not "at the left," as the calf, but he is over all three faces. For in another passage the eagle is declared [Ezek 1:4, 10], so that through the eagle he signifies the presiding spirit of the soul. But I am speaking of the "spirit of man who is in him" [cf. 1 Cor 2:10]. And thus all things are led by the will[65] of God, "the heavenly things, the earthly things, the things below" [Phil 2:10], and the things that are above the heavens. And we all become Cherubim that are under God's feet, to which the wheels of the world are connected, and they follow these things [cf. Ezek 10:9]. For we are not now found under the wheel nor under the domination and affairs of the world, since we have already been delivered through the passion of Christ from the occupations of the world [cf. Gal 1:4].

(2) "And the wheel was in the midst of the wheel" [Ezek 1:16]. If you consider how the universe rolls on to contrary outcomes, whether in those who are thought to go astray, or in those who are said to be estranged from error, you will see how the wheel is in the midst of the wheel. But the God of the whole universe rules all these things, and he turns all things wherever he wills, in Christ Jesus, "to whom is the glory and power for ages of ages. Amen" [1 Pet 4:11].

HOMILY 2

Against the False Prophets (Ezekiel 13:1–19)

For Universal Healing

1. There is no kind of sin about which Scripture is silent or fails to instruct its readers. For the Word of God had to be sent to heal those who were listening. It had to touch upon every kind of sin and to speak to all men, so that no one would be deprived of salutary remedies and of these cures that could bring help to the wounds that need to be healed. So then, some things are said about the people, other things about the chief priests, certain things about the elders, and some things about the leaders. And indeed Scripture praises the good leaders, but ascribes blame to the evil ones, so that some receive exhortation to better things, but others are exhorted not to fall into worse things. In the same way, it is necessary to proclaim the divine instruction concerning the false and the true prophets, so that prophets might indeed be received in that part whereby they minister to the words of God;[1] but certain teachers of the churches should be called false prophets who, whether in words or life, do not match up rightly with the instruction that they preach. This is why we are glad if the Scripture warns us and says that we should withdraw from vice, and more still if the word of God touches some of our rank, who want to be healed and converted from our sins.

In Israel, in the Church

2. "The word of the Lord came to the prophet Ezekiel, saying to him: Son of man, prophesy for me against the prophets of Israel" [Ezek 13:1–2]. There were indeed even other prophets of Israel, in name more than in truth. And even today there are in the true Israel, that is, in the church,[2] certain false prophets and false teachers to whom these words are making an advance announcement. If the word of God rebukes me, I will strive to be converted. Nor is it the case that, because some things are said against me, I should be silent, I who seem to be a doctor of the church. On the contrary, I will not spare myself, but I will reveal everything that is said, so that I may be converted from vice. I do not want to become one of those whom the Scripture is now chastening, but one of those who stand forth as teachers in the church, who preach the word of God in all its truth.

(2) "Prophesy against the prophets of Israel who prophesy out of their own heart, and say to the prophets" [Ezek 13:2]. Just as the one who was commanded these things had need of the Holy Spirit, so there is need of the same Spirit in the one who desires to explain the things that are being signified in a hidden fashion,[3] that he may now show that there is a prophecy against the one who teaches contrary to the will of God, against those who prophesy out of their own heart. To be sure, according to the simple understanding there are some prophets who speak from the divine Spirit and who have not spoken "out of their own heart." Rather, they speak from the mind of God. But others have arisen as false prophets, who feign themselves to be prophets and say: "Thus says the Lord," though the Lord is not speaking in them.[4]

(3) But the present words can also be applied to those who teach in the churches, if they teach otherwise than as the truth demands. For if someone has this passage refer to those things that Jesus Christ the Lord has spoken, and if he interprets them in such a way that, when he teaches, it is clear that he is speaking not out of his own heart, but from the Holy Spirit, then he is speaking the words of Jesus the Son of God. If he agrees with the intention of the Holy Spirit, of him who has spoken in the apostles, he speaks not out of his own heart, but from the heart of the Holy Spirit who spoke in Paul [cf. 1 Cor 7:40], who spoke in Peter [cf. Acts 11:12], who spoke in the other apostles as well. But if someone, when reading the Gospel, applies his own meaning to the Gospel and fails to understand it in the way in

which the Lord spoke it, he is a false prophet.[5] He speaks about the Gospel "out of his own heart." And indeed, there is no absurdity in understanding these statements about the heretics. For as though it were from the Gospels and as though it were from the apostles, they discuss their fables of the αιώνων (aeons).[6] They set these things forth from their own heart, not from the heart of the Holy Spirit. For they are unable to say: "But we have the mind of Christ, that we may see the things that have been given to us from God" [cf. 1 Cor 2:16, 12].

(4) Now when he comes upon me, I, who am spoken of as a man of the church,[7] I who receive the Holy Book and who depend on him for the interpretation, to determine what should be understood about the heretics, I request that the hearers pay diligent attention and receive the grace of the Spirit according to what has been spoken: "the discernment of spirits" [1 Cor 12:9–10]. Thus, when they have become approved money changers,[8] they may carefully notice when I am a false teacher, when I truly speak things that are of piety and truth.[9] And so, if I find the mind of Christ in Moses and in the prophets, then I am speaking not out of my own heart but from the Holy Spirit. But if I do not find any agreement, I am fabricating for myself what I am saying. In the words that pour forth that are estranged from God, I am speaking out of my own heart, rather than from the thoughts of God.

I Am Being Addressed

3. "Prophesy, and say to the prophets who prophesy." He does not say simply "from the heart," but "from their own heart. And you will prophesy and say to them: Hear the word of the Lord" [Ezek 13:2]. These things are being said to me; these things are being said to him who promises to be a teacher, in order that a greater fear of God arise within us. Thus, when we take the risk of setting forth these words, we should do so in such a way that this commentary would be written as it were not by men, but by the angels of God. For I know that when that [angelic] order "sits down in the judgment," of which Daniel prophesied, "and the books are opened" [Dan 7:10], all my attempts, all my expositions, will be set forth into public view, whether to my justification or condemnation. What has been said well will indeed be for my justification, but the things that have been explained not as well as the truth

requires will be for my condemnation. "By your words," he says, "you will be justified, and by your words you will be condemned" [Matt 12:37]. He says this as it were to one who does not have all the words by which he deserves to be justified, nor, on the other hand, all words by which he deserves to be condemned. If anyone becomes pure from foreign words and from those which must later be reprehended, he will be justified by his words and will not be condemned. But if he has never spoken rightly, but has always brought forth bad things, he will be condemned by his words and he will not be justified. But because we who are not "perfect in every way" [Eph 4:15; 6:13] do not speak in such a way as always to be justified, nor on the contrary are we such sinners that we are always condemned, and we have some words by which we will be justified and others by which we will be condemned, God puts both on his scales and weighs them carefully. And he judges in what words I am just and in what words I am to be condemned.

(2) And what he does with our words he will also do with our deeds. For necessarily there are some deeds for which we will be justified, and others for which we will be condemned. For I am not so perfect that I have all the deeds for which I should stand forth as a just man, nor am I such a sinner that I do all such things that would condemn me on every side. That there are some of the one kind of deeds and some of the other kind is manifest from what is said: "The sins of some men are manifest, preceding them to judgment, but the sins of others follow; and similarly the good deeds are manifest and what they have otherwise cannot be hidden" [1 Tim 5:24–25]. This applies equally with intellectual matters. That is why even "for the thoughts, whether mutually accusing or making satisfaction between them" [Rom 2:15], a judgment awaits me for everything I do, understand, and speak.[10] And I wait in uncertainty about what there may be in store for me at that judgment. To the degree that the fear of God inspires me the more to receive approval for everything that I have done, so much the more do I need to watch myself. Though I cannot keep myself from all sins, would that I might at least keep away from the most serious ones.

The Heart, the Spirit

(3) The words we have set forth: "Who prophesy from their own heart," are spoken to those to whom it is said: "Hear the word of the

Lord, thus says Adonai the Lord: Woe to those who prophesy from their own heart, who walk after their own spirit" [Ezek 13:2–3]. There are two sins, one of the heart and one of the spirit. Let us first look at the better part, that we may be able to consider likewise the things that are contrary. The apostle says: "I will pray with the spirit, I will pray also with the mind" [1 Cor 14:15]—for the mind has its seat in the heart—"I will sing with the spirit, I will sing also with the mind" [1 Cor 14:15]. Therefore there is both a spirit and a mind in us. And just as the saint prays with the spirit, so he prays also with the mind; he sings with the spirit, he sings also with the mind; so he who is a false prophet prophesies from his own heart and he walks not after the Spirit of God but after his own spirit.[11] For there is a spirit of man that lives in him—far be it from me that I should walk after it!—but I understand the Holy Spirit of God and will walk after the Lord my God.

(4) These prophets, then, who prophesy from the heart and walk after the spirit, not so much God's as their own, "they do not see *at all* (*omnino*)" [Ezek 13:3]. In Greek this latter word is καθόλου. Its meaning in this expression is ambiguous. For either they do not see things that are *universal*, that is, καθολιχά, though they may see, as it were, "in part" [1 Cor 13:9], or (and I regard this as a better interpretation) they do not see *at all*, though to themselves they seem to see "in part" [cf. 1 Cor 13:9], as it were. For there are eyes within us that are better than those that we have in the body. These [inner] eyes either see Jesus the Lord, who created them for seeing him, or, on the other hand, they are completely (*omnino*) blind. If I am a sinner, I see nothing, nor can I view the light of the truth. For it says: "I have come into the world for judgment, that those who do not see may see, and that those who see may become blind" [John 9:39].[12] But if I am just, I receive grace from God, and as a seer it is said of me too: "For prophets were previously called seers" [1 Sam 9:9].[13] He says: "Go, seer, go down to the land of Judah, and live there and prophesy there. But in Bethel you will not continue to prophesy" [Amos 7:12–13]. And again it is said elsewhere: "The vision that Isaiah the son of Amos saw" [Isa 1:1]. Blessed is the one whose eyes the Lord will open to see marvelous things from God's law, according to the prayer of the prophet who said: "Open my eyes and I will consider marvelous things from your law" [Ps 119:18].

Like Foxes in the Desert

4. Now let us consider the other words by which the false prophets and false teachers are rebuked. In order for me to do this, I ask that you pray that I may be found pure. What then is the rebuke? "Your prophets, O Israel, are like foxes in the desert" [Ezek 13:4]. A fox is a bad animal—it is crafty, it is untamable, it is wild.[14] The Savior says: "Tell that fox: Behold I perfect healings today and tomorrow and on the third day I am completed" [Luke 13:32]. Samson had need of these foxes against foreigners. He caught thirty of them, tied torches to their tails, and sent them for the destruction of the enemies' crops [cf. Judg 15:4–5]. False teachers are like that, crafty, wicked, and like wild animals [cf. Jude 10].[15] If I am like that, I am a fox, but not simply a fox, but a fox in the desert, a fox among the ruins, a fox among the rocks. For these variants are contained in different versions.[16] These hypocrites and rascals stay always in the desert; they are always in the solitudes. For whenever a soul is indwelt by God and is full of the Holy Spirit, the teaching of the heretics cannot penetrate it. Their words are not strong enough to break through. But where there is a solitude that is without Christ, when the soul has been deserted by justice [cf. 1 Cor 1:30], there the most evil and poisonous doctrines live.[17] That is why it says: "Your prophets, O Israel, are like foxes in the desert."

(2) "They have not stood in steadfastness[18]" [Ezek 13:4–5]. If you want to consider false teachers, you will see that they are weak, unstable, and unable to say: "He set my feet on the rock, and he directed my steps" [Ps 40:2]. And since they are the sort that do not stand up strongly, well rooted, and founded, therefore "they have not stood in steadfastness," but they have preferred to move their feet. But even this is a great sin, to move the feet even a little, as David the Psalmist sings: "How good is the God of Israel to those who are upright in heart. But my feet almost moved" [Ps 73:1–2]. Blessed and very happy is the one to whom it has been given to have firm feet of the soul for standing very strongly, who is worthy to hear from God: "But you, stand with me" [Deut 5:31]. But false prophets are not like that, nor are false teachers; for "they have not stood in steadfastness."

False Visions

5. "And they were gathering flocks[19] against the house of Israel" [Ezek 13:4–5 LXX]. The flocks refer to those who are taught and instructed, whether by the heretics who preach impious doctrine, or by false teachers who deceive those whose ears they tickle [cf. 2 Tim 4:3]. They gather flocks of schisms against the Church of God,[20] against the house of Israel. "Those who said: 'On the day of the Lord,' though they see false things, have not risen" [Ezek 13:5–6]. They have not risen; but the just, when they rise, say: "We have been buried together with Christ through baptism, and we have risen together with him" [Rom 6:4]. For we have "the pledge of the Holy Spirit" [2 Cor 1:22], whom we will receive in fullness, "after what is perfect comes" [1 Cor 13:10]. Thus [we have] the pledge of the resurrection, since no one has as yet risen from us in the perfect resurrection. And yet, as Paul says, we *have* resurrected: "We have been buried together with Christ through baptism, and we have risen together with him" [Rom 6:4]. Therefore, the false prophets and the false teachers who "said: 'On the day of the Lord,' while seeing false things," have not resurrected; that is, they have not yet attained the baptism of the resurrection. Everything they see is false, nor are they able at any time to see the truth. Take an example. The one who reads the Scripture and takes it in a different sense than it is written, sees the Scripture falsely. But the one who hears the Scripture and, since he has the understanding of the truth within him, interprets it in this way, sees the truth.

(2) Now saints of course do not practice divination. "For there is no divination in Jacob" [Num 23:23]. But sinners practice divination and say false things: "Thus says the Lord, and the Lord has not sent them" [Ezek 13:6]. Listen to the heretics, how they claim to have the tradition of the apostles. Listen to the false teachers, as they affirm that their doctrine is the Lord's doctrine, that their sense agrees with the sense of the prophets, and they say: "Thus says the Lord, and the Lord has not sent them, and they have begun to raise the word. You have not seen a false vision" [Ezek 13:6–7]. For they even want to raise a word in their own defense, on behalf of themselves, but the Lord refutes them and says: "[Is it] not a false vision you have seen, and have you not spoken vain divinations and said: Thus says the Lord, and I have not spoken? Therefore say: Thus says the Lord; because your words are false" [Ezek 13:7–8].

(3) Pray for us, that our words may not be false. Although certain men, by their ignorance of judgment, assert that my words are false, the Lord does not say so, and he will act rightly with us. But if thousands of men said that my words were true, and yet in God's judgment they were false, what good would it do me? The Marcionites[21] say as well that the words of their teacher are true; and those who receive the fictions of Valentinus's fables say that his sect is the strongest. What advantage is there that very many churches have been deceived by heretical depravity and have conspired in their judgment? What is sought is this: that the Lord stand by as a witness of my words, that he approve the things I say when I cite the Holy Scriptures.

Divine Threats

(4) "Therefore behold, I the Lord Adonai speak to you, and I will stretch out my hand against the prophets who see false things" [Ezek 13:8–9]. These threats are against the false teachers and those who speak false things. But let us see what he threatens them for. "They will not be in the instruction of my people" [Ezek 13:9]. The Lord does not chasten sinners in a single manner. God's people are rebuked in one way, and he rebukes foreign people in another way: "Son, do not despise the Lord's instruction, do not grow weary while you are being rebuked by him. For whom the Lord loves, he chastises, and he scourges every son whom he receives" [cf. Prov 3:11–12]. "Rebuke" us, "O Lord," but "in judgment" [Ps 72:2], and not in fury. This is the chastening of God's people. But the chastening of the sinner and of the foreigner is what the just man refused by saying: "Lord, do not rebuke me in your wrath, do not chasten me in your fury" [Ps 6:1]. And so, it is said of false teachers and false prophets: "They will not be in the instruction of my people, nor will they be written in the Scripture[22] of the house of Israel" [Ezek 13:9].[23] Just as it also says elsewhere: "Let them be blotted out of the book of the living, and let them not be written with the just" [Ps 69:28], so now it says: "They will not be written in the Scripture of the house of Israel, and they will not enter into the land of Israel" [Ezek 13:9]. Heretics will live outside the land of promise, which is "an exceedingly good land" [Num 14:7]. We pray that we will be led into it, having first been inscribed into the book of the living [Ps 69:28] by Christ Jesus, "to whom is the glory and power for ages of ages. Amen" [1 Pet 4:11].

HOMILY 3

Against the False Prophets and Elders (Ezekiel 13:1, 17–22; 14:1–8)

SET YOUR FACE

1. First of all, we need to seek the meaning of his words: "Set your face" [Ezek 13:17]. Then, if the Lord grants, we need to investigate: "the daughters of the people prophesying from their own heart" [Ezek 13:17], and who do things for which the "word of God" [Ezek 13:1] chastises them. That there is another face besides this face of our body, though this is clear from many sources, yet it is indicated even from the things that the Apostle records: "But we all with unveiled face, beholding the glory of the Lord, are being transformed into the same image from glory to glory, as from the Spirit of the Lord" [2 Cor 3:18]. All of us human beings have this physical face unveiled, unless we happen to be oppressed by calamities and difficulties. But that face of which the Apostle speaks is covered in many people and unveiled in few. For the person who has confidence in a spotless life, in a sound mind, and in true faith, not only does not have the veil of fraudulent shame and sin, but, because of a pure conscience, "he contemplates the glory of the Lord with an unveiled face" [cf. 2 Cor 3:16, 18]. But far be it from us that we should let this face be veiled! [cf. 1 Cor 11:4].

(2) These few things have been said about the face, that we might be able to understand what the words that follow mean: "Set your face on[1] the daughters of your people" [Ezek 13:17]. This face, that is, the master faculty of our heart, if it is not set on what needs to be understood, so that just as it sees, so will it declare to the hearers,

it does not see what is being viewed. For it is impossible for anyone who fails to set his face, who wanders and wavers and is "borne about by every wind of doctrine" [Eph 4:14], to see what he ought to see, to see as he should see. Therefore, the one who wills to understand must have his face fixed on what he is striving to understand. This is why the first command given to those who would prophesy is always that they set their face. But in order for us too to be able to set our face on the Gospel, on the law, on the prophets, on the apostles, we must set it on Christ and not on the affairs of the world [cf. Matt 13:22]. But when our soul is involved in worldly cares, when it always burns with the hunger to have more, we are not setting our face on the things that God has commanded, but on things that are opposed to God's precepts. Who among us do you think is free from setting his face on things that are forbidden? Who is so careful and cautious that day and night he sets the face of his heart on the things that are commanded?

On the Daughters of Your People

2. Here, too, if we are to understand the present Scripture and the sense in which it is said to the prophet: "Set your face on the daughters of your people," [Ezek 13:17], so that he sees the things he is about to speak, we need to set our understanding and hold a full investigation into the intention of our heart [in order to determine] what it is that is signified. Thus let us draw back from the letter and at last be overcome by reason. Now to be sure, according to the common understanding,[2] there were some "daughters of the people" who are seen "prophesying" the things that follow and who committed sin. "Taking pillows, they sewed them, and having sewn them," they put them not under the head, but "under the elbow" of the hearers. And they "covered the heads of every age" [Ezek 13:18] with veils. These are the things that are reckoned as great sins to the daughters of the people who were prophesying. But who is there who rests on the words, who can say that a person is delinquent and is chastened by God, if he sews pillows and places what has been sewn under the elbow of another? Who can assert that someone is behaving impiously if he makes veils for covering the head of every age? Necessity is imposed upon us by the Scripture itself, though we are unwilling, to draw back from shapes of the letters and to ask that his word, wisdom,

and intention disclose what is closed off and illuminate what is obscure. Thus we may be able to become free from this curse, while we learn what it means for the one against whom the cursed is pronounced.

THEY SEW PILLOWS

3. "Woe," he says, namely "to those who sew pillows under every elbow of the hands" or "of the hand" [Ezek 13:18]. Some people are preoccupied with the life of the body. Not even in a dream do they behold those spiritual delights that the word wishes us to possess when it says: "Delight in the Lord, and he will give you the requests of your heart" [Ps 37:4]. They have no knowledge of the pleasure of the blessed ones, of which it is written: "You will make them drink from the river of your pleasure" [Ps 36:8]. Being lovers of comfort, not lovers of God, they are always seeking to enjoy the delights of the body. Now the "pillow sewed under the elbow of the hands" seems to me to be a symbol of carnal pleasure. For since, when one reclines to take refreshment in the things of the body, we seem to be using things that have been sewn and embroidered with a needle "under the elbow of our hands," perhaps by this figure and token the divine word is laying blame on those teachers who by their empty rhetoric and repeated promises of bliss encourage the crowd of their hearers in their lust, vice, and pleasure. For the Word of God and the God-man[3] should utter what leads to his hearer's salvation, what encourages him to self-control, to a life of sound conduct, to everything in which a man intent upon labor, and not upon lust, should exert himself. Thus he may succeed in obtaining what God has promised. When, therefore, anyone who is well in sympathy with the morals of the people, in order to charm the people who have itching ears, makes the kind of speeches they gladly welcome, speeches that border on pleasure, a teacher of this kind "sews pillows under every elbow of the hand."

(2) It follows that the one who has this sin also makes "cloths for veiling the head of every age" [Ezek 13:18]. Let us also more carefully consider of what the veil is a figure. The man who has confidence and is truly a man wears no veil upon his head. Instead, he prays to God with his head uncovered, he prophesies with head uncovered [cf. 1 Cor 11:4, 7]. In a hidden way he manifests his spiritual reality by the

sign of his bodily attire. Just as he has no veil over his physical head,[4] so he has no veil over the master faculty of his heart. But whoever does the deeds of shame and of sin, he, so to speak, wears womanish veils upon his head. And so, when a man teaches the things that soothe the ears of the people and arouse the applause of his hearers rather than their groans, if like a seductive enemy he has soothed rather than cut out the wounds, a man of this kind weaves cloths for the head. And when the speaker's oration is wasted on exuberant rhetoric, when it prances about in licentious eloquence, he is weaving a veil over the head of every age, not alone of boys and young men, but even of the old. For just as "the false Christ and false prophet will do signs and wonders to deceive, if it be possible, even the elect" [cf. Mark 13:22], similarly these men discharge their elaborated incitements to pleasure. They are ever seeking for things that will charm their hearers rather than convert them from vice. They make veils on the head not only of boys and young men only, but, "if it be possible," of old men and fathers too. This goes on to the point that they deceive even those who through their soul's effort have advanced in spiritual age and maturity.

(3) Well, the prophet could have said: On the *sons* of your people who prophesy. But, as though all who weave veils and sew pillows under every elbow of the hand are women,[5] and none of them deserves the name of man, the prophet says: "On the *daughters* of your people who prophesy out of their own heart," and do the things that follow. Effeminate indeed are the souls and wills of their teachers, who are ever putting together fine-sounding and melodious speeches. Indeed, let me be perfectly honest: There is nothing manly, nothing strong, nothing worthy of God, in the men who preach according to the pleasures and wishes of their hearers. Therefore he has said that all the *daughters* rather than sons are sewing pillows.[6] And note the appropriateness of his term. Sewing, he says, not weaving. Or do you not know that the robe of your Lord Jesus had nothing in it sewn, but "was woven throughout" [cf. John 19:23]? It is these women, then, who with craft and cunning patch word to word, sewing rather than weaving. They make pillows for the repose not of the head but of the elbow, that is, so that the hands may not be at work or grow weary in labor, but be at rest, be at ease, be occupied in those actions that serve our pleasures.

THE LORD WILL TEAR UP THE PILLOWS

4. The following words of the prophet show more clearly that what we are saying really does bear the meaning we have given. He says: "Thus says the Lord Adonai: Behold I am against your pillows on which you turn souls toward destruction" [Ezek 13:20]. He has revealed the enigmas he was concealing by clearly showing that the sewn pillows were for the destruction of souls. Who, then, can hesitate about the words that are read, when he hears that God threatens to tear up such a patchwork and such a pillow? For he says: "Behold"—not I command but—"I myself will tear up the sewn pillows under every elbow of the hand" [Ezek 13:20, 18]. It is God's duty to rebuke every fabric and to destroy all things that are very badly sewn, which are harmful to those who are unwilling to work with their hands, but make use of these leisures. "And I will tear these things," that is, the pillows, "from your arms" [Ezek 13:20]. Now God threatens as one who is mild, that he will tear away the pillows from the arms, so that we will no longer possess things that are put underneath our elbows. "And I will send forth the souls, the souls of those that you are subverting" [Ezek 13:20]. What, then, is the subversion in sewing pillows and in putting them underneath the elbows? But that you may understand the mystery of the words, you will see that the great subversion is in making the man soft in body.

(2) The words of the heretics are like this, where a hard way of life does not exist.[7] You will find that the disciples of Valentinus are dissolute in morals. They aim for nothing strenuous, nothing manly. The sectarians attached to Basilides are the same way. His teaching goes so far as to shamelessly deny the command pertaining to martyrdom.[8] They do not teach what men of the church point out: Be prepared "to take up the cross and follow" the Savior [Matt 16:24]. Therefore, the Word, the Son of God, who speaks these threats, tears away these very badly sewn things. Grant to me, O Christ, that I may tear up every pillow that has been sewn for the luxury of souls.

AND THE VEILS

5. But what else follows? "And I will tear up the veils" [Ezek 13:21]. What does he testify that he is going to tear up? Not only the

pillows but the veils as well. Now the reason he is going to tear them up is so that the head may become bare. In this way, with assured confidence and with not only the face uncovered [cf. 2 Cor 3:18] but also the head, the man of the church will be able constantly to pray. "I will tear up your veils, and I will deliver my people out of your hand" [Ezek 13:21]. Though you subvert the souls with pillows and veils, I, by tearing up these things, will deliver my people. Now God delivers the people by means of a severe way of life that withdraws them from pleasures. "And they will no longer be in your hands for subversion" [Ezek 13:21]. These pillows will no longer be in your hands, you who deceive the hearers. "And you will know that I am the Lord" [Ezek 13:21]. If the pillows had not been ripped to pieces, if I had not torn up the veils, you would not know that I am the Lord. For delights, leisure, and relaxation do not allow him to be known who says: "I am the Lord. Because you wickedly pervert the heart of the just" [Ezek 13:21–22].

(2) Just as in the passage about the signs it is said that they may deceive even the elect [Matt 24:24], so it often comes to pass that heretics trip up even the just. For men love pleasure since, as is immediately obvious, it is tranquil and lascivious and enticing to the senses. It provokes us to its enjoyment. We flee from what is bitter, even though these things may be salutary, and we do not want to exert the effort to be coaxed away from pleasures. We are not aware that it is impossible for the same person to be a lover of pleasure and a lover of God [cf. 1 John 2:15]. That is why the apostle says of the wicked that they are "lovers of pleasure rather than lovers of God" [2 Tim 3:4].

He Will Deliver His People

6. "And I did not turn away to strengthen the hands of the wicked" [Ezek 13:22]. I did not turn away, but I have dispensed everything that was for edification.[9] But these prophetesses, being effeminate souls, "turned away to strengthen the hands of the wicked," that is, that their hand might become stronger in wickedness. "That he should not at all be turned from his evil way and be made alive" [Ezek 13:22], that is, that absolutely no one be converted from his wicked way and made alive. "Therefore you will not see the false things" [Ezek 13:23]. You who teach false things, I will bring it about that you not

advance any further in the prosperous attempt to be able to insinuate what you say. "You will no longer speak by divination, and I will deliver my people out of your hand" [Ezek 13:23]. We pray that God would deliver us as well out of the hand of such teachers who, wherever they are, speak to the pleasures of the hearers. They tear and divide the church, since the majority of them are lovers of pleasure rather than lovers of God. "And you will know that I am the Lord" [Ezek 13:23]. If I convert your divinations, if I silence your lies, then you will know that I am the Lord. This is the first prophecy.

Against the Elders

7. And other things follow that are composed as follows: "And there came to me men of the elders of Israel, and they sat before my face" [Ezek 14:1]. The word of God touches on everything. It leaves unscathed no kind of orders that have been constituted in the church. On the contrary, passing through to all, it desires to heal all, just as now it says some things to the elders.[10] For the things that preceded this were said of the teachers. Therefore, let us also consider what is said of the elders, and strike our very selves, lest any elder among us should be like those that are described below. "And there came to me men of the elders of Israel, and they sat before my face. And the word of the Lord came to me, saying: son of man" [Ezek 14:1–3]. Let us look at the accusation, that we may be able to know whether we can detect it in ourselves. "Have not these men set their thoughts in their hearts and set a punishment of their iniquities before their face? Shall I not indeed answer them?" [Ezek 14:3]. "Blessed are the pure in heart" [Matt 5:8]. For those who have a pure heart do not put their own thoughts into their hearts, but they have them rather in the Word of God. But those who labor in worldly cares, and seek for nothing else but how they may pass the present life, put their own thoughts into their hearts. For example, if you see a man thinking about nothing else except the business of the world and physical gains and abundance of food, of those things that he lacks, of those things for which he is anxious, for which he sighs, who seeks only future nourishment with grief, he has put the penalty of his own thoughts into his heart.

(2) Therefore he is rebuking certain elders who are like this, and the divine word says to the prophet: "These men"—that is, the

previously mentioned elders—"have put their own thoughts into their hearts and they have put the penalty of their iniquities before their face" [Ezek 14:3]. Let none of us think that torments are inflicted upon us by anyone but ourselves. God does not make punishments, but we ourselves prepare the things that we suffer. And so, here again we can appropriately use the citation that we have frequently used:[11] "Walk in the light of your fire and in the flame that you have kindled" [Isa 50:11]. The fire is not someone else's but "yours," for you who have heaped up the wood, the straw, and the material for the fire that is coming [cf. 1 Cor 3:12].

MAN, MAN

8. So then, he says of the elders—and may this be far from us!—"These men have put their own thoughts into their hearts, and they have put the penalty of their iniquities before their face; should I not indeed respond to them?" [Ezek 14:3]. For is it not fitting for me to respond to those who came to you, prophet, wanting to learn my words? "Therefore speak to them and say to them: Thus says the Lord Adonai: Man-man[12] from the house of Israel" [Ezek 14:4]. All men are born men, but we are not all "men-men," just as I have very frequently noted what is written in Leviticus: "Man-man of the sons of Israel, or of the strangers who are among you" [Lev 17:8]. *Be* men-men, namely, because not all *are* men-men. Let us show from the Scriptures why some are not men-men. "When the man was in honor, he did not understand; he has been compared with foolish beasts and he has been likened to them" [Ps 49:12]. That is not a man-man but a beast-man. "Generation of vipers, who warned you to flee from the coming wrath?" [Matt 3:7]. This type is not a man-man but a serpent-man. "The horses have become mad for the females, each one was neighing for his neighbor's wife" [Jer 5:8]. That one is not a man-man but a horse-man.[13] Far be it from us, then, to be the sort that deserve to hear that we are not men, but something other than men. For if we are good and gentle, we double the term *man*, so that among us one would not simply be a man but a man-man. Consider whether we are strong enough to find what that is that doubles the name of man. When that man who is outer is a man, while that which is inner is from the serpent man, there is no man-man in us, but just a man. But when

the inner man has persevered in the image of the Creator, then a man is born, and he thus becomes, according to the outer and inner man, a double man-man.[14] Further, whenever someone who has been called to become a man-man puts his own thoughts into his heart and puts his own punishment before his face and comes to the prophet, it says: "I, the Lord, will respond to him about those things in which his mind is detained" [Ezek 14:4].

Appropriate Remedies

(2) The present words teach us how it is necessary to respond to each person. We are not to employ inappropriate medicines, but to bring forth each one matching the condition of the diseases. Pay attention to what we are saying. Ten men go to a physician having ten kinds of illnesses. He does not cure them all in the same way, but he heals one, for example, by this or that medicated plaster; to another he gives some medicine; to several he applies what is called cautery; another he soothes with a bitter potion; another by a sweet one; and on someone else's wounds he smears a very heavy ointment. This is how the Word of God addresses the conditions of men. He does not cast the mysteries of his wisdom everywhere. And so it says: "I will respond to him for the things in which his mind is detained," namely, as I cure those things "in which his mind is detained, so that he not cause the house of Israel to turn aside" [Ezek 14:5]. Whoever does not present himself as an example of a good life, but has "walked perversely" [Lev 26:40], that one by his own depravity, while he is inclined toward things that he should not be, in some way causes even the people of God[15] "to turn aside according to their hearts that are estranged from me" [Ezek 14:5]. And the one who does this does it "in accordance with a heart that is estranged" from God "in their thoughts" [Ezek 14:5]. Therefore, a response is given to them for these things in which their heart is detained, and it is said: "Speak to the house of Israel: Thus says the Lord Adonai: Be converted and turn away from your practices" [Ezek 14:6]. Since he had promised to speak to those for the things in which their heart is detained, therefore now he speaks as if to sinners, saying: "Be converted and turn yourselves away from your practices, and turn away your faces" [Ezek 14:6]. Is it not clear to you that he does this? Your faces are set on

things that they ought not to be. Convert them and set them on things that are for your benefit.

(3) "Therefore the man-man[16] from the house of Israel and from the proselytes who come to Israel, whoever has been estranged" [Ezek 14:7]. It can happen that a man-man, either the created man-man, or the one who has become a man-man through his own progress, is estranged, if indeed according to the same Ezekiel even the just is converted whenever "from his justices he even sins" [Ezek 3:20]. If, then, a man like this "has put his own thoughts into his heart and the penalty of his own iniquities before his face, and he comes to the prophet to ask him about me, I," he says, "the Lord, will respond to him for that in which he is detained, and I will set my face against that man" [Ezek 14:7–8]. Consider how in the beginning he promised to respond mildly, and then how, if again he does not get cured by the first words, he said, "I will set my face against that man, and I will put him in the desert" [Ezek 14:8]. For if he did not obey the words of warning, but persevered in transgression, "I will put him in the desert and in banishment, and I will remove him from the midst of my people" [Ezek 14:8]. Do not remove us, Almighty God, from the midst of your people, but preserve us in your people. But justly is he cast out who acts in a manner worthy of rejection, so that he is removed from the people of God, and he is uprooted from it and "is handed over to Satan" [1 Cor 5:5].

(4) Now to be sure, at present one who departs from the people of God can again return by means of penitence; but if he is uprooted from that people, it is with very great difficulty that he returns to his original place. I base this on what is said in one of the parables, that a certain man came and entered and reclined who did not have wedding clothes. The householder said to him: "Friend, how did you enter here without wedding clothes?" and then he commands the attendants "to bind his hands and feet and to cast him into the outer darkness" [Matt 22:11]. But we will not be uprooted, on the contrary, both in the present and in the future age we will be planted in our Lord Jesus Christ and in him we will bear fruit in superabundance, "to whom is the glory and the power for ages of ages. Amen."[81]

HOMILY 4

The Famine and the Ferocious Beasts (Ezekiel 14:12–22)

Threats

1. "The word of the Lord," which came to the prophet, speaks about "the sinful[1] earth[2]" [Ezek 14:12–13]. On account of its transgressions it is tormented by various punishments, by famine, evil beasts, the sword, death—indeed sudden death, which either is created from the problem of corrupt air or happens by some event. And it is said: "But even if I send my four vengeances upon the sinful earth, and though these three men, Noah, Daniel, and Job should be on the sinful earth, they alone will be saved" [Ezek 14:21, 16].[3] In the first threat in which he separated the penalty of famine from the other penalties, he was silent about the terms *sons* and *daughters;* but in these words in which he has threatened evil beasts on the earth [Ezek 14:15], he says: "Will their sons and daughters be saved? On the contrary they themselves alone will be saved , but the earth…"—and since he was somewhat reticent, he added: "And [the earth] will be for destruction" [Ezek 14:15]. Again, in the threat of the sword, he says: "They will not deliver sons or daughters" [Ezek 14:18]. And likewise with death he has said: "Their sons or daughters will not be left, but they themselves alone; Noah, Daniel, and Job will deliver their souls" [Ezek 14:19–20].

Sinful Earth

(2) I am overwhelmed with great anxiety concerning the explanation of this passage. And for that reason, let us pay diligent attention. I plead with the hearers to focus the acuteness of their intelligence, as if they were poring over some grand spectacle.[4] Otherwise, an obscure detail may slip past when your senses are relaxed. In the present text he did not say: If the inhabitants of some city or place sin, but: "If the earth sins."[5] Now I know that when a more simple person hears: "If the earth sins," he arrives at once at a facile interpretation and thinks that the earth he has named is said for those who live on the earth;[6] but the Scriptures that follow immediately rule out this explanation. For "when the earth sins," and falls into its own sins, "the hand is stretched forth," not on those inhabiting the earth but "on the earth" itself, and it is laid waste in the first chastisement, so that "the support of bread is removed from it" [Ezek 14:13]. That is to say, it is as if the punishment is on the earth, whenever a famine occurs on it, as seed crops are denied to it. For it is similar to the way a sinful *man* is punished when he has no offspring and is among the cursed when he is sterile. This accords with what is written in a certain passage, where it is said of the just man: "He will not be without offspring nor sterile among you" [Exod 23:26]. For contraries are understood from contraries. Thus, sinners are condemned with eternal infertility when they are without children and without their own posterity. This is what happened to the house of Abimelech and to those for whom "God closed the womb" [Gen 20:18] on account of the sin that was committed in connection with Isaac. In the same way, the earth is somehow left without offspring and becomes sterile, when a famine has been sent against it.

(3) Do you think it is true that what the word begins to affirm is being said not about the inhabitants of the earth but about the earth itself? By ascending briefly to higher things, I can prove through scriptural testimonies how the earth may be called a sinner.[7] For it is said to Adam: "You are earth and you will go into the earth" [Gen 3:19]. We can say that even now the earth, by transgressing, is a sinner (*peccator*). But conversely, when I survey the very extensive forest of Scripture, I am compelled to surmise that this earth that we see is a living being. For if we want to understand what is written: "He who looks over the earth and makes it tremble" [Ps 104:32], as it is written,

we understand that the movements of the earth are occasioned by the sight of God. It is not as the Jews surmise. For they assert that a tremor of the earth is its own movement. This is far removed from the truth. For even we ourselves are anxious and trembling on the earth on account of our sins, yet our trembling does not occasion a trembling of the body. As it says in another place: "Upon whom shall I look," says the Lord, "if not on the one who is humble and quiet and who trembles at my words?" [Isa 66:2]. From this it is manifest that the one who serves God meekly also trembles humbly at his words, mentally rather than physically. And these things have been said openly in order to give a satisfactory explanation of the reference we have brought forward: "He who looks at the earth and makes it tremble" [Ps 104:32]. But you should take the other statements as having been said about the earth as well: "The earth is offended by those who occupy it" [Isa 24:5]. How is the earth offended, and when does it turn away from those who live in it? When they become sinners.

Sabbaths

(4) Take another example: "The land[8] will enjoy itself on its Sabbaths" [Lev 26:43]. For on the contrary, one speaks of Sabbaths of the land in which it enjoys itself and rejoices. I say nothing for the moment about: "Attend, O heaven, and let me speak; and let the earth hear the words of my mouth" [Deut 32:1]; nor this: "Hear, O heaven, and with the ears, perceive, O earth" [Isa 1:2]; nor the prophecy of Jeremiah: "Land, land, hear the word of the Lord: Record this man as disinherited" [Jer 22:29–30]. Many things are concealed from us on account of the poverty of our memory and the dullness of our wits. There are many things that God created as rational and that are capable of receiving, not only the "principalities and powers, and rulers of this darkness" [Eph 6:12], but also, in their better part, "thrones, lordships" [Col 1:16], and the other things that the Apostle left to our understanding, when he says: "And over every name that is named, not only in this age but also in the future" [Eph 1:21]. The air too is full of living beings according to the testimony of the same Apostle, when he proclaims: "In which you once walked according to the age of this world, according to the ruler of the power and of the spirit of the air, which is now at work in the sons of faith-

lessness" [Eph 2:2]. So then, there is the earth and all the living things and varieties of animals by groups. For when the earth is offended and again enjoys itself on its Sabbaths, it is not entirely offended, nor does it entirely exult. For in some manner, it is instructed with its inhabitants, and it learned to celebrate the Sabbaths, whether in shadow or in truth, according to the condition of its nature. This is why, by a more mysterious interpretation, the Sabbath is practiced after seven years of holy earth, until it pleases God to dwell in it; but if they become sinners on it, the land no longer bears the Sabbath every seven years, but seventy. We have the word about seventy years certified in the sacred literature, both in Jeremiah and in Daniel [cf. Lev 25:4; Jer 25:11; Dan 9:2].

On the Day of Judgment

(5) And it will happen in the future that on the day of judgment not only man but also all creation will be judged. For "every creature groans together and suffers grief together" [Rom 8:22]. If every creature groans and suffers grief together, but there is a portion of creatures, earth and heaven and those in the air, some of which are under the heavens and some of which are above the heavens, and "all creation will be set free from slavery to corruption into the freedom of the glory of the sons of God" [Rom 8:21], then who knows also about the earth, whether it is held accountable for any sin according to its own nature? For if it is a living creature, if it is rational, if it needs to hear the prophetic words saying: "Attend, O heaven, and let me speak; and let the earth hear the words of my mouth" [Deut 32:1], and: "Listen, O heaven, and perceive with the ears, O earth" [Isa 1:2], why should we not say that, just as among men there is a man who hears and does the words that he has been commanded to do, and there is another who hears and does not fulfill what is commanded, so also an angel may transgress. For "the angels who did not keep their rulership but deserted their own abode, he will reserve in eternal chains under the darkness for the judgment on the great day" [Jude 6]. So then, even angels transgress, and there are some who keep God's commands. Not only do men await the judgment, but so do the angels of God, as we have frequently said. This is the case for those who are described in the Apocalypse [cf. Rev 12:7–9] and of the others who are too numerous

to count [cf. Rev 7:9]. Why, then, I repeat, will there not be a future judgment of earth and air? But if you think there is need to be in agreement with this argumentation, by which we have asserted that every creature must be judged, hear even another testimony about the earth. God asks Cain who killed Abel his brother. And after many words that we read in Genesis, at the end he says of the earth: "Cursed is the earth that opened its mouth to receive from your hand the blood of your brother" [Gen 4:9, 11]. I do not pass over the following: "Cursed is the earth in your works" [Gen 3:17]. And conversely, if at some time it is blessed, we read indeed in God's words both of a "cursed" and a "blessed earth" [Rom 8:22]. You see, then, that it is deservedly said: "Every creature groans together" [Rom 8:22].

Like a Mother

(6) Let me return to the preceding example: "The earth is offended by those who inhabit it" [Isa 24:5]. I think that the earth is like a mother who sustains us. It rejoices over good sons, and it grieves over sinners. For "a foolish son is anger to his father, and grief to her that bore him" [Prov 17:25]. This applies not only to that father and mother from whose seed we descend, but also to that mother which is truly our mother. And "God took the dust of the earth and formed man" [Gen 2:7]. Therefore, the earth is our mother. It rejoices, when it sustains a just son. The earth rejoiced in bearing Abraham, Isaac, and Jacob; the earth rejoiced at the coming of my Lord Jesus Christ, when it saw that it was worthy of sustaining the Son of God. What need is there to speak of the apostles and prophets, since it is written about the coming of the Lord: "All the earth shouts with joy" [Isa 24:14]? Even the wretched Jews admit that these things are predicted about the presence of the Christ, but they foolishly ignore the person, when they see the fulfillment of the things that were spoken. For when, before the coming of Christ, did the land of Brittany[9] agree with the religion of the one God? When did the land of the Moors[10]? When did the whole earth ever do this? But now, thanks to the churches that possess the ends of the world,[11] the whole earth shouts with joy to the God of Israel, and it is capable of good deeds in accordance with its own boundaries. "And he appointed the boundaries of the nations accord-

ing to the number of the sons of Israel[12], and his people Jacob became the Lord's portion, Israel is the line of his inheritance" [Deut 32:8].

Culpable

(7) It is capable, I say, as a living being, in accordance with the characteristics of its portions, of both good and evil actions for which it earns either praise or punishment. So then, when it is said: "the earth that sinned against me when it committed transgression" [Ezek 14:13], this is indicating a certain mystery. For one speaks one way about inhabitants, another way about that which is inhabited. "Heaven and earth shall pass away" [Matt 24:35]. Why is the heaven passing away, why is the earth passing away, unless they committed certain acts that made them worthy of passing away? And in another passage it says: "The whole earth is corrupt" [Gen 6:11]. When did it become corrupt? Before the flood, not that it was corrupted through the inundation of the flood. That is why he says: "The earth that sinned against me when it committed transgression, I will stretch forth my hand and I will crush its support of bread" [Ezek 14:13]. God "stretches forth his hand against the sinful land, he sends famine into it" [Ezek 14:13].

Our Soul

(8) There is also another way in which I can interpret the words "The earth" at some time "commits transgression" [Ezek 14:12]. For the earth is our soul, just as the soul in the parable of the Gospel is signified by "rock," "good earth," and "fertile through much patience."[13] Therefore, this earth frequently sins, frequently it does not sin.[14] And if it sins, God stretches out his hand against it, and he crushes the whole support of its bread. Almighty God, do not crush the support of bread from this earth, that is, from our soul, but rather enlarge your seed for us that it may become one hundredfold fruit in us [Matt 13:8, 23; cf. 2 Cor 9:10].

Famine

2. "And I will send forth famine upon it, and I will remove from it man and beast" [Ezek 14:13]. How can I bring out such hidden matters into the public? From what source will I be able to explain the reasons why famine, fertility, abundance, and scarcity occur on earth? "O the depth of the riches of the wisdom and knowledge of God!" [Rom 11:33]. Is the famine sent because of men and the evil in their souls, or on account of angels? Are the things that we see happening the effects of the earthly things that the angels committed when they sinned? But if there are certain attendants of heavenly providence who preside over the crops, perhaps also because of them the earth's infertility occurs.[15] For most of his works "are hidden" [Sir 16:21]. We cannot declare the greatness of his wisdom. "Who will number the sand of the sea and the drops of rain and the days of the age? Who will search out the height of heaven and the breadth of the earth and the depth of wisdom?" [Sir 1:2–3]. Therefore, famine is sent against the sinful earth in different ways.

Man and Beast

3. He says: "And I will remove from it man and beast" [Ezek 14:13]. Earth is one thing; man is something else (for he is not now naming the inhabitants of the earth for the earth, as some think).[16] For if he wants the inhabitants of the earth to be understood for the earth, it would have been superfluous to say: "I will remove from it man and beast." For the earth rejoices when it is full of inhabitants; it grieves when that which is said to it comes to pass: "I will remove from it man and beast." We want to explain a few things about these things, if the Lord will administer the meaning while you pray—but only if we become capable of receiving the Lord's meaning. Just as there is punishment of the mother who was destined for exile, that she be deprived of her sons, or at least that she see her sons destined for another province, so in some way our mother, the earth, is scourged by God for its sins, when man and beast are removed from her. She rejoices, when she has men, but even more when she has the best men and those who live in the practices of God, as we have explained above. Therefore, it is said: "When the earth sins," as if it is being said:

"If, when the mother sins, I will remove her son from the house, so also now "I will remove the man from her." For the earth does not rejoice over rabid and wild beasts, but over domesticated animals, since she loves animate beings that are placid and gentle.

Three Men

4. "And I will remove from her man and beast. And though these three men were in her midst" [Ezek 14:13–14]. How can the number of these three equally live in the sinful land? How can the lives of those who lived in such diverse times be joined among them? At present we read that they exist equally in the sinful land: that is, Noah, who lived during the flood; and Daniel, who lived during the Babylonian captivity; and Job, who is testified to have lived during the times of the patriarchs and of Moses. For we have discovered that this was when Job lived. What then can we say? We need to remember, as we have already said repeatedly, that as a man begets a man, so Israel begets Israel; for when Israel was Jacob [Gen 32:28], it begot the people of Israel. And in the Scriptures we have found that the name of Israel is given both to a single man and to the whole people. Thus, not only does Israel beget Israel, but also Reuben begets Reuben, and Simeon Simeon, and Levi Levi, and Judah Judah, and all the rest who are in the tribe of Judah are declared to come from the stock of Judah, and the Scriptures are replete with names of Judah for the tribe of Judah. What is said in Moses, in the section about the blessings of Jacob, concerning Reuben, Simeon, Levi, and Judah [Gen 49:3–12], does not really correspond to the other patriarchs as much as to those who bore their names on account of the root of their family.

Spiritual Descent

(2) "Benjamin is a ravenous wolf. He devours in the morning and will give food in the evening" [Gen 49:27]. That Benjamin was never a ravenous wolf, that Benjamin never gave food in the evening. But he who was born "from the tribe of Benjamin, a Hebrew of Hebrews, according to the law a Pharisee, circumcised on the eighth

day" [Phil 3:5], he was predicted to be a Benjamin, a ravenous wolf, devouring in the morning (when he was a young man), and giving food in the evening (when as a believer he offered spiritual food from himself to the churches he had established). Therefore, Benjamin begets a Benjamin. And so, just as a man is born from a man, and a Benjamin from Benjamin, so a Judah is born from Judah, a Reuben from Reuben. For "let Reuben live and not die, and let him be many in number" [Deut 33:6]. This shows how much the word was not about the patriarch but about the people who would descend from the patriarch.

(3) Why have I said these things? Obviously so that I might explain the present passage about Noah, Daniel, and Job. For just as Israel begets Israel, and Jacob Jacob, and Reuben Reuben, and the rest the rest, so Noah begets a Noah. And I would say that from the sons of Noah, Seth[17] was of Noah [cf. Gen 4:25], but Ham was not of Noah [Gen 5:31]; for he did not have the likeness of his father. And just as not all who are *from* Abraham are Abraham's sons [cf. Gal 3:7]—though they may be from his seed, they are not his sons, since they are sinners—so those who have the likeness of the deeds of Daniel are Daniel's, those who imitate the patience of Job become Job's. So do not say: "Blessed is Noah, since he alone was worthy to be chosen by the Lord at the time of the flood. And while the rest perished in the inundation, he was preserved unscathed with his own." Rather, consider that you too will be Noah's, if you do the things that Noah did. Hear the Savior saying: "If you were sons of Abraham, you would do the works of Abraham" [John 8:39]. Therefore, to be a son of Abraham is to do the deeds of Abraham; to be a son of Noah is to do the work of Noah; to be a son of Daniel is to do what Daniel did.[18] The imitator of Job is the one who follows the things by means of which Job became glorious [Job 40:5, 10]. For example, this applies to anyone who loses his property, and who patiently endures the loss of the family's goods as well as the deaths of children, and says: "The Lord gave, the Lord has taken away, as it has seemed good to the Lord, thus it has been done, may the name of the Lord be praised in the ages" [Job 1:21]. It applies to the one who is burned by physical evils and is scourged by different kinds of grief over these evils and who nevertheless glorifies God in the midst of these punishments. It applies to the one who can give a response that is worthy of God and who can utter prophetic words in the midst of excruciating torments,

such as Job uttered. And so also, in this manner, Noah and Daniel and Job can be found at the same time.

5. But we will attempt to prove out of another passage as well that Ezekiel has not spoken here about those men of whom we repeatedly read in the Scriptures, namely, those whom either transfer[19] or death removed from the present life. Daniel, who was handed over to the leader of the eunuchs with Ananias, Azariah, and Mishael, was a eunuch [cf. Dan 1:3, 6], and in the present passage it is said: "Noah, Daniel, and Job will not deliver the sons and daughters" [Ezek 14:14, 18], etc. Now obviously Noah had sons, but let us try to imagine how Daniel will be shown to have had sons, since the Jews have the tradition that he was a eunuch.[20] Well, since his soul was fertile and holy, and since by prophetic and divine words he procreated many children, therefore it is said: "If for instance Noah and Job and Daniel were present at this time or that, they alone will be saved" [Ezek 14:14, 18]. So then, even we can become a Daniel, and lest I enumerate all the saints, I can be a Paul, if I become an imitator of him who says: "Be imitators of me" [1 Cor 11:1]. This will happen if I have the cautery by which Paul was marked [cf. Gal 6:17], if I possess the same form by which he was formed in Christ, through which he said like a good father: "My little children, for whom I suffer birth pains again until Christ is formed in you" [Gal 4:19]. But if I am exposed for bearing a counterfeit resemblance, since Paul had a different form than I have in my soul, then I am deceiving myself when I say: You are his son, you are Paul's seed.

(2) Do not be amazed that you may become the apostle's son. If you possess the virtues, you will even become Christ's son.[21] For he says: "Little sons, I am with you still for a little while" [John 13:33]. But when you become Christ's, you will also belong to the Almighty Father, since they are of a single and united nature. The just man labors to this end; he turns all his effort unto this, that he may ascend to the adoption of God as a son of Daniel, Job, Noah, and Abraham; that he may no longer be called by the names of men, but by the designations of the sons of God. "If then these three men were [here]" [Ezek 14:14]. The Holy Spirit does not now require to point out as well Noah, Daniel, and Job.

6. "These three men in the midst of it" [Ezek 14:14]. A learned hearer says to me: three are named in the present passage, but you speak of many Daniels, Jobs, and Noahs. Let me respond to this person as follows. Every multitude of things that are similar is one, and

many who are similar are not many bodies, but they are all one body, according to what is written: "But you are the body of Christ and members in part" [1 Cor 12:27]. And our Savior came to seek and to save what was lost [cf. Luke 19:10], in the mystery of the ninety-nine sheep who were not astray and of the one that was lost [cf. Luke 15:4–7; Matt 18:12–14]. "For the Son of man came to seek and to save what was lost" [Luke 19:10]. For just as many bodies are one body, and the many sheep that were lost are one sheep, in this manner all Noahs, Daniels, and Jobs are reduced to one Noah, Daniel, and Job.

7. "They will be saved by their own justice, says the Lord Adonai" [Ezek 14:14]. God's proper name[22] consists of four letters and is naturally translated "God." Therefore, "famine is sent on the earth on account of sins" [Ezek 14:13]. This refers to the earth according to all the meanings of which we have spoken above, and whatever we have left to the understanding of the hearers. Thus, from our statements they may discover other interpretations for themselves.

Ferocious Beasts

(2) But let us see even another work of divine wrath that "sends evil beasts upon the sinful land" [Ezek 14:13, 15]. Even the Jews say: if at some time wolves and other beasts devour men and make an attack upon homes—as history relates that one time lions were sent against the human race [cf. 2 Kgs 17:25], and at another time bears [cf. 2 Kgs 2:24]—maulings like that proceed from the indignation of God. And when we follow the letter and hold back from the deeper meaning, we see that the prophet follows this sense for the time being. But "he who is spiritual, who judges all things, and is judged by no one" [1 Cor 2:15] confidently says that there are many beasts that God sends against the sinful land, but only if our land sins: "Our adversary the devil roams about like a roaring lion, seeking whom he may devour" [1 Pet 5:8]. Even in the historical narrative that offers a plain interpretation to those who carefully observe the Scriptures, there is this kind of signification, when "two bears were sent against the little children, who were insulting the prophet, saying: 'Come down, baldy, come down baldy'" [2 Kgs 2:23–24]. For those bears were a symbol of other beasts that are truly ferocious, truly savage, which are sent against this sinful earth. But far be it from us that beasts be

sent against us for God's vengeance. Rather, may we say in prayer: "Do not hand over to beasts a soul that praises you" [Ps 74:19]. I have known just men who persevered in the faith who were handed over to wild beasts and were torn to pieces by them. They consummated martyrdom, and yet they did not cease to be blessed. For they were not handed over to the spiritual and invisible beasts that tear apart the souls of sinners and fasten their teeth into the hearts of the impious. For "as when a shepherd removes from the mouth of lions two legs or a piece of an ear, so shall the sons of Israel be removed" [Amos 3:12]. At times, then, the land is handed over to beasts for destruction "so that man and beast may be removed from it" [Ezek 14:13].

Different Threats

8. Observe carefully the differences in the threats. In the first threat he speaks of famine: "They alone shall be saved, Noah, Daniel, and Job" [Ezek 14:14]. But in the second one, where it is reported that beasts will be sent, it speaks of sons and daughters [Ezek 14:15]. "Nevertheless they alone will be saved, says the Lord Adonai" [Ezek 14:16]. This passage is understood in two ways. Let us explain the first, in accordance with the common meaning. We need to do this on account of the folly of many who identify the interpretation of their own mind with the truth of God. They frequently say: "It will happen that each of us by his own prayers will snatch anyone he wants from Gehenna" [cf. Jas 5:20], and they introduce iniquity to the Lord, for they do not see that "the justice of the just man will be upon him and the iniquity of the unjust will be upon him," and each one "will die in his own sin and will live by his own justice" [Ezek 18:20, 22, 24]. Having a father who was a martyr does me no good, if I do not live well myself and adorn the nobility of my descent.[23] That is, I must adorn his testimony and confession by which he was illustrious in Christ [cf. Rom 16:7, 13]. It does not profit the Jews when they say: "We have not been born from fornication, we have one father, God" [John 8:41]; and a little later: "Abraham is our father" [John 8:39]. Whatever they may have said, whatever they may have wanted to assume for themselves, if they do not have Abraham's faith, they boast in vain. For they will not be saved simply because they are sons of Abraham. Since then some do not think rightly, by necessity we have

inserted the meaning of the letter as well, which says: "Noah, Daniel, and Job will not deliver the sons and daughters, but they themselves alone will be saved" [Ezek 14:18, 14]. Let none of us put trust in a just father, in a holy mother, in chaste brothers. "Blessed is the man who has hope in himself" [Ps 34:8] and in an upright life. But to those who have confidence in the saints, it is not unfitting for us to bring forward a citation: "Cursed is the man who has hope in man" [Jer 17:5], and the following: "Do not trust in men" [Ps 146:3], and even another: "It is better to trust in the Lord than to trust in princes" [Ps 118:8–9]. But if it is necessary to hope in anyone, when all others have been forsaken, let us hope in the Lord, saying: "Though they set up encampments against me, my heart will not fear" [Ps 27:3].

Why Three?

(2) Since these things are so, another question arises for us that we should carefully investigate in order that the truth of the Scriptures might shine forth. Seeing that there are so many just men, why are only three named now, Noah, Daniel, and Job? Once I heard a Hebrew[24] who was explaining this passage say that the reason these men are named is because each of them had seen three periods of time, a joyful period, a sad one, and again a joyful one.

(3) Picture Noah before the flood. Consider the world when it was intact, and then afterward the same Noah alone with his sons and animals was saved in the ark from the shipwreck of the entire world. Consider how after the flood he went forth and planted a vineyard, standing forth again as it were as a creator of a second world.[25] Such is the just man. He sees the world before the flood, that is, before the consummation.[26] He sees the world during the flood, that is, during the corruption and destruction of sinners, which is coming on the day of judgment. Then he will again see the world in the resurrection of all sinners [cf. John 5:28–29; Dan 12:2].

(4) Someone may say to me: I grant that Noah saw three periods of time. But what will you respond about Daniel? Before the captivity he flourished here in his native land in nobility, and then he became a eunuch when he was transferred to Babylon, as can be understood plainly from that book of his. He also saw the return to Jerusalem [Dan 1:3]. Now in order to prove that he was in Jerusalem before the

captivity and became a eunuch after the captivity, we cite what is said to Hezekiah: "They will take your sons and make them eunuchs in the house of the king" [Isa 39:7]. Then, after seventy years, he is found "praying to God," so that when the time of captivity is completed, he might again enter Jerusalem [cf. Dan 9:2–4]. We have his prayer written in his own book [cf. Dan 9:4–19], yet we cannot find where he died. Therefore, he saw three periods of time, before the captivity, during the captivity, and after the captivity. Such is the just man.

(5) But let us see whether Job too had three time periods. Certainly he was rich, for he had "seven thousand sheep, three thousand camels, fifty yoke of oxen and exceedingly many household goods, seven sons and three daughters" [cf. Job 1:3, 2]. Then the devil received power against him. See how the times changed. A father rich with children suddenly becomes bereft of them; a lord rich in fortune is reduced to extreme poverty [cf. Job 2:12]. Behold two time periods. After these things, the Lord appears to him and speaks to him from a cloud, and Job himself responds in the things that are written in his book [cf. Job 38:1]. Therefore, in the first time period he is recommended by the praises of God; in the second he is handed over to temptation, and, "having been struck by a very horrible ulcer from head to foot" [cf. Job 2:7], he experiences hard and grievous sufferings. In the end, there came fourteen thousand sheep, six thousand camels, a thousand yoke of oxen, a thousand pasturing she-asses and seven sons and three daughters are born to him [cf. Job 42:12–13]. And thus even in Job we find the three periods of time that we find in just men. The just see three time periods, the present, the time of change when God will judge, and the future after the resurrection of the dead, that is, the perpetuation of heavenly life in Christ Jesus, "to whom is the glory and power for ages of ages. Amen" [1 Pet 4:11].

HOMILY 5

Sword, Death, Vine (Ezekiel 14:13–21; 15:1–4)

The Sword

1. The famine that is inflicted on account of the sinful land has been discussed to the best of our abilities.[1] After the famine, we spoke about the evil beasts that God will send against sinners.[2] For at the beginning we set forth the four vengeances, of which the remaining two are the double-edged sword and death. Now in the first, the term *sons and daughters* is passed over in silence. In the second, however, and in the third, which we are now trying to explain, the term *sons and daughters* is added, that is, to the "double-edged sword" by which those fall who have done things worthy of slaughter. What, then, is this sword—that is, the double-edged sword—which we need to fear, lest it be sent against our land, against the land that we have explained figuratively, lest we have to pass through the sword, but through the sword that punishes in two ways? For it is of the nature of a sword to divide and cut the one against whom it is applied. But if, in addition to the sharpness of the point, its very touch also inflicts pain, the one who has to be punished by this sword is tormented in two ways. For it is written: "He placed a flaming double-edged sword and cherubim and to guard the way to the tree of life" [Gen 3:24]. And just as when a sharp and red-hot sword is thrust into a body, it causes two kinds of pain, burning and cutting, so also does the double-edged sword that is recorded to have been set up to guard paradise, which we have now cited for the sake of explaining the present sword. It inflicts torments in two ways, as it burns and cuts.

The Iron and the Fire

(2) Now in order that we might insert something essential in the present passage from the things with which God enlightens our mind, take an example. Experts in the art of medicine say that some bodily cures require not merely cutting with a knife but also burning. For to those who are deteriorating with an advanced cancer, they apply either a heated metal plate to a razor, or some kind of extremely sharp iron instrument, in order that by means of fire the roots of the cancer may be removed. Through the incision, the putrid flesh is cut out, and the way stands open for medicines to be introduced. Who among us, do you think, has a sin—dare I say it?—like cancer? Well, for him the simple edge of an iron instrument is not enough, nor a solitary burning with fire. Rather, both need to be applied, so that the man is both burned and cut into. Hear the Savior indicating the rationale for fire and sword[3] in two passages. In one passage he says: "I have not come to cast peace on earth, but a sword" [Matt 10:34]; and in another passage: "I have come to cast fire on the earth, and would that it were already burning!" [Luke 12:49]. Therefore the Savior brings both sword and fire; and he baptizes you with sword and fire. For those who are not cured by the baptism of the Holy Spirit he baptizes with fire, since they were unable to be purged by the purification of the Holy Spirit.

Divine Mysteries

(3) Divine mysteries are ineffable and known to God alone, yet they consist more in the giving of gifts than in different kinds of torments. For physicians are not acting rationally by the practice of their art, when they cut, burn, and give a potion of extremely bitter nature, and the many other things they do, as the case demands. But the God and Lord of the universe does not merely inflict punishments on sinners, without any rational wisdom and without a providential care that is worthy of his majesty.[4] For it is not as they think,[5] that he applies penalties only for the purpose of tormenting; but as a Father he knows the wounds of all of us, he knows from what cause a given ulcer has arisen, what deterioration is produced in a wretched soul and

from what commencement this comes, and what sort of grief comes from a given sin.

(4) He also knows the forms and modes and numbers of sins, he who sins once, twice, and three times; he who frequently falls into one kind of transgression; he who goes astray in various sorts of vices; he who goes astray only in specific kinds. He wants us to seek out all these things in accordance with the wisdom of God, in accordance with what is written: "God searches hearts and reins" [Ps 7:9], and to understand the penalties that are inflicted by him in a way that is worthy of God and befitting his providential care. It is not that he wants us only to be tortured. "For he created everything for this, that they would exist, and he made the generations of the world healthful, and there is no medicine of destruction in them" [Wis 1:14]. But since out of contempt [for him] we have not done what he wanted, he also did not work in us what he desired. The discussion forced us to say something about the kinds of punishments that are inflicted on the earth.

Suspended Sentence

2. Now we need to know that when there is famine, death does not follow at once. For it can happen that one who endures a famine continues to live, though he is violently tormented by the lack of food, squalor, and emaciation. It can happen that when evil beasts are sent in, it is not at once that all who preserve themselves by the aid of flight perish. It can come to pass that when the double-edged sword falls, destruction delays. Now some are wounded and cut and, so to speak, pierced through by repeated blows, and yet they do not perish. Therefore, now the last punishment in the list of punishments that is inflicted is that of death. The most holy apostle was thinking of something of this sort when he said: "The last enemy will be destroyed, death" [1 Cor 15:26]. I will be so bold as to say: If the last enemy, death, will be destroyed, there was an enemy before death, that is, the double-edged sword; there was an enemy before death,[6] evil beasts; there was an enemy before the evil beasts, famine. All these things are inimical to the enemies of religion. For if you do not want to become a friend of God, who invites you to reconciliation, and who says through the apostle: "I beg you through Christ to be reconciled to

God" [2 Cor 5:20], why do you plead from God, when you yourself are the cause, you who wanted to be under the power of the enemies?

(2) Or do you not know that the reason God sent his fury and wrath [cf. Exod 15:7] and anguish [cf. Rom 2:8–9] against Egypt, a mission through evil angels, was that they were his enemies and were being ruled by his adversary? But may the four penalties of these punishments be far from us, famine, evil beasts, sword, death. For whichever of these things was inflicted, it came to those who are God's enemies; it passes by his friends, nor did it dare to touch those who boast of their close relationship with him. And just as it is well believed concerning fire, since the Scriptures testify to this, that the just pass through it and are not burned—"For fire will test the quality of the work of each one" [1 Cor 3:13]—so also in these penalties, some Daniel, Noah, and Job may be found, who will experience none of these punishments.

Against Jerusalem and Us

3. We have offered this exposition especially for each of the penalties, which in the final part the prophet joins together into one [unit], when he says: "Thus says the Lord Adonai: But even if I send my four evil vengeances, the double-edged sword, famine, evil beasts, and death" [Ezek 14:21]. Where? Not against the land, but "against Jerusalem" [Ezek 14:21]. For if the land is punished, a single chastisement suffices for it. But if Jerusalem is chastised, over which is invoked the name of God, four torments are inflicted upon it at the same time. It would have been much more to our advantage not to have believed the divine words, than after expressing belief in them, to be converted again to those sins that we previously committed [cf. 2 Pet 2:21].[7] For consider how Scripture speaks of single penalties being inflicted against the land, and it does not add which land. But when it comes to Jerusalem: "But even if I send my four evil vengeances, the double-edged sword, famine, evil beasts and death, into Jerusalem" [Ezek 14:21]. This indicates that we are Jerusalem, since we, when we sin, are indeed the Jerusalem that is being destroyed, but when we abide in the commands, we are called the Jerusalem that is being saved. All the lamentations that we read about Jerusalem, all the complaints with which God bewails it, pertain to us,

we "who have tasted the word of God" [Heb 6:5] and afterward do things that are contrary to his commands. One is not beaten in this way for despising Solomon's laws, one is not punished in this way for abandoning Lycurgus's decrees.[8] The penalty is different for the one who tramples on and despises God's law that was handed down through Moses.

(2) Greatest of all is the punishment for him who regards the precepts of the Son of God as nothing. For "one who has violated the law of Moses dies without mercy at the testimony of two or three witnesses. How much more do you think he earns worse penalties who has trampled upon the Son of God?" [Heb 10:28–29]. Those, then, whom we have enumerated have not trampled upon the Son of God, but they have merely transgressed the law of God. This applies especially to those who lived before the coming of the Lord. But not even those who crucified my Savior have a punishment as enormous as those have to whom the apostle is speaking: "the one who tramples on the Son of God and insults the Spirit of grace" [Heb 10:29]. And he indicates something else in that passage in which he describes the sins of those who have sinned after [coming to] faith in God [cf. Heb 10:26].

In the Church

4. These things were said on account of these "four evil vengeances" that are brought "against Jerusalem" [Ezek 14:21]. And indeed all of us who learn the divine Scriptures are Jerusalem, whether we live well or badly. If we live badly, we are that Jerusalem that is punished with torments and that endures four vengeances. If we live well, we are that Jerusalem that rests in the bosom of God [cf. Gal 4:26]. And there is a great difference, both in the rest of the land, and in Jerusalem itself. For all who are sinners in the church, who have tasted the word of God [cf. Heb 6:5] and transgress it, deserve penalties, to be sure; but each one will be tormented according to the rank they occupy. The one who presides in the church and commits sins will have a greater punishment.[9] Or does not a catechumen deserve more mercy in comparison with one of the faithful? Is not a layman worthy of more pardon if he is compared to a deacon? And again, in comparison with a priest, does not a deacon have a better right to pardon? What follows from that you know even if I am silent

about it. Therefore, I fear God's judgment and I keep before my eyes this ordering of the judgment that is contained in the Scriptures. I bear in mind the saying: "Do not lift a weight that is too heavy for you" [Sir 13:2]; and also the following: "Do not seek to be judge, since you may not be able to take away iniquities" [Sir 7:6]. What good is it to me[10] to be enthroned on the master's seat, to receive the honor of a prominent person, if I cannot do the works my position demands? Will I not be tormented by a greater punishment, since the honor of a just man is conferred on me by everyone, though I am a sinner?

To Jerusalem

(2) It was necessary to treat anew rather carefully the things that were said about the four vengeances on the land, and to add that Jerusalem was indeed in the tribe of Benjamin, and the priests of the temple and the Levites who were serving the ministries of God, and the other orders were living in it that the word of the Scriptures includes. It receives four evil vengeances, which are not similar for those who dwell in it; for the threat is not directed in the same way both to the people and to the Levites. For the Israelite who sins falls into an Israelite transgression. But the one who is greater than an Israelite will endure correspondingly greater penalties, to the degree that he is of a more noble order, that is, a Levite and priest. But if a chief priest sins, Eli, his fellow priest, says to him: "If a man transgresses and sins against a man, they will pray for him; but if he sins against the Lord, who will pray for him?" [1 Sam 2:25]. These things have been said in explanation of his words, whereby the individual vengeances were particularly threatened against the sinful land and likewise those were threatened who were gathered together in wretched Jerusalem.

The Wood and the Vine

5. But let us look at the Scriptures that follow. We should explain only the meaning of the things that the prophet heard in the parable and omit speaking about the ordering of the testimony. For that we send the hearer himself to the book. Just as among fruit the wood of

the vine is more noble than all woods, especially of those that bear fruit in a forest, so is it less useful than all woods for other tasks. And certain vessels can be made to serve a necessary use in diverse works; but from the branches of a vine not only is it not possible for a vessel to be made even for a useful task, but not even can a useful peg be made.[11] Therefore, the divine word says that, just as the branch of the vine, if it bears fruit, becomes more honorable than the other woods, so, if it does not have the means to excel, it is judged to be inferior to all the others, and in this manner those who are imbued with the utterances of God, when they bear clusters of the fruit of salvation, are more noble than everyone and in every way in their position of dignity on the vine. Of this it is written: "But I have planted you as a fruitful vine, entirely true" [Jer 2:21]; and elsewhere: "The vine of the Lord is the house of Israel" [Isa 5:7]; and again: "You have transferred the vine from Egypt" [Ps 80:8]; etc. But if they do not bear fruit, to the point that God could say: "How is it that you have converted into the bitterness, O foreign vine?" [Jer 2:21] then they are found to be much worse than those woods which, though they are more common, nevertheless bear their own fruit.

(2) For just as the woods of the forests surpass sterile vines, in the same manner, according to a certain dispensation of divine wisdom, things that are indispensable to any house are produced out of more common kinds of woods. Nor should you be disturbed and think that in what we are saying, we are asserting things that go beyond the Scriptures, that it will happen that from the woods of the forest something useful is made, that is, from myself, if I shall not bear fruit proper to my nature. For indeed even the Apostle picks up an image of these vessels, which are commonly used in human life, when he says: "Now in a large house there are not only golden and silver vessels, but also wooden and clay ones" [2 Tim 2:20]. Note what he says of the wooden vessels: "and some are for honor, but some are dishonor" [2 Tim 2:20]. These wooden vessels that the Apostle proclaims are in a large house are not made from vines, nor from the branches of vines, but from other woods of a more common kind, which bore fruit in their groves. What a great evil is it, then, and how perilous that the woods that are in the householder's large house one day be found to be worthless, and that the branch of my vine be of no use in the house and be cast into the fire! [John 15:6]. For this is what is written: "Fire consumes that which is yearly pruned" [Ezek 15:4; cf. John 15:2, 6]. This is in Ezekiel.

The Vine and the Branches

(3) But the Savior has touched on the meaning of this parable in the Gospel when he speaks as follows: "I am the vine, you are the branches, my Father is the vine-dresser. Every branch that abides in me and bears fruit, my Father prunes, that it might bear greater fruit. The branch that remains in me and does not bear fruit, my Father cuts off and throws into the fire" [John 15:1–2]. Do you see the resemblance of the two passages? Do you see how "the Father cuts off and throws into the fire"? But we, being foolish and irrational, as if the Scripture deserves to be ignored, do not want to hear things that strike fear into us. Instead we desire to listen to things that strike pleasure into our prurient ears. Gladly do we hear things that subvert and deceive us. He who says to his neighbor: "God forgives us our sins, since indeed we enjoy such mysteries," and those who promise this to us in turn: "God will drop a napkin."[12] And: "since he is good and absolves the sins of all, it would have to be the case that we can rest and say with an undisturbed heart: If we sinned yesterday, let us do penance today." But to this branch—for it is a living being—who says: "God is powerful and he is a good vine-dresser, he will not cut me off and cast me into the fire," the vine-dresser will say: "But if the branch is such that it is on the vine to no purpose, can it be left there? If it is not allowed to drop off, will it not hinder the vine from bearing green and fruitful branches of fruit, in place of this dry branch?" For just as it is the duty of a good vine-dresser to cut off and amputate things that are dry, and to hand over unfruitful branches as material for fire, so it is the duty of the good God to amputate fruitless branches from all vines and to hand them over to fire for destruction. But we indulge ourselves contrary to ourselves, and having been deceived we equally deceive and prefer to go astray with the majority than to be converted from error. Instead we should seek that which edifies, that which increases the fear of God, that which calls us back to repentance, that which leads to the confession of sin, that which makes us day and night think about how we may please the Lord [cf. 2 Cor 5:9].[13] Thus may we become fruitful branches on the true vine, Christ Jesus, and cleave to his root, "to whom is the glory and power for ages of ages. Amen" [1 Pet 4:11].

HOMILY 6[1]

Iniquities of Jerusalem (Ezekiel 16:2–16)

The Free Choice of the Prophets

1. I am struck with amazement when I consider the constancy of the prophets, how those who truly believed in God rather than men despised death, dangers, insults, and everything that they suffered from those by whom they were being accused, while they served the will of God in their prophesying. Quite recently, before I compared Ezekiel, I was admiring Isaiah. I was astounded at how he said, "Hear the word of God, rulers of Sodom[2]; attend to the law of the Lord, people of Gomorrah. Of what value to me is the multitude of your sacrifices? says the Lord" [Isa 1:10–11]. For he said this when he could have either spoken or kept quiet. For it is not the case, as some people surmise, that the prophets were out of their minds and spoke by the Spirit's compulsion.[3] The Apostle says: "If a revelation is made to another who is sitting there, let the first one be silent" [1 Cor 14:30]. That shows that the one who speaks has control over when he wants to speak and when he wants to be silent. Also, to Balaam it is said: "But there is a word that I am sending into your mouth, take care to speak this" [Num 23:5, 16]. This implies that he has the power, once he has received the word of God, to speak or to be silent.

(2) Well then, what is it that I admire in Ezekiel? It is that when he was commanded to give witness and to make known to Jerusalem her iniquities [Ezek 16:2], he did not put before his eyes the danger that would come from the preaching, but only to obey God's precepts. Thus he spoke whatever he was commanded. So be it, let it be a mys-

tery, let it be the revelation of a sanctified understanding about Jerusalem and about all the things said of her. And yet he prophetically accuses her of fornication, since she "spread her legs[4] to everyone who passed by" [Ezek 16:15–25]. He attests this with a condemnatory voice; he rebukes the city for its wickedness. But because he was confident of doing the will of God, he spoke boldly, as one who was ready either to live or die.

2. Let us therefore look at the prophecy itself and, first of all, consider how it was really put within the prophet's control whether to speak or not. "The Word of the Lord came to him saying: Son of man, testify to Jerusalem her iniquities, and you shall say: Thus says the Lord" [Ezek 16:2–3]. The Lord laid it down that he was to testify to Jerusalem her iniquities not by the compulsion of inspiration but by the will of the one speaking; and he says: "You shall say." What shall you say? The things that follow. It was left to the prophet who heard "you shall say" whether he would speak or not, just as it was laid down in Jonah's case. For it was within the control of him who heard: "Say: Yet three days, and Nineveh shall be overthrown" [Jonah 3:2, 5], if he wants to speak or to keep silent. And because it was placed in his choice, and he did not want to speak, see how many things happened to him afterward: "The ship was endangered" because of him; through the casting of lots he was discovered in his hiding place, and "the great fish swallowed him up when he was thrown overboard" [Jonah 1:4–7, 15; 2:1]. So then, these prophets who came after Jonah, considering perhaps what happened to him or to other prophets, saw how they were hemmed in from all sides: persecution from the world if they spoke the truth, an offense to God if, for fear of man, they said what was false instead of the truth.

Origins

3. Therefore Ezekiel has testified and made known to Jerusalem her iniquities and has said: "Thus says the Lord: Your root and your origin are of the land of Canaan; your father was an Amorite, and your mother a Hittite" [Ezek 16:3]. What city was raised so high or was so elevated in thought as the city of God? And yet this very city, which promised such great things, as one that was very close to God and was his city [cf. Rom 11:20; Heb 12:22], because it sinned, it is convicted

by the Holy Spirit as degenerate and foreign. For its father is an Amorite, no longer God. As long as she did not sin, God was her father; but when she sinned, an Amorite became her father. As long as she did not sin, the Holy Spirit was her father; but when she sinned, a Hittite woman became her mother. As long as she did not sin, she had a root in Abraham, Isaac, and Jacob; when she sinned, her root became a Canaanite. I have often marveled at what was spoken by Daniel to the old sinner, to whom he gives a name according to his sin. He says: "You are the seed of Canaan, not Judah" [Dan 13:56].[5] Great indeed is the most steadfast Daniel when he names the old sinner the seed of Canaan and not Judah; but in comparison with him, Ezekiel is greater, who does not reproach the disgraceful origin of one old man or of two men, but who says: "Your root and your origin are from the land of Canaan, your father was an Amorite and your mother a Hittite" [Ezek 16:3]. Since Jerusalem had committed many sins, therefore when the prophet rebukes it, he marks it out not with one or two, but with three names. Seven nations are listed in Genesis by God in one passage that he handed over to the sons of Israel. And these are the seven: He says: "In the land of the Canaanites and the Hittites and the Amorites and the Perizzites and Evaeans[6] and the Girgashites and the Jebusites" [Gen 15:20–21]. It was impossible to gather these seven nations together in order to reproach the disgrace of sinful Jerusalem by means of them. Otherwise the prophet would have surely done so. But now what has he done? He selects from the seven the Amorite and the Canaanite, and he says that sinful Jerusalem has a relation, to be sure, with the Canaanite according to her root and origin, specifically with the Amorite according to her father, specifically with the Hittite according to her mother.

(2) If such grave things are spoken against Jerusalem, about which so many great and marvelous things are written, which are promised to it, what will happen to a poor wretch like me, if I sin? Who will be my father or mother? Of the great and noble Jerusalem it is declared that her root and origin are from the land of the Canaanites; her father is an Amorite and her mother a Hittite. If I sin, I who believe in Christ Jesus and have entrusted myself to so great a master, who will be my father? Certainly not an Amorite, but a worse father. Who is he? "Everyone who commits sin is born of the devil" [1 John 3:8]; and again: "You are of your father the devil" [John 8:44]. If, then, Jerusalem is said to be from the root and origin of the land

of Canaan, what will be said to us? Fathers will also be found for us, who beget us in sins. For example, if I become good and am established in excellent conduct, Jesus says to me: "Son, your sins are forgiven you" [Matt 9:2]. Paul the disciple of Jesus says to me: "For in Christ Jesus through the gospel, I have begotten you" [1 Cor 4:15]. In this way, if I become a sinner, the devil who begets me in sins will assume that voice with which God the Father spoke to the Savior and say to me: "You are my son, today I have begotten you" [cf. Ps 2:7].[7] And I will have a great number of additional fathers to whom I will go. Each one goes to his fathers. If someone is from Abraham, it is said to him: "But as for you, go to your fathers in peace, having been raised to a good old age" [Gen 15:15]. But if someone leaves this world not in peace but in a war with sins, and not in good old age, "having grown old in the days of evil" [Dan 13:52], assuredly it is said to him: But you are going to your fathers in war, nourished in evil old age. With other designations God shows us what we ought to do.

The Umbilical Cord

4. "On the day you were born they did not bind your breasts," or: "your umbilical cord was not cut" [Ezek 16:4], for in Hebrew the text says: "Your umbilical cord was not cut."[8] Allegorically, this presents Jerusalem under the image of a newborn baby girl. But we should know that what is said about Jerusalem applies to all people in the church. Its first moment [of life] is as described here; but far be it from us to have as a third moment what is said to Jerusalem. For God calls all of us "Jerusalem," we who at first were sinners. And our beginning was as described here. But if we persist in sins after God's visitation and his taking note of us, the second moment also applies to us. The third evil moment, which we deeply abhor, we will take up in due course.

(2) Now, let me return to the first moment. It is written as though about Jerusalem: "On the day you were born, your umbilical cord[9] was not cut" [Ezek 16:4 Hebrew]. We need God's assistance to be able to find the uncut umbilical cord of sinful Jerusalem, or at least to explain the cord that was cut from that which did not sin. Therefore, from another Scripture I am looking either for Jerusalem's umbilical cord or for the one of some other city, so that by "compar-

ing spiritual things with spiritual things" [1 Cor 2:13], I may find out how the umbilical cord of Jerusalem was not cut. It is written in Job about the dragon: "His power is in his navel[10], and his strength is in the navel of his belly" [Job 40:16]. I know from the things that divine grace granted to me that when I explained the current passage, I said that the dragon represents contrary strength.[11] For he is "the dragon, the ancient serpent, who is called the devil and Satan, deceiving the whole world" [Rev 12:4]. His strength is in his navel, no doubt, for the commencement of all evils resides in the loins. And that is why it is related that the one who would be born was still in the loins of his father [cf. Heb 7:10]. For human seed is collected in the loins. There is contrary strength, then, wherever there is seed, and that is where he tries to display the force of his ambushes. Against males his power is in the loins; against females his power is in the navel of the belly. And behold how becomingly the Scripture has named the genitalia of man and woman with concealed designations, lest it signify what is shameful by the terms that are at hand. If the reference that we have brought forth from Job has been understood, understand with me that just as in a man the foreskin is circumcised, so in a woman the umbilical cord is cut off. For when the woman was chaste, and employed clean feminine lingerie that she not fall into sordid affairs and disgraceful sins, at that time her umbilical cord was cut off. But if she sins her umbilical cord is not cut off. Therefore he rebukes Jerusalem as if she were a woman for whom the umbilical cord is not cut.

(3) The LXX translated this passage: "They have not bound your breasts" [Ezek 16:4], expounding more on the meaning of the expression than expressing it word for word. Now in the Song of Songs breasts are employed in place of your thoughts and way of thinking: "For your breasts are better than wine." And: "he reclined on the chest of Jesus" [John 13:25], where your breasts are, because he would have communion of his intellectual understandings. Therefore when the mind is rigid and the thought is constricted, and firm words do not flow, it is plain that your breasts are bound. But when the things that are said loosen up and begin to flow, the breasts are not bound up.

5. "You were not washed with water unto salvation" [Ezek 16:4]. Let us see what happens to Jerusalem lest the same fate befall us. It may be said, for example: A woman has now been washed, but one asks whether this leads to salvation, in order that we too may have fear.

This is why the words are added: "Unto salvation." Not all are washed "unto salvation." We who have received the grace of baptism in the name of Christ have been washed; but I do not know who has been "washed unto salvation." Simon was washed, and "after being baptized he continued in the company of Philip" [cf. Acts 8:13]. But because he was not washed "unto salvation," he was condemned by him who said to him in the Holy Spirit: "Your money perish with you!" [Acts 8:20]. It is immensely difficult for someone who is washed to be washed unto salvation. Pay attention and listen to what is being said here, you catechumens; prepare yourselves, while you are catechumens, while you are not yet baptized, and you may come to the washing and be washed "unto salvation." May you not be washed like some who are washed but not "unto salvation." Such a one receives the water but does not receive the Holy Spirit [cf. John 3:5]. The one who is washed unto salvation receives water and the Holy Spirit.[41] Since Simon was not washed "unto salvation," he received water, but he did not receive the Holy Spirit, "thinking that the gift of the Spirit could be acquired with money" [Acts 8:20]. He was not washed with water unto salvation [Ezek 16:4].[12] To every sinful soul which seems to believe, these things are said which we now read as being said to Jerusalem, so that I do not climb to higher levels to search out meanings that are beyond my power and ability.

Salt

6. "Nor [were you] salted with salt" [Ezek 16:4]. And this is a charge against Jerusalem, because it was not worthy of the salt of God. If I believe in my Lord Jesus Christ, he will make me to be salt and will say to me: "You are the salt of the earth" [Matt 5:13]. If I believe in the Spirit who has spoken in the Apostle [cf. Acts 13:9], I am seasoned with salt and am able to keep the precept that says: "Let your speech always be gracious, seasoned with salt" [Col 4:6]. It is a great work to be salted. The one who is seasoned with salt is full of grace. For even in the common proverb, "salty" means gracious, and conversely unsalty means without grace.[13] If therefore grace comes to us from God and we are filled with his gift, we are salted with salt.

Swaddling Bands

(2) Further, sinful Jerusalem "was not wrapped in swaddling bands" [Ezek 16:4]. Observe what we are saying. A soul that is reborn and has first come forth from the washing is wrapped in swaddling bands. My Lord Jesus himself was "wrapped in swaddling bands" [Luke 2:7, 12] as it is reported written in the Gospel according to Luke. There is need, then, for the one who is reborn, assuredly reborn in Christ, "to long for the rational and sincere milk" [1 Pet 2:2]. And before he desires the rational milk that is without deceit [cf. 1 Pet 2:2], he needs to be salted with salt, and to be bound and wrapped in swaddling bands. Otherwise it would be said to him: "You were not salted with salt, and you were not wrapped in swaddling bands" [Ezek 16:4]. But since these are charges against Jerusalem, that her umbilical cord was not cut, she was not salted with salt, she was not wrapped in swaddling bands, she was not washed with water unto salvation, the remaining words that are woven into the context point out the following: "Nor was your eye sparing toward yourself, that I should do for you one of all these things" [Ezek 16:5]. Therefore "I did" none of these things "for you, that I should suffer anything for you" [Ezek 16:5], says the Lord.

The Suffering of Divine Love

(3) Let me offer a human example; then, if the Holy Spirit grants it, I will move on to Jesus Christ and to God the Father. When I speak to a man and plead with him for some matter, that he should have pity on me, if he is a man without pity, he does not suffer anything from the things I say. But if he is a man of gentle spirit, and not hardened and rigid in his heart, he hears me and has pity upon me. And his feelings are softened by my requests. Understand something of this kind with regard to the Savior. He came down to earth out of compassion for the human race.[14] Having experienced our sufferings even before he suffered on the cross, he condescended to assume our flesh. For if he had not suffered, he would not have come to live on the level of human life. First, he suffered; then he came down and was seen [cf. 1 Tim 3:16]. What is this suffering that he suffered for us? It is the suffering of love. The Father, too, himself, the God of the uni-

verse, "patient and abounding in mercy" [Ps 103:8][15] and compassionate, does he not in some way suffer? Or do you not know that when he directs human affairs he suffers human suffering? For "the Lord your God bore your ways, as a man bears his son" [Deut 1:31]. Therefore God bears our ways, just as the Son of God bears our sufferings. The Father himself is not without suffering.[16] When he is prayed to, he has pity and compassion; he suffers something of love and comes into those in whom he cannot be, in view of the greatness of his nature, and on account of us he endures human sufferings.[17]

Unmerited Compassion

7. Therefore, "your eye was not sparing toward you," he says, "that I should do for you one of all these things, that I should suffer anything over you." And since you became like this, "You were cast out on the face of the field" [Ezek 16:5]. God, do not suffer us to be like this, that we too be cast out by you from your church on the face of the field, but instead let us go out to the field from the narrow places of meanings! "And you were cast out on the face of the field." Why? "For the depravity of your soul on the day on which you were born" [Ezek 16:5]. Can anyone have depravity of soul on the very day of birth? So then, he is describing our passions and human vices and customary depravities. For through our depravity, if our heart is not right, we are cast out onto the field on the day on which we are born. If, after the rebirth of the bath,[18] after [receiving] the word of God, we sin again, on that day on which we are born, we are cast out.[19] All too often we find people like this who have been washed in the "washing of the second regeneration" [cf. Titus 3:5] and do not "bear fruits that are worthy of repentance" [Luke 3:8]. They do not rejoice in the mystery of baptism with a greater fear of him whom they held in regard when they were catechumens, nor do we find them having a deeper love than they practiced when they were only hearers of the word, nor do they have holier deeds than they did before. For men of this sort there follows what is spoken of here: "You were cast out on the face of the field because of the depravity of your soul on the day on which you were born" [Ezek 16:5].

(2) But consider the mercy of God; behold his singular clemency! Although Jerusalem was "cast out on the face of the field,"

he does not despise her to the extent of casting her out forever, nor does he abandon her to her depravity so as to forget her totally, so that he never lifts up again her who was lying there. Note what follows: "And I passed by you" [Ezek 16:6]. You were cast out, nevertheless I came back to you; you were not deprived of my visitation even after your fall.

8. "And I saw you bespattered with your blood" [Ezek 16:6]. It is as if he is saying: He sees a land of murderers, a land guilty of bloodshed and mortal sins. "And I said to you: Be filled with life from your blood; rise up from your blood and be filled with life; I have given you as the springing of the field" [Ezek 16:6–7]. I had pity on you after you were cast out; I saw you bespattered with blood and sins; I made you like the springing of the field. "And you were multiplied" [Ezek 16:7]. Because I came to you and visited you when you had been cast out, I became the cause of your being multiplied. "And you were multiplied and increased" [Ezek 16:7]. I gave you for a multitude and increase, that is, to grow and to be multiplied. For through the fact that we increase, we are multiplied.

Young Daughter

(2) "And you entered into the cities of cities" [Ezek 16:7]. Again he is setting forth the errors of Jerusalem who enters into the cities of cities. But let us consider how it culpably entered into the cities of cities. Suppose some man of the church enters the individual "cities" in which there are heresies and doctrines that are estranged from God. If he becomes a participant in such cities, then he hears: "You have entered into the cities of cities."

(3) "Your breasts were set" [Ezek 16:7]. After such great crimes, again you flourished and "your time came and the time of those who lead astray" [Ezek 16:8]. It is said to me: Do not allegorize, do not explain things figuratively. Let them answer: Jerusalem has breasts, and there is a time when they are bound up, there is a time when they are set, and she has an umbilical cord, and she is convicted because "it was not cut" [Ezek 16:4]. How, pray, can these things be understood without an allegorical exposition?

(4) "Your breasts were set and your hair had grown" [Ezek 16:7]. With all decency the divine word describes the things that usually hap-

pen to the bodies of virgins. "And your hair had grown, yet you were naked and indecent" [Ezek 16:7]. Whoever has not "put on Christ Jesus" [cf. Rom 13:14; Col 3:12] is naked; whoever has not "put on the feelings of compassion, kindness, humility, meekness, patience, that he might bear with his neighbor" [cf. Col 3:12–13] is indecent. "But you were naked and indecent. And I passed by you" [Ezek 16:7–8]. A second time he comes to her, sees her sinning, goes away again because of the sins, and he still comes back. Once again the clement and kind God comes to visit her.

(5) "And I came to you and saw you and behold, it was your time and the time of those who lead astray" [Ezek 16:8]. What is the meaning of "your time"? It signifies puberty at which time one becomes old enough to commit fornication. And again he says: "and the time of those who lead astray." Who are "those who lead astray"? While we are children [cf. 1 Cor 13:11], those who want to lead us astray and are trying to destroy us are, namely, bad Christians, unclean demons, and the angels of the devil. But they do not have the means by which they can lead us astray. But when we get a little older and are now able to sin, they seek for an opportunity to turn us aside.[20] Both the angels of God and the angels of Satan do this. Now it is impossible that both of them turn us their way. If we sin, the angels of the devil are turning us their way. If we stand firm, the angels of God are turning us their way.

(6) Therefore, "your time came and the time of those who lead astray" [Ezek 16:8]. For the time of those who lead astray had come, and our Lord and God Jesus Christ again visits pitiful Jerusalem, that is, our sinful soul. "I spread my wings over you" [Ezek 16:8]. Scriptural usage speaks of the edges of garments as "wings," as in Ruth, who "went secretly and uncovered a place at the feet of Boaz" [Ruth 3:7], and she slept under the "wing" of his garment [cf. Ruth 3:9]. So God is speaking as one who is wearing a garment: "I have spread my wings over you and have covered your shame" [Ezek 16:8]. Blessed is the one whose shame God covers with his wings, but only if he perseveres in the blessedness in which Jerusalem did not wish to persevere. "And I swore to you in covenant and I entered into covenant with you" [Ezek 16:8]. After so much for which he returns again, turns away again, after such frequent visitations, now for the first time he "enters a covenant" with her.

Outfit and Finery

9. "And you became mine. And I washed you with water" [Ezek 16:8–9]. After all these things I took you and I myself washed you unto salvation. "And I washed off your blood from you" [Ezek 16:9]. In our understanding of these things, let us pray that the mercy of God come upon us and that he might wash away the blood from our souls; for if we have done anything deserving death, that is our blood. "I washed your blood from you, and I anointed you with oil" [Ezek 16:9]. God wants to make us christs[21] as well. "And I clothed you in various colors" [Ezek 16:10]. How great is the kindness of God for each of the souls in Jerusalem! To those who believe in him, he gives a tunic not of a single color, but of much variety. Even then Jacob made this "tunic of various colors" as a sign, putting it on his son Joseph, "and he clothed him in various colors" [Gen 37:3]. If you consider the mysterious interpretations, you will truly see that the varied tunic stands for good works [cf. Matt 22:11–13; Rev 19:8]. The visitation of God gives this tunic to those who have been called to salvation [cf. Matt 22:14]. I understand the law, I comprehend the prophets, I recognize the Gospels, the Apostle is not hidden from me, I am cautious, I am just, I am merciful, and still you seek another tunic of various colors that God puts on Jerusalem when he says: "And I have clothed you in various colors and I have shod you with hyacinth (crimson)" [Ezek 16:10]? He wants our footwear to be brilliant and finely colored. But which footwear? Hear Paul proclaiming quite openly: "Having shod the feet in readiness for the gospel of peace" [Eph 6:15].

10. "And I girded you with fine linen" [Ezek 16:10]. The Apostle speaks of this girding more clearly: "Standing with your loins girded in the truth" [Eph 6:14]. For truth is taken for fine linen.[22] "And I have covered you with a fine hair garment (*trichaptum*)" [Ezek 16:10]. Since I have not found the meaning of *trichaptum*, I looked at another version and in place of *trichaptum* found "blooming"; in another version I found "garment."[23] So then, after the varied clothing, God clothes us with a blooming tunic. "And I adorned you with adornment, and I put bracelets around your wrists[24]" [Ezek 16:11]. When he gives me opportunities to do good deeds, he puts bracelets around my wrists. "And a chain around your neck" [Ezek 16:11]. If, after works of justice, he adorns me with understanding of truth, then a wedding adornment is put around me, then a lovely chain is placed around my

neck. "And I put a pendant[25] on your nostril" [Ezek 16:12]. When I am able truly to receive the sweet and fragrant mysteries, then God adorns my nostril with pendants. "And rings (*rotulas*) in your ears" [Ezek 16:12], so that not merely earrings but even a large golden ring (*rota*) would be around my hearing. Now the wheel (*rota*) is golden that rolls around the sacred mysteries. "And a crown of glorification on your head" [Ezek 16:12]. Almighty God, grant to us that we may become worthy of a crown of glorification on our head. "And you were adorned with gold" [Ezek 16:13], that is, with divine meanings, "and silver," with sacred words.[26] "And your covering was fine linen" [Ezek 16:13]. The fine linen refers to the depth of concealed meanings. "And blooming," in place of the word the LXX recorded, τρίχαπτα, which signifies an exceedingly fine cloth and a garment that is refined, as it were, in the likeness of hair. "And of various colors." Behold, Jerusalem is washed, covered with wings, diversely clothed, adorned with gems.

Transgressing Again

(2) What does God, the great lover of humanity, do after these things? He nourishes her with delicate foods. "You ate fine flour and honey and oil" [Ezek 16:13]. He does not say merely flour or barley bread; we are now speaking to you about fine flour. But after the fine flour, after the honey, after the oil, this wretched Jerusalem is again reviled as a whore. And so we must really be on our guard lest we too should again transgress, after the clean words of fine flour, after the sweetest words of the prophets, after the oil that "gladdens the face" and with which we wish to anoint our head to make our fast acceptable [cf. Matt 6:17]. But we do not merely anoint ourselves with this oil; we eat it too. "And you grew exceedingly beautiful." He praises her beauty, he praises her appearance, he proclaims her beautiful figure. "And you came to regal estate." What progress, that she came even to the royal state! "And your name went forth among the nations" [Ezek 16:14]. This applies to one who, after beginning to be free from the world, and whose manner of life is advancing toward the blessed life, also gains a famous name in the world.

(3) But don't let happen what now takes place; it is written to strike fear into the hearers. After the beauty, after the great name,

wretched Jerusalem commits fornication. Therefore, "Do not boast about tomorrow, for you do not know what the coming day may bring forth" [Prov 27:1]; and elsewhere: "Brothers, even if a man is overtaken in some sin, you, as spiritual men, endure such a one in a spirit of gentleness" [Gal 6:1]; and again: "Watch yourself, lest you too be tempted" [Gal 6:1].

11. "And your name went forth among the nations for your beauty, for it was perfect through the splendor which I had appointed for you, says the Lord God; but you trusted in your beauty" [Ezek 16:14]. The beautiful Jerusalem thought great things and was set in the awareness of her beauty. And because she "thought high things" [cf. Rom 12:16] and did not humble herself and glorify God, listen to what is said to her: "You committed fornication against your name, and poured out your fornication on every passerby" [Ezek 16:15]. What do these words mean: "You poured out your fornication on every passerby"? The opposing power "goes around" observing our souls in various ways and seeking an opportunity by which it can break through [cf. 1 Pet 5:8].[27] Anger wants to commit fornication with me in its own name, by attaching itself to my character. Grief too wants to make me sorrowful in its own name; for its part desire for silver and gold and of things like that do the same thing. If I do not guard myself and close my opening, but receive every speech of the enemy, it is said to me: "You have poured out your fornication on every passerby. You have taken your garments and have sewn them into idols for yourself" [Ezek 16:15–16].

(2) You took the things with which "I adorned you," with which "you had become beautiful," and "you sewed them into idols for yourself." I still want to explain what these sewn idols are, which some sewed from their clothes. These clothes are the divine Scriptures and the meaning that lies within them. The heretics tore up these clothes and sewed together expression to expression, linking word to word, but without the proper and fitting connection. And in sewing together impious things, they made idols for themselves with which they led some astray, to believe and agree with their cult and to accept an artificial church order.[28] But may God deliver us all from these and other idols, that we might grow in Christ Jesus, "to whom is the glory and power for ages of ages. Amen" [1 Pet 4:11].

HOMILY 7

The Beneficial Effects of God's Turning Away (Ezekiel 16:16–30)

Lists Are Instructive

1. A listing of Jerusalem's sins, when it is understood, edifies the hearer. For example, if a master chastises some household member in his home and sets forth his sins, another slave who was recently purchased, upon seeing the discipline of the father of the family—that is, what he finds fault with, what he praises—is instructed not to do the things that his fellow servants did previously. And with all effort he will hasten to do the things by which the others earned honor and liberty from the master. In the same way, we too receive no small benefit when we hear about what things God finds fault with, whether in Jerusalem or all of Judea or some individual from the tribes who sins in some particular way. And this can prevent us from falling into the things that the others fell into.[1]

The First Fault

(2) Now here is how today's reading begins: "Jerusalem received clothes from God and from them she sewed certain idols and she fornicated with them" [Ezek 16:17]. I explained these things to the best of my ability in the preceding homily,[2] where I showed that those who tear apart the Scriptures and sever word from word sew these things together and compose invented dogmas. They are serving the idols

that they wear as their clothes. "You will not enter my tabernacle, you are outside and you will remain outside." Scripture knows that the saints are inside, sinners are outside.[3] Therefore, since Jerusalem committed such sins so that she does not deserve to enter into the promises of God and it is said to her: "And you will not enter," let us beware lest perchance at some time it may be said to us: "You will not enter, nor will it happen" [Ezek 16:16]. The phrase "nor will it happen" is incomplete, and therefore something needs to be supplied in addition so that the meaning can be completed. The good things that were promised to you that you were to receive "will not happen."

Another Transgression

2. Another transgression follows. "And you took the vessels of your boasting from your silver and of your gold, from the things which I gave you, and you made for yourself male images" [Ezek 16:17]. According to the common understanding, this can be understood as follows. "Vessels of boasting"—from the things that Moses wrote in Numbers, "dishes, phials, golden candlesticks, an ark gilded on the inside and outside,"[4] etc.—"you took" and you melted these things, and "you made male effigies and you fornicated with them." But according to allegory it will be explained as follows. In the sacred literature we have golden and silver vessels, that is, dishes, phials, and other things of this sort. Therefore when we twist the meaning of the Scripture into another sense which is contrary to the truth,[5] we melt the divine words and we change the things of God into other effigies. By doing this, we fall into the sin that Jerusalem has now committed. The vessels of our boasting are the law and the prophets. We exult over these; we take pride in them. When we explain them otherwise than the truth regards them, we convert the vessels of our boasting from the rational silver and the sensible gold that God gave us, and we make for ourselves male images and we fornicate with them.

Varied Apparel

3. Here is what follows: "You took the varied apparel and you covered them" [Ezek 16:18]. The "varied clothes" is here as well as

one passage in the Scriptures with which we are clothed, "putting on affections of mercy, kindness, humility, meekness, and patience in bearing with one another" [Col 3:12]. If we tear and rend these varied garments and beautiful clothes that God has given to us, and we surround ourselves with false teaching in order to deceive men, it is scarcely to be doubted that we are covering idols with varied clothes. But you will understand what is being said, if we describe this matter more clearly. Behold with me some follower of Marcion, or a disciple of Valentinus, or indeed a defender of any heresy you like. Now consider how he clothes his idols—that is, the fabrications that he has composed—with meekness and chastity,[6] so that words that have been adorned with a good life may more easily penetrate the ears of those who listen. And when he has done this, understand that he has put on the varied clothes of morality and of an excellent way of life. He has thrown this over the idols that he himself constructed. But to my way of thinking, the heretic with a good life is much more dangerous. For he has more authority in his doctrine than the one who defiles his doctrine by his way of life. For the one with a bad way of life does not easily entice men to false doctrine, nor can he deceive the simplicity of the hearers by the shadow of his sanctity. But the one who is perverted in his words and contrary to salvation in his doctrines, but who has an ordered and honorable morality, does nothing but take varied garments of a well-ordered and tranquil way of life and put them around his idols, so that he deceives more hearers.

(2) Let us then be especially on our guard against those heretics who lead an excellent life. Perhaps they have been brought to this life more by the devil than by God. For just as bird-catchers put out tasty bits of food as bait so as to capture birds more easily by pleasing their appetite, so too, if I may speak so boldly, the devil has a certain chastity, that is, deceptions for the human soul, that enables him to capture it more easily by a chastity and meekness and justice of this kind, and lead it astray with false words. The devil fights with different kinds of snares to bring pitiful human beings to ruin. He gives a good life to evil people to deceive observers, and he sears a bad conscience in good people [cf. 1 Tim 4:2].

(3) He often sets traps for me, because I preach in the church, in order to confuse the whole church by my way of life. And that is why those who hold public positions are subject to special attack by the enemy so that, by the fall of one man, which cannot be hidden, a

scandal may come to all, and the faith is hurt by the evil life of the clerics. The devil is at work in all things, as we have said, and the things that seem to be good are not, and things that are evil by their own nature, he devises all things against the human nature. This is why the one who is concerned for his way of life is neither taken in by the meekness of the heretics to agree to their doctrine, nor will he be scandalized by my sins, I who seem to preach in the church. Rather, by weighing the doctrine itself and by thoroughly investigating the faith of the church, he will indeed turn away from me, but he will accept the teaching according to the Lord's command, who says: "The scribes and the Pharisees sit on Moses' seat; so hear and do whatever they tell you, but according to their works, do not do; for they speak, but do not do it" [Matt 23:2–3].[7]

(4) Those words are about me. For I teach what is good but do the opposite. And I am the one sitting on Moses' seat like a scribe and a Pharisee. The command is for you, O people, though you may not have an accusation of evil doctrine and of dogmas that are estranged from the church, but if you notice my blameworthy life and sins, do not order your life after the life of the speaker, but do the things I say. Let us imitate no one; or, if we wish to imitate someone, Christ Jesus is put before us to imitate. The Acts of the Apostles have been described, and we know the deeds of the prophets from the sacred books; that is a safe model, that is a solid proposal. The one who desires to follow such models enters securely. But if we seek out blameworthy people for us to imitate, as when we say: "he teaches, and he himself acts contrary to what he teaches," we are acting contrary to the Lord's precept. For he commanded us to consider the doctrines of the teachers rather than their lives. We have said these things about what is written: "You took your various-colored garment and you covered them" [Ezek 16:18], that is, "the vessels of boasting," which you changed into "idols."

Oil and Incense

4. It follows: "And you set before their face my oil and my incense" [Ezek 16:18]. When Scripture teaches, we learn that incense stands for the prayer of the saints. For it says: "Now the incense is the prayers of the saints" [Rev 5:8]. If, then, we who have been appointed

for prayer, though we ought to offer it to God—that is, to the God of the law and the prophets, "to the God of Abraham, to the God of Isaac, to the God of Jacob" [cf. Matt 22:32], and to the Father of Jesus Christ—we offer to those things that we ourselves have fabricated, to the point that we set God's incense before idols, we are doing what is said in the present passage: "And you set before their face my oil and my incense."[8] Now let this be the interpretation of the incense. What account shall we give of the oil? Oil is that by which a holy man is anointed, the oil of Christ, the oil of holy doctrine. So then, when someone receives this oil that the saint makes use of, that is, the Scripture that lays down how he ought to be baptized in the name of the Father and of the Son and of the Holy Spirit [cf. Matt 28:19], and by making a few changes he anoints someone and says some such thing as: You are no longer a catechumen, you have attained to "the washing of the second birth" [Titus 3:5], such a man takes the oil and incense of God and puts it before the face of idols.

Bread

(2) "And my bread that I gave you, I fed you with fine flour and honey and oil" [Ezek 16:19]. Behold our bread, the purest fine flour in the Scriptures and the honey from the bees of the prophets.[9] God gave all this to us, and he fed us from the bread of the prophets, from the fine flour of the law, from the honey of the Gospel. Having been fed on these, we place them before idols. For when in our desire to undertake a defense against false doctrines we say: "It is written in the prophet, Moses bears witness, the Apostle says," what else are we doing but taking the bread of truth[10] and placing it before the idols that we ourselves have created? Marcion made an idol and set the bread of the Scriptures before it. Valentinus, Basilides, and all the heretics acted similarly. "And you have set them before their face for a sweet-smelling fragrance" [Ezek 16:19]. The things that God has granted to us by nature are the sweetest in fragrance. The one who either acts or interprets contrary to the authority of the Scriptures sets this very sweet fragrance before idols.

Sacrifice of Children

5. "And it came about, says the Lord Adonai, and you took your sons and your daughters to whom you gave birth, and you sacrificed them for consumption" [Ezek 16:19–20]. When sinful Jerusalem gave birth to sons and daughters, the end of those who are born is slaughter; for salvation is not the end of the wicked. That is why it is written: "You sacrificed them for consumption. As little things, you committed fornication, you killed my children and you gave them" [Ezek 16:20–21]. In proper terms he says: "You took *your* sons," and he expressly adds: "You killed *my* children." For whoever is born into the doctrines of the heretics, and there has received the elements of his faith, these are sons of fornicating and sinful Jerusalem. The one who is born in the church, and who is deceived later by heretical falsity, that one, though he is a son of God, is seized by sinful Jerusalem and places victims before her idols.

(2) "This is beyond all your fornication and your abominations" [Ezek 16:22]. To take the sons of the church and to sacrifice them to idols—this is beyond every one of your sins. "And you did not remember the day of your infancy, when you were naked and acting basely" [Ezek 16:22]. He has spoken before about the nakedness and baseness of Jerusalem. In the midst of iniquity, therefore, it was necessary to remember how "I stretched forth my wings over you and took you from your blood and washed you" [Ezek 16:8–9]. But you, oblivious of all these things, did these things that befit one who is naked and acting basely and bespattered by her own blood.

House of Prostitution

6. "And it came about after all your evils; woe, woe to you, says the Lord Adonai, and you built for yourself a house of prostitution, and you made for yourself a place of exposure on every street" [Ezek 16:23–24]. If you consider the soul that is exposed to its lovers, you will see how it makes a house of prostitution and receives all whom we have previously declared were its lovers.[11] But understand what we are saying from what follows, that is, those who are Jerusalem's lovers. The human soul is very comely and has an admirable beauty. For its maker, when he first created it, said: "Let us make man in our image and likeness" [Gen 1:26].

What is more beautiful than this beauty and likeness? For this reason certain adulterers and sordid lovers, enticed by her beauty, desire to corrupt her and to commit fornication upon her [Ezek 16:16]. This is why the wise man Paul says: "But I am afraid that just as the serpent deceived Eve in its malice, so your minds may be corrupted" [2 Cor 11:3]. In carnal fornication bodies are corrupted, but in spiritual debaucheries the mind is corrupted and the soul itself is wounded.

Defilement

7. "And you defiled your beauty" [Ezek 16:25]. Even if a man is not entangled in the greatest sins, nevertheless, since the beauty of the soul is extremely great, he may be disgraced by the association with lesser sins as well. Consider the virtues of the soul. When these are implanted by God, behold its beauty, its faculty of invention, disposition, expression, memory, delivery; consider the nature of its innate genius, how it first understands, then decides on things that have been understood, how it may be incited by the senses, how it may adapt the things it has perceived by the senses to the mind, which impulses it may hold on to, which thoughts are from God. The one possessing these things possesses great beauty, but it is corrupted among the sects of the heretics and among additional systems of religion.

(2) "And they spread their legs at every crossing, and you multiplied your fornication" [Ezek 16:25]. There is a fornication that is different from fornication, and just as in the fornication of the flesh, there is someone who is polluted by fornication but not by excessive fornication, and there is another who multiplies his fornication, so also in this fornication, which defiles the soul and mind: one person falls into a multitude of fornications, but another is no longer separated from fornication. This is why it is said: "by the measure with which we measure, it shall be measured back to us" [Matt 7:2].

Sons of Egypt and Sons of Assyria

8. "And you fornicated with the sons of Egypt, your neighbors" [Ezek 16:26]. The sons of Egypt are the opposing powers.[12] It is no

wonder that our neighbors (*confines*) are called Egyptians, since the borders (*fines*) of Egypt and Jerusalem are set very near each other. Those who are "great of flesh" [Ezek 16:26], not because these Egyptians have enormous flesh—and indeed it seems to have signified their shameful parts in a decent way by changing the designation, that is, by saying "great of flesh"—but because the fleshly understanding makes us "great of flesh," just as on the contrary there is a flesh, the face of God, of which it is said: "Just as my flesh is in the desert land, in the roadless and waterless land, so have I appeared to you in the holy place" [Ps 63:1–2]. Therefore, Jerusalem commits fornication with the sons of Egypt, her neighbors and those great of flesh. "And multiple times," he says, "you committed fornication to provoke me to anger" [Ezek 16:26]. You committed many forms of fornication to incite me. "And if I stretch out my hand against you, and I remove your legitimate part, and I hand you over to the souls of those who hate you, the sons of foreigners" [Ezek 16:27]. You see that she who is unworthy of using the law and the words of God is handed over to the souls of foreigners.

(2) "Who turned you aside from your way. You acted impiously and you fornicated with the sons of Assyria" [Ezek 16:27–28]. First, [she fornicated] with the sons of Egypt, then with the sons of Assyria. These refer to kinds of sins. For even when the Assyrians took the sons of Israel captive, what the historical narrative relates did indeed happen, but it was written down [cf. 1 Cor 10:11; Rom 15:4] on account of our repeated captivity, which is perpetrated by the spiritual Assyrians,[13] of whom the apostle says: "For our battle is not against flesh and blood, but against the spiritual forces of wickedness" [Eph 6:12].

Insatiable Fornication

9. "And not thus were you satisfied; and you committed fornication and you were not satisfied" [Ezek 16:28]. When a transgressor is not fulfilled, but always adds new sins to former sins, "tying together iniquities as with a long rope and as with the thong of the heifer's yoke" [Isa 5:18], never converting himself to better things, nor doing penance for his evils, it is said to him: "And you were not satisfied. And you have multiplied my covenants with the land of Canaan[14]" [Ezek 16:29]. When God makes covenants with us and we agree with him,

we are blessed; but when we commit fornication with the spiritual forces of wickedness [cf. Eph 6:12], then we convert God's covenants to the land of Canaan, and we set up a pact with it. But understand this with me: when we are reprehended for any other sin, [we are regarded as being] both among the Chaldeans and among the other nations. "And covenants with the Chaldeans, and not thus were you satisfied."

THE DIVINE DECISION

10. After the listing of sins, he speaks to sinful Jerusalem: "What should I appoint for you, says the Lord Adonai, when you do all these things, the works of a shameless harlot?" Let us rise a little above this utterance. For it is not always advantageous to speak about acts of fornication, and far be it from us that anyone in the Church should be in need of exhortations and words that dissuade from fornication! For if anyone needs to hear: "You shall not commit fornication" [Exod 20:13], and again: "If anyone violates the temple of God, God will destroy him" [1 Cor 3:17], he is like those of whom the apostle says: "Law is not laid down for the just, but for the unjust and insubordinate, for the impious and for sinners" [1 Tim 1:9]. So then, just as law is not laid down for the just but for the unjust and insubordinate, so this teaching that warns us to stay away from fornication is not laid down for the chaste but for the unjust and for fornicators and for the disobedient.

(2) And so, we do not need to learn to stay away from fornication, but let us strive for what is more perfect from the principles of the elements of Christ. For he says: "Though by this time you ought to be teachers, you yourselves need to be taught again what are the beginning elements of God's words. And you have become those for whom there is need of milk, not solid food" [Heb 5:12]. Every word that has commanded, "You shall not commit fornication, you shall not commit adultery, you shall not steal" [Rom 13:9], is not solid food, but as it were milk that is offered to infants. There is the food of athletes from the Almighty God, from his mysteries that are covered and that are signified in a hidden manner in the Scriptures. See how Paul speaks to the Corinthians: "I gave you milk to drink, not food, for you were not yet capable of it; nor are you now capable"

[1 Cor 3:2]. And since they still needed milk, they learn the things that small children typically learn: "It is good for a man not to touch a woman; but because of fornication" [1 Cor 7:1–2], etc. And again, they are instructed not to eat things that have been sacrificed to idols [1 Cor 8].

(3) All this instruction is the milk of little children and of those who are still infants in Christ. But when he writes to the Ephesians, he offers them solid food [cf. Heb 5:12–14]. For "there is" no "talk of fornication" [cf. 1 Cor 5:1] in Ephesus, nor is there talk of idolatry and of eating things that have been sacrificed to idols. From this we are shown what solid food consists in, and that the "rational milk that is without deceit" [cf. 1 Pet 2:2] refers to moral subject matter. Solid food refers to the mystical understanding. It is then a blessed thing for us to hasten toward things that are more perfect, passing on from beginning principles. And the apostle shows that milk refers to moral subject matter when, after he had already spoken about milk, he adds: "Not again laying a foundation of repentance from dead works" [Heb 6:1]. Everyone who still drinks milk is like this, but the perfect man needs other instructions. These things had to be spoken openly, since I had ascended above the wording. In the explanation of the one kind of fornication, I wanted to avoid dealing with the other kind of fornication, which I shall now explain.

Threefold Fornication

(4) For it is said to Jerusalem: "And you committed a threefold fornication in your daughters" [Ezek 16:30]. What do his words mean when he says that Jerusalem committed a threefold fornication in her daughters"? We need God's help, that he himself may explain the obscurity of this passage. And just as Moses heard God and then set forth before the people what he had heard from God [cf. Exod 25:1ff.; 35:1ff.], so we need the Holy Spirit to speak mysteries in us, that, by your prayers, we might be able to hear the Scripture and again announce to the people what we have heard. What, then, is the meaning of "You committed a threefold fornication in your daughters"? You will see Jerusalem committing a threefold fornication when you understand fornication of the flesh, of the soul, and of the spirit, that is, if you see someone committing fornication in these. But the one

who is chaste threefold is he who deserves to hear the Apostle say: "But may God sanctify you through all things, and may he preserve your whole spirit and soul and body without fault at the coming of our Lord Jesus Christ" [1 Thess 5:23], "to whom is the glory and power for ages of ages. Amen" [1 Pet 4:11].

HOMILY 8

Brothels, Head and Base of Streets, Gifts (Ezekiel 16:30–33)

Where to Fix Your Heart?

1. We have explained the things that were read first. Today let us begin with what is written: "Where shall I establish your heart, says the Lord Adonai, when you do all these things, the works of a shameless harlot, and you committed a threefold fornication in your daughters" [Ezek 16:30]. We have already spoken about the things that come up to this point. It follows: "When you built your brothel at the head of every way, and you made your base on every street. And you have not acted as a harlot gathering gifts (*mercedes*). The woman who commits adultery similar to you received gifts (*mercedes*) from her husband, she gave gifts (*mercedes*) to all her lovers; and you have given gifts (*mercedes*) to all your lovers, and you have honored them that they should come to you in a circuit for fornication with you" [Ezek 16:31–33].

(2) A man can establish a man, an evil man in evil, a good man in good. For "bad company corrupts good morals" [1 Cor 15:33]. There is no doubt that the words of the one speaking incite the hearer to worse things, as when a heretic speaks and establishes his hearer in heretical depravity. And when we come to better things, if the one who speaks can do good, and his life agrees with his words, he establishes his hearer in good things. We who are in the least place, if we hear words that recommend chastity, we try to be established on them. If we ourselves speak about purity, we also as hearers establish ourselves in purity; if we preach about justice, we impel unto justice; if about faith, we inspire faith, that we might obey the Lord in a way

that is worthy of the divine majesty. If, then, we human beings, though we are evil [cf. Matt 7:11], are accustomed to establishing the hearer's heart, whether in good things, if we are good, or in evils, if we do evilly, do you think that God does not have the ability to establish someone in better things, or even to abandon him, so that there comes to him an occasion by which he is established in evils? According to the present utterance, wretched Jerusalem sinned much. How often indeed did God wish through his prophets to establish her in better things, but because she was unwilling to hear his counsels and accept God's commandments, God hesitates and says he does not know what to do: "Where shall I establish your heart? says the Lord Adonai" [Ezek 16:30]. What shall I do? Where shall I establish you? You are bound by many chains of sins; your crimes prevent your life from being established by my words. I often wanted to establish you by speaking through my saints, and you did not listen. Now I don't know what to do, and I say to you: "Where shall I establish your heart, says the Lord Adonai, when you are doing all these things, the works of a shameless harlot?" [Ezek 16:30].

(3) We have often said[1] that the opposing powers love the beauty of the human soul and, when a human soul receives the seed of her lovers, in some way she commits fornication with them. But because even in the common life there are certain prostitutes who commit fornication with shame, desiring to be unnoticed, but others who not only do not veil their transgressions with shame but prostitute themselves with all shamelessness, therefore for this sinful Jerusalem he has taken the example of a soul of a prostitute. And he says that in her fornication she has become like a shameless prostitute. Often such things are committed even by us. For those who have not completely withdrawn from religion but are conquered by sin and want to remain unnoticed in their sinning are acting like a blushing prostitute. But those who are completely turned away from religion to such an extent that they don't care about the bishop, the priests, the deacons, or the brethren, but sin with all shamelessness, are like the prostitute who prostitutes herself with effrontery. God complains, then, in this passage about the sinful Jerusalem, because she is doing the works of a shameless prostitute, and he says to her: "And you committed a threefold fornication in your daughters" [Ezek 16:30]. We have explained this when it was said to us: "You built your brothel at the head of every way, and you made your base on every street" [Ezek 16:31].

At the Head of Every Street

2. Now we want to interpret the meaning of "to build a brothel," not simply "on every way" but "at the head of every way." Nor was it adequate "to build the brothel at the head of every way," but beyond this, "to set up her base on every street." Well, then, she committed two general sins, when "she built her brothel at the head of every way," and when "the harlot Jerusalem made a base" and established it "on every street."

(2) What are these ways? "Stand in the ways and ask for the eternal paths of the Lord, and see what is the good way and walk in it" [Jer 6:16]. Many are the eternal ways. If you hold to this explanation that I have often set forth, you know that Moses too is a way, as is each of the prophets. And just as there are many pearls, which it is necessary for one to possess who is about to come upon "the one pearl of great price" [Matt 13:46], so it is necessary to enter upon the many ways of Moses and all the prophets for the one who is about to come to the one who says: "I am the way" [John 14:6]. But someone says to me: How does what you have said pertain to the subject? I will respond to this person as follows. Jerusalem built her brothel on every way. If you consider all the heretics who are estranged from the truth as the ones who are building a house from these words that are read in Moses, from those they have found that are in Isaiah, Jeremiah, and the rest of the prophets, then you will understand that the new doctrines are the fornication of Jerusalem, who builds her brothel not on every way but at the head of every way.

(3) For if, after the starting point of Moses, after the commencement of the prophets, someone has been prevented from reaching its depth and the knowledge of all, that prostitute who builds a brothel on every way cannot do anything. She seeks the one who is first making an entrance into the church, who has received the beginning elements of the faith, who is a raw recruit in the mysteries. She wants to introduce into her brothel the one who is at the beginning point of the faith, as she builds her house of prostitution. And since fornication is frequently named in the Scriptures, I want to explain the reason for this word. Ecclesiastical men who are teachers in the church purge morals, both their own and those of their people, and by their diligence they build up the house of God, the church, and their task is the building of God. Heretics build a brothel on every

way, as, for example, the teacher of Valentinus's training school, the teacher of Basilides' band, the teacher of Marcion's tavern,[2] and of the other heretics. They build a prostitute's home. For a brothel is a gathering of all evils. But what does Scripture say? "Son, give no heed to an evil woman; for honey drips from the lips of a prostitute" [Prov 5:3]. From what source does the honey drip for her? "For honey drips from the lips of a prostitute." She entered unto Moses, to Isaiah, to Jeremiah, and from their writings she gathered honey for herself. Go to the heretics who say: Thus says Moses, thus says Isaiah, [thus says Jeremiah], and you will see how the honey does not flow from their lips, but it drips from those who pick a few words from these writings. And therefore honey drips from the lips of a prostitute. So then, "At the head of every way she builds a brothel" [Ezek 16:31].

On Every Street and Way

(4) So be it, the brothel should be so understood. We should also interpret the base that the prostitute Jerusalem set up on every street. It is written in another passage how: "A prostitute openly calls to those passing by on the streets" [Prov 9:15]. For sin strives to attract us to itself in various ways, whether through heresy or through a pagan way of living. And through heresy, indeed, when she builds a brothel on the head of every *way*; through a pagan way of living, when she sets up a base on every street. "For broad and open is the *way* that leads to destruction" [Matt 7:13]. Since, then, it is out of the Scriptures that she asserts the things that she is saying, and in which she is trying to instruct the hearers, "she builds a brothel on the head of every *way*." But when the moral subject matter has been destroyed, and by instructing things of luxury, she made the hearer lascivious, what else has she done but set up a base on every *way*?

Gifts

3. "It was not done like a prostitute gathering gifts (*mercedes*)" [Ezek 16:31]. Let us consider the prostitute who gathers gifts and again another who does not gather them. For from this it is asked as

if about the prostitute not gathering gifts. When I consider that there is a prostitute who does not gather gifts, and I read that it is said to her that she has acted as a prostitute not gathering gifts, I would say that to gather gifts is to become wealthy by sinning, to confer glory in secular affairs by sinning, to live happily in this world by sinning. When, as I have said, these things arise through sin, the soul is committing fornication and gathering gifts of its fornication, it is gathering glory, wealth, and the other things, which it has acquired for the destruction of its own soul. But when it commits fornication and does not live prosperously in secular affairs, but through what it has sinned it likewise lives unhappily in the world, then it is a prostitute not gathering gifts but doing the opposite, that is, fornicating and beyond that paying out gifts.

(2) "And you gave gifts to all your lovers" [Ezek 16:33]. Sometimes the soul enriches her lovers who rejoice because they have received gifts from her. But a hearer says to me: Explain how a soul commits fornication by paying out gifts from the goods of her husband. For thus the divine Word says, both in the present passage and in other passages, that the prostitute Jerusalem took her husband's things and gave them to her lovers. What is this that her husband has given to her that later, when she has become an adulteress, she gives all that she had received to her lovers?

(3) The soul's husband is the Word of God, a true bridegroom and lover,[3] who gave chastity to her; he gave justice, he gave the other good things. So then, when the soul wants to follow the opposing powers—that is, to say it more plainly, when the soul has lived chastely for ten years but in the end commits fornication—she takes her husband's goods, which he had acquired over much time with effort, and she gives these things to her lovers. These bloodthirsty lovers seize to themselves the virtues of the wretched soul and move on, boasting over her riches, and they say: I have taken from her a chastity of ten years, I have snatched from her five years worth of justice [cf. Ezek 18:24], I have laid claim for myself to her powers. God has forgotten all her goods which at one time she had done, since she has been seized in sin and he has forgotten her [cf. Ezek 18:24]. For our female friend has confessed to us the secrets that she heard, and she handed over all the goods to us, her lovers. By learning these things, "Let us preserve our heart with all watchfulness" [Prov 4:23], and let us pay attention, lest at some time the things that belong to

the husband may be handed over to evil lovers. Instead let us invite the bridegroom, the Word and the truth, to make for us golden adornments imprinted with various signs by means of various commands. And having become adorned, let us make preparations for our husband Christ Jesus, "to whom is the glory and power for ages of ages. Amen" [1 Pet 4:11].

HOMILY 9

Iniquities, Pride, Relative Justification (Ezekiel 16:45–52)

ORIGINS

1. At the beginning of the prophecy, we read that Jerusalem too is rebuked as one who has her "root and birth from the land of Canaan, an Amorite father and a Hittite mother" [cf. Ezek 16:3]. If one reads this together with the things that we are now trying to interpret, one will think that the same things are being repeated, that one set of words is being preached twice. But the one who is a diligent reader and who applies his attention to the significance of the divine Scripture and relates the things that have been passed over to the present things, and compares word with word, will see a difference that is not fortuitous. For in the former passage he says, "your (*tua*) root and your (*tua*) birth are from the land of Canaan." This is not said in the present passage. Also: "your (*tuus*) father is an Amorite, and your (*tua*) mother a Hittite" is not presently signified. And again, there it is first set down: "Your (*tuus*) father is an Amorite," secondly: "Your (*tua*) mother is a Hittite"; but here: "Your (*vestra*) mother is a Hittite and your (*vester*) father an Amorite" [Ezek 16:45].[1] There the words are, as it were, addressed to one person; here as if to many. For he does not say, as he had said higher up, "Your (*tua*) mother," but "your (*vestra*) mother."[2] Therefore, when sin is diffused and evil goes forth more widely and sinners share their sins among themselves, then there is not a single sinner, but in one there are many, just as in the beginning when there was a commencement of transgressing, there were not yet so many as the multitudes that now exist. This is

why it seems useful to me to back away from the present words to consider the nature of sin and virtue.

Multiplicity, Unity

(2) Where there are sins, there is multiplicity[3], there are schisms, there are heresies, there are dissensions; but where there is virtue, there is the solitariness and unity from which there was "one heart and one soul" in all the faithful [Acts 4:32].[4] That I might speak more clearly, the beginning of all evils is multiplicity, but the beginning of goods is limitation and withdrawal from the crowds into solitariness. For example, if we are to be saved, we must in unity "become perfect in the same mind and in the same thought" [1 Cor 1:10]. We must be "one body and one spirit" [Eph 4:4]. But if we are such that unity does not circumscribe us, but it could even be said about us: "I am of Paul, but I am of Apollo, I am of Cephas" [1 Cor 1:12], and we are still being torn apart and divided by evil; we are not going to be where those ones are who are drawn back into union. For as the Father and the Son are one [cf. John 10:30], so those who have one Spirit are confined into a union. For the Savior says: "I and the Father, we are one" [John 10:30], and: "Holy Father, just as I and you are one, that even they may be one in us" [John 17:11–12]. And one reads in the Apostle: "Until we all attain to the perfect man and to the measure of the age of fullness in the unity of Christ" [Eph 4:13]; and again: "Until we all attain to the unity of the body and spirit of Christ" [Eph 4:13]. From this it is signified that virtue makes one from many, and that we need to become one through it and to flee from the multitude.[5] And let these things indeed be said since it was recorded in the reading that we passed over: "Thy (*tuus*) father and thy (*tua*) mother and the root of thy (*tuae*) birth" [Ezek 16:3], but in the present: "Your (*vestra*) mother and your (*vester*) father" [Ezek 16:45].[6]

The Sisters of Jerusalem

(3) There, although the words were about an Amorite father and a Hittite mother, we did not learn that Jerusalem has sisters; but

here he made this addition, saying: "Your mother was a Hittite and your father an Amorite, and your elder sister was Samaria, she and her daughters, who dwell on your left, and your younger sister was Sodom, who dwells on your right" [Ezek 16:45–46]. Just as virtue makes me a son of Abraham, if I live in accordance with it—for "the one who does the works of Abraham is a son of Abraham" [John 8:39]—so vice makes me a son of the devil; for "all who commit sin are born of the devil" [1 John 3:8]. Virtue also causes me to have Christ for a brother, so that when I become good and when I live well, he says to his Father: "I shall declare your name to my brothers, in the midst of the church I will sing of you" [Ps 22:22]. And to her who was able to announce his words, he says: "Go, and tell my brothers" [John 20:17]. But just as virtue makes the Lord Jesus my brother, so evil acquires many brothers and these sinners, and then this evil, when it grows, generates brothers for me.

(4) Indeed, when sinful Jerusalem was at her beginning, she had no sister Samaria, nor did she yet have Sodom as a sister; but as she advanced in wickedness, as the past words showed, she took up the middle place between the two sisters, the elder one Samaria and the younger one Sodom. Who are these two sisters of sinful Jerusalem? A schism and division of the people created Samaria. For indeed, at that time, when the ten tribes withdrew, saying: "For us there is no portion among David nor an allotment among the son of Jesse" [1 Kgs 12:16], then two golden calves were set up by Jeroboam [cf. 1 Kgs 12:28], and Samaria became a schism. The schism grew all the more after the captivity of the ten tribes, when guards were sent by the Assyrians to the land of Israel, who are called Samaritans; for in the Hebrew language "guard" is translated as *somar*. Therefore, as I began to say, Samaria is not yet my sister as long as I am far from sin; but when I sin, two sisters are produced for me, the elder Samaria and the younger Sodom. Let us consider what figure they contain.

(5) Whoever promises divine words and does not have the truth of the proclamation in themselves, as they promise, these are figuratively called Samaritans in the Scriptures. "Woe," it says, "to those who spurn Zion and to those who trust in the mountain of Samaria; you have harvested the rulers of the nations" [Amos 6:1]. It is as if he had said: Woe to those who spurn the church and trust in the arrogance and inflated words of the heretics! For this is what it means to spurn Zion and to trust in the mountain of Samaria. Therefore, if we men

of the church sin, the heretics with their perverse doctrines are not estranged from us. For whoever sins is a bad believer. If we have a bad way of life, Sodom is our sister; for the pagans are Sodom. Thus, when we transgress we are brothers both of the heretics and of the pagans, for Samaria is understood for heresy, and Sodom stands for paganism.

(6) But "Samaria dwells on the left" of sinful Jerusalem, "Sodom on the right" [Ezek 16:46]. For with her the sin is more honorable that is committed in deed, and therefore Sodom is on her right. And again, Samaria is not far away, since she dwells on her left, and is rebuked because "she walked with her daughters and sisters in all iniquities," and she walked to such an extent that a comparison of her transgressions "made the iniquities of those [cities] justice" [cf. Ezek 16:47, 51]. This is why one needs to become acquainted with the iniquities of Sodom, so that, having been instructed, I might guard myself from them and not be caught in ignorance of what Sodom's iniquities consisted in.

PRIDE

2. "Yet the iniquity of your sister Sodom" [Ezek 16:49]. What iniquity? "Pride; she and her daughters were affluent in sufficiency of bread and in abundance; and they did not take the hand of the poor and needy" [Ezek 16:49]. It is doubtful to no one that sins are not qualitatively equal, since the Scriptures show this. For some are said to be great; some are said to be less than these. But since they are not equal, whether they are small or very great, perhaps someone may inquire about which sins among the universal sins are greater. It is easily understood that among all the sins the greatest is either fornication, uncleanness, or any kind of defilement associated with lust. These indeed are truly abominations and sources of pollution, but these are not the kind of things that are now being condemned by the Scripture as greatest of all and against which we must be on our guard.

(2) What sin, then, is greater than all sins? Assuredly it is that on account of which even the devil fell. What is that sin into which such a great sublimity fell, so that the Apostle says: "having been puffed up he falls into the judgment of the devil" [1 Tim 3:6]? Haughtiness, pride, arrogance—this is the sin of the devil. It is on account of these transgressions that he emigrated from heaven to earth. This is why it

says: "God resists the proud, but he gives grace to the humble" [Jas 4:6], and: "why are earth and ashes proud?" [Sir 10:9]. By this a man is lifted up by arrogance, forgetful of what will be, and how he is contained in a fragile vessel, and what filth he is immersed in and what sort of purgings he constantly casts forth from his flesh. For what does the Scripture say? "Why are earth and ashes proud?" and: "In his life he cast forth his bowels" [Sir 10:9]. Pride is greater than all sins, and is the principal sin of the devil himself. If at any time the Scripture describes the sins of the devil, you will find that these emanate from the font of pride.[7] For it says: "I will act in strength, and in the wisdom of [my] understanding I will remove the boundaries of nations, and will consume their powers; and I will shake the inhabited cities and I will seize the whole globe of lands as a nest, and I will remove them as broken eggs" [Isa 10:13–14]. Notice how proud are his words, how arrogant, and how he regards the universe as nothing. That is what everyone is like who is puffed up with boasting and pride. The material of pride is wealth, rank, and worldly glory.

(3) Very often the priesthood and Levitical rank are a cause of pride in men who do not realize that they have ecclesiastical positions. How many who have been raised to the priesthood have forgotten humility! As if the purpose of their ordination was for them to cease being humble! Instead, they should have pursued humility all the more,[8] and precisely because they have been raised to this position, since the Scripture says: "The greater you are, the more you must humble yourself" [Sir 3:18]. The assembly[9] has selected you. Then lower your head more humbly. They have appointed you as a leader: Do not be lifted up, but become among them as one of them. We must be humble, we must be cast down, we must flee from pride, which is the source of all evils. Think of the Gospel: with what severity are the pride and boasting of the Pharisee condemned! "The Pharisee stood and prayed thus with himself: 'God, I thank you that I am not like other men, extortioners, unjust, adulterers, and like this tax collector. I fast twice a week.' But the tax collector," humbly and meekly "standing far off, did not dare even to lift up his eyes, and he said: 'God, be merciful to me a sinner!' And the tax collector went down to his house justified" [Luke 18:11–14]. He was not simply justified, but justified in comparison with the Pharisee.

(4) For the entire wording of Scripture, the order, and connections must be most diligently observed. It is one thing to be justified,

something else to be justified by another. That the tax collector was justified by the Pharisee is similar to the way Sodom and Samaria were justified in comparison with a sinful Jerusalem [cf. Ezek 16:51]. For we must know that each one of us, on the day of judgment, will be justified by one and condemned by another. Even when we are justified by another, that justice is less an object of praise than of blame. If, for example, I am found guilty of Sodomitic sins and someone else is brought forward who has committed twice as many serious sins, I am justified, to be sure; but I am justified not as a just man, but as it were in comparison with one who has committed more sins. I am judged to be just, although I am a long way from justice.

(5) Woe to that man who is justified by many sinners. Conversely, blessed by far is he who is shown to be just in comparison with the just. We have found among the praises of Scripture that one who is better is recorded to be among the good; for example, [when it says that] no one acted so rightly before the face of the Lord as this one and that one. "No one celebrated the Passover in the way that Josiah did" [2 Chr 34:2; 35:18]. From this it is shown that a comparison with the just is being made, and that one is truly just who deserves to be justified in this way. Would that I might be found to be wise when I am compared with the wise, and that I might be judged to be just by the just. For I do not wish to be justified by the unjust, because such justice is blameworthy.

INIQUITIES

3. I have said these things in anticipation, because in the things that have been read it is said: "You have justified your sisters by all your iniquities that you have done" [Ezek 16:51]. For Samaria and Sodom have been justified by the iniquities of Jerusalem. "By all your iniquities that you have done, you have justified them over yourself" [Ezek 16:51–52]. Therefore, let us pay more careful attention, that we might be able to know that all of us must be justified on the day of judgment by those who are worse than us, and on the other hand others are justified by us. There is only one who is justified by everyone and he justifies no one. For example, Sodom is justified by Jerusalem, since Jerusalem committed graver crimes than she did; and perhaps Jerusalem will be justified by some other city worse than herself. Thus,

there is someone who is going to be justified by the Antichrist, who is compared to him and is found inferior to him in his iniquity and crimes. But he is the worst demon and, as they say, wretched is the one who is justified by him [cf. Ps 1:1]. Perhaps even the father of that one will not be justified by him, who has been found to be much more guilty than that one.

(2) But in accordance with the dispensation of the flesh, which he bore for the sake of our salvation, my Lord Jesus Christ is justified by Abraham, by Isaac, by Jacob, and by the rest of the prophets. For I glorify our Savior all the more when all the just, the prophets, and blessed men have been placed in comparison with him and one finds the contrary to that which is said of Sodom and Jerusalem. But what I am saying is of the following nature, and as God grants in answer to your prayers, I will offer an explanation from the Scriptures.

(3) Sodom committed sin, Samaria too sinned, Jerusalem was covered with iniquities; but lesser sins are justified by greater ones according to the example by which Sodom is justified by her sister Jerusalem. Therefore just as iniquity justifies, so sometimes justice condemns. But wait a little bit, I pray, until you are shown how justice may be said to condemn. My iniquity is justice in comparison with greater iniquity. So also, my justice is reckoned as iniquity in comparison with a more complete justice. This is why it says: "no man living will be justified in your sight" [Ps 143:2]. Although Abraham may have been just, and Moses was just, and each of the illustrious men was just, but compared with Christ they are not just; their light, when compared with his light, turns out to be darkness [cf. Matt 6:23]. And just as the light of a lamp becomes dark before the rays of the sun, and it becomes dark like all other blind matter, so too the light of all the just: it may be bright "before men," but it is not bright before Christ.[10] For it is not said simply "let your light shine," but "let it shine before men" [Matt 5:16]. The light of the just cannot shine before Christ. As the splendor of the moon and the glittering stars of heaven sparkle in their places before the sun rises, but as soon as the sun rises they go into hiding, so too before the true light "of the sun of justice" [Mal 4:2] rises, the light of the church, like the light of the moon, is bright and clear before men; but when Christ comes it fades before him.[11] And elsewhere it is written: "The light shines in the darkness" [John 1:5]. Which light is it that shines in the darkness? The light of the just ones shines in the darkness. But in which darkness? In that one where

"our struggle is against the rulers of this darkness" [Eph 6:12]. Whoever gives this long and diligent consideration will hardly be able to get puffed up when he sees his own light considered as darkness in comparison with that greater light. What is my justice, even if I should be the Apostle Paul? [cf. Phil 3:6]. What is my chastity, even if I be a Joseph? [cf. Gen 39:6–12]. "What is my courage, even if I stand out as a Judas Maccabeus? [cf. 1 Macc 2:66; 2 Macc 15:10]. In comparison with God, what other virtue of wisdom do I have, even if I appear as a Solomon? [cf. 1 Kgs 4:29]. Therefore, as we began to say, iniquity justifies and justice condemns in comparison with others.

(4) This is why it is said to God: "that you may be justified by your words, and you may conquer when you are judged" [Ps 51:4; Rom 3:4]. If God wants to save me, he does not bring his own light into the judgment; if he wants me to be unscathed, he does not bring the light of his Christ—otherwise he will punish me—but he brings the light of lesser ones; he compares those who are inferior to me. To the extent that he compares me with those who are greater and better, so much the more just will I be, if they are found inferior to me. What the Apostle says is to be understood similarly to this: "There is one glory of the sun, another glory of the moon, another glory of the stars; for star differs from star in brightness; so also the resurrection of the dead" [1 Cor 15:41–42]. For example, such and such a star sparkles not in the presence of a brighter star, but of one that is dimmer. Who among us can shine like the moon, who can glitter by the light of brighter stars, according to what is written in Daniel: "They will shine like the stars for the ages" [Dan 12:3]?

Pride (continued)

4. We have discussed these things indeed out of necessity that we might distance ourselves from pride. For pride is the sin of Sodom. "This is the iniquity of your sister Sodom, pride" [Ezek 16:49]. He goes on to speak of the source from which pride arises and what are its roots. "They were affluent in the sufficiency of bread and in abundance" [Ezek 16:49]. If you look at the letter alone, the meaning is that there was great abundance among the Sodomites of antiquity. For their land was "like the Paradise of God and like the land of Egypt" [Gen 13:10].

(2) But if you ascend from the carnal to the spiritual understanding in order to see how "the pride of the Sodomites flowed in the sufficiency of bread and in abundance," you will receive a benefit both for the task of living and for certain other very great things that need to be chastised. Let us first present what was read many days ago:[12] "There was a rich man clothed in fine linen and purple, rejoicing daily" in delights and luxury, and "Lazarus" who was wasting away with decaying wounds and with filthy vermin, who sought relief from his hunger by "the crumbs that fell from his table" [cf. Luke 16:19]. That reference is suitable now for this passage. For it clarifies the iniquity of the rich man. He was rich, he abounded in delights. Scripture did not accuse him for possessing his riches by iniquity. The divine word did not incriminate him as one who had surrendered himself to prostitutes or as a murderer or as one who had committed any other wicked acts.

(3) But if you consider what is written in the present passage, and what is said in the Gospel, you will see that the rich man's greatest sin, among all his sins, was pride. For he was "affluent in the sufficiency of bread and in abundance" [Ezek 16:49]. He did not have any feeling of pity toward him who "was lying before his gates, wasting away with ulcers" [Luke 16:20–21]. On the contrary, he was puffed up with such great pride that he despised the poor man. He did not take into account either the supplications of inferiors or common human rights. For in view of his similar [human] condition it would have been befitting for the man to think human thoughts and somehow to have pity on the calamities of others. So then, even that rich man was from Sodom. For if there were such sins in Sodom—that is, that it was "in sufficiency of bread and in abundance," but even the rich man who is described in the Gospel is such a man—then it should be doubtful to no one that the rich man is from Sodom. But just as Sodom and the daughters of the Sodomites were proud, so are all arrogant souls. And the daughters of Sodom, whosoever they may be, are ignorant of the statement: "Everyone who exalts himself will be humbled, and whoever humbles himself will be exalted" [Luke 18:14].

Another Sin

5. "This was her portion and that of her daughters" [Ezek 16:49]. Next follows another sin of Sodom that we ought to mention,

lest we be found to be guilty of the same charge: "And she did not take the hand of the poor and the needy" [Ezek 16:49]. Consider carefully the enumeration of Sodom's sins. I myself have the sin of Sodom, if I do not help the hand of the poor and needy in accordance with my resources [cf. 2 Cor 8:3]. Another accusation follows: "And she was boasting arrogantly" [Ezek 16:50]. Vain boasting is another Sodomitic charge. Now there are certain Egyptian sins, certain Sodomitic sins; there are others that are Babylonian, others Assyrian, others Moabite, others Ammonite. "Who is wise and has understanding of these things, or who understands and will know these things?" [Hos 14:10].

(2) When we read the description of the destruction of the Sodomites, we should not say: "Oh, the poor Sodomites, whose descendants the earth no longer bears! How pitiful and lamentable are those who suffered such sad and fearsome things!" Rather we should apply these words to our own hearts (*corda*). "Let us examine our hearts (*renes*)" and thoughts [cf. Rev 2:23]. Then we will see that those for whom we are mourning are contained within us, and that the Sodomitic and Egyptian and Assyrian and all the other sins that Scripture castigates and enumerates are found in ourselves.

(3) Higher up we promised that we were going to say something greater from the Scripture. To Sodom, who had transgressed in the sufficiency of bread and in abundance and in pleasures and sins of that sort, the law says: "Watch yourself, lest you eat and drink when filled up, and build good homes, and your oxen and sheep are multiplied to you, and when you are made to abound in silver and gold, you should forget the Lord your God" [cf. Deut 8:11–14]. And in another passage: "And the beloved ate and drank and was satisfied and grew fat and balked" [Deut 32:15]. Solomon says things similar to these in the Proverbs: "Establish for me what is necessary and adequate, that I may not become a liar when I am filled up and say: Who sees me? or being in need I may steal, and I will swear by the name of God" [Prov 30:8–9]. Let it simply be said that nothing rises into arrogance so much as wealth, sufficiency and the nourishment of having abundant resources. One's station in life also contributes to this, as does prestige.

(4) But it is even possible to see here a means of passing to a higher level. Very often I nourish pride when I come to understand the divine word, when I become wiser than the rest. For "knowledge puffs up" [1 Cor 8:1]. It is not I who say this, but the Apostle. And therefore I fear lest even I may be lifted up. Charisms are given for that which

is useful. If they are given for that which is useful, who is he for whom it is not useful? And listen to why it would not be useful. To the inferior it inspires swelling up and a certain complacency, while he thinks that he is eminent among the others. Often, then, sufficiency of bread and abundance feeds arrogance, and often even from spiritual gifts the charge of arrogance arises, and there is danger in both. So great a man as the Apostle Paul needed the "blows of a messenger of Satan to harass him, to keep him from being too elated" [cf. 2 Cor 12:7]. For by praying and pleading with God he procured for many what he often asked for; but when he likewise asked for this, he did not obtain what he asked for. It was said to him: "My grace is sufficient for you; for virtue is perfected in weakness" [cf. 2 Cor 12:8–9]. And so, it is necessary for the one who still lives among the human race and in this present light to fear not only the things that are thought to be good things in the world but also the things that are truly good, since we are not able to endure great things.

(5) To prove my current opinion I shall exhibit the story of David, where it is recorded that he committed a sin against Uriah [cf. 2 Sam 11:2–27]. Before Uriah, no sin is found in David; he was a blessed man and "without blame in the sight of God." But because he became conscious of his spotless life, he said what he should not have said, when he said: "Listen, Lord, to my justice, attend to my petition; give ear to my prayer that is not with deceitful lips. Let my judgment come forth from your face, let your eyes see equities. You have proven my heart, you have visited at night; you have examined me with fire, and iniquity has not been found in me" [Ps 17:1–3]. And he said these things because God's visitation was presented to him on account of his conscience and beatitude of life. He was tested and deprived of help, that he might see what human weakness can do. For when the help of God withdrew, he, the very chaste one, was not able to persevere. For he was the one who was admired for his modesty, who had heard: "If your young men are clean especially from women" [cf. 1 Sam 21:4–5], and who had received the Eucharist[13] as one who was clean. Instead he was caught in the very sin for which he had prided himself on being continent.

(6) If, then, someone is conscious of his own purity and boasts in himself, forgetful of the statement: "But what do you have that you have not received? But if you received it, why do you boast as though you had not received it?" [1 Cor 4:7] he is deserted. And once aban-

doned, he learns by experience that in these goods in himself of which he was conscious, it was not so much he himself who stood forth as the cause, but God who is the font of all virtues. From this it appears that both the sufficiency of bread and the spiritual gifts generate pride in him who is not able to sustain these things. Therefore let us flee from Sodom and its sins. Let us flee from Samaria and the charges for which wretched Jerusalem is rebuked, so that in all things, as God supplies the strength to us, we might attain to humility and justice in Christ Jesus, "to whom is the glory and power for ages of ages. Amen" [1 Pet 4:11].

HOMILY 10

Shame, Return, Restoration (Ezekiel 16:52–63)

Shame

1. Now the first thing is to do no shameful work,[1] but only the kind that can look upon God with an open face. But because, as human beings, we often sin, we should know that there is a second ship,[2] so to speak, after shameful works, namely, to be ashamed and modestly to lower your eyes because of your misdeeds, instead of walking around with a look of effrontery, as if you had not sinned at all. For it is good to be ashamed after committing shameful works. For often the maker of evil is at work in keeping the sinner from returning to repentance, so that the sinner acts as if he is still persevering in justice. From daily life we can see and learn that many men, after their sins, not only do not mourn for what they have done, but they even defend their own failures with a look of effrontery. And so, a great benefit is being reserved for Jerusalem, if she will only believe the Lord who says: "And you, be ashamed" [Ezek 16:52].

(2) Do not think that these things are said only to Jerusalem, and do not apply to each of us who are held liable for transgressions. "For each one should consider himself" [cf. 1 Cor 4:1], what he has done that is worthy of being ashamed of, what he has spoken that is disgraceful, of what statement he is not proud in the way that he is when he makes a good statement, what he thinks that seems worthy of being ashamed of before him "who considers the secrets of the heart and of the inner being" [Ps 7:9]. And when he carefully looks into his thoughts, deeds, and words,[3] he is ashamed when he hears the

prophet saying: "And you, be ashamed." After this it is added by the prophet: "And bear your dishonor for having justified your sisters" [Ezek 16:52]. Dishonor follows shame, and God gives dishonor to him as well as who has done things worthy of being ashamed of, and he says to him: "And bear your dishonor."

In the Cities

(3) But you can understand what is said if you consider what happens daily in the cities. It is a dishonor for a citizen to be exiled from his native land. It is a dishonor for a councilman to be erased from list of the senate, and for a man of whatever other condition to be left alive, to be sure, but with dishonor, whether sentenced to public works or to be left alone on some island [cf. Rev 1:9]. But understand with me that the just judge says to him who did things worthy of dishonor: "O you who deserve to be punished, do not endure your exile with grief, for you will not deserve pity, if you get angry at the punishment; but rather understand that you are suffering deservedly what you suffer." And when you have humbled yourself and say that the judgment that has been carried out against you is just, perhaps you may attain mercy from him who can call you back to your original status after your condemnation. For just as it is allowed for a great ruler to liberate someone from an island and from exile and from public prison, how much more is it allowed to God to restore to former honor him who was dishonored. But this will happen only if, when he thinks about his sin, he confesses that he deserved to endure what he has suffered [cf. Luke 23:39–43].

In the Church

(4) I will give another example from ecclesiastical custom. It is an infamy to be separated from the people of God and from the church. It is a disgrace in the church to leave the congress of the priesthood or be expelled from the rank of deacon. And indeed, of those who are thrown out, some cause dissensions, but others accept with all humility the judgment made against them. Those, then, who

out of indignation over their deposition are incited to gather people together in order to make a schism, and who stir up a multitude of evils,[4] are not "bearing their disgrace" [cf. Ezek 16:52] in the present. On the contrary, they are "storing up for themselves a treasure of wrath" [Rom 2:5]. But those will gain mercy from God who, with all humility, leave the judgment to God and patiently bear the judgment made about them, whether they have been rightly or wrongly deposed. And frequently men even call them back to their earlier office and to the honor they had lost. The lesson is excellent, then, both what is said: "And you, be ashamed," and that which follows: "And bear your dishonor" [Ezek 16:52].

Dishonor

(5) Now I am saying these things in order to introduce a more profound meaning concerning the coming dishonor. For even there [in the future life], there will be a certain dishonor for those who have done a work worthy of dishonor. For indeed "some will rise unto eternal life and others unto reproach and eternal shame" [Dan 12:2]. But what else does this refer to but that they will endure the punishment of dishonor? Therefore, while it is still possible for us, we ought patiently to endure our abasement [cf. Sir 20:11], so that when we have endured this grief bravely here, in the future age we may arouse, so to speak, "the bowels of the mercy of God" [Luke 1:78] and his kindness. Thus he may call us back to our original status from dishonor and shame.

(6) Conversely, it is impossible for anyone who has a heart of stone, who does not deep down feel his sin, to attain to the surpassing mercy in the presence of the Almighty God. For we do indeed see certain good men who willingly endure the sentence passed on them, and for the sake of their salvation they justify God's judgment; but evil men blaspheme against the providence of God and say: I have been adjudged of this infamy undeservedly, I am enduring these things unjustly. If we justify Providence, we pay off our infamy; but if we do not receive God's judgments, we multiply our infamy. And what happens to the infamy also happens to the penalties, and to the other things that are often accustomed to happening likewise with this to those who have been condemned by God for their sins.

RETURN

2. "And you, be ashamed and bear your dishonor for having justified your sisters" [Ezek 16:52]. We are more deserving of dishonor when we do such things by which other sinners are justified, so that by comparison with my sins, mercy would absolve the wicked deeds of evil men condemned long ago, for my having subsequently committed worse things. That is why it is said to sinful Jerusalem: "Bear your dishonor for having justified your sisters." Then, if someone has fulfilled what is written: "Be ashamed," if someone has carried out the following sentence of God: "Bear your dishonor for having justified your sisters" [Ezek 16:52], let him also see the grace, how in exchange for his shame, a change to clemency is restored. For he did not despise the judgment of God [cf. Rom 2:4]. Instead, with all humility he endured what had been judged for him.

(2) What, then, is promised? "I will turn away their turnings away with the turning away of Sodom and her sisters, for your having justified your sisters Sodom and Samaria" [Ezek 16:52–53]. This refers to Sodom, as the younger, and Samaria, as the elder, as we have said in the preceding.[6] "I will turn away their turning away." This means, of the three whose turning away he had turned away, he will convert to better things, first that of Sodom, then of Samaria, and third of Jerusalem. Now he says, when I turn away the turning away of Sodom and of Samaria and of Jerusalem, then they will be restored to their ancient state, first Sodom, whose prior turnings away he has turned away; second Samaria, which he converted in the second place; third Jerusalem, whose turnings away were third. Therefore healing is granted to those sinning in the turning away of Sodom and her daughters, and in the turning away of Jerusalem herself. And it is granted later to those who are more loved by God. For Sodom, having been justified by Jerusalem,[7] is the first to receive mercy; these are the Gentiles; but Samaria, that is, the heretics, receive their healing in the second place; but third (as if they are unworthy of a more rapid healing), those who were in Jerusalem are restored to their former estate. The Gentiles will be granted clemency first, before us, and the heretics come before us, but only if we have become impious, and if sins have overwhelmed us.

(3) For the nearer we have been to God and the closer we have been to beatitude, the farther we put ourselves from it when we sin,

and the closer we put ourselves to terrible and very great punishments. For God's judgment is just, and "the powerful suffer powerful torments" [Wis 6:5–6]. But whoever is least [cf. 1 Cor 15:9] earns mercy more quickly. Sodom is the least, and after her, by comparison, Jerusalem is least; but Samaria is not as small as Sodom. And therefore, first he turns away their turnings away, and afterward that of Jerusalem, saying: "And I will turn away your turning away"; for this is said in the third place to Jerusalem. But when does he turn away my turning away, if I have been found to be a Jerusalem and a sinner in the midst of my sisters? It will be when I hear: "That you may bear your torment" [Ezek 16:54]. Therefore in the third place he says: "I will turn away your turning away," and after everyone: "That you may bear your torment, and be dishonored for all that you have done" [Ezek 16:53–54].

(4) There is a certain measure of sin that each one will receive in proportion to what he has sinned. If I have fifty sins, I have fifty dishonors; if one hundred, the punishment for my deeds will be doubled and dishonor will be given to me for the magnitude of my sins. A great torment is attached to the greatest sins. But God alone, the true judge, can discern the magnitudes of sins and the characteristics of dishonor and the number of sins. And so, it is said to Jerusalem: "That you may bear your torment and be dishonored for all that you have done in provoking me to anger." Conversely, you can see God making satisfaction and in some way testifying through these words that he himself does not have wrath, but that the sinner incites God to wrath against himself. This is also why the Apostle says: "Or do you despise the riches of his goodness and his gentleness and patience, not knowing that the goodness of God leads you to penitence? But according to your hardness and impenitent heart you are storing up wrath for yourself" [Rom 2:4–5]. These words separate wrath from God. For in fact wrath is something alien to God. It is not connected to him as something innate. This is why it is said of sinners: "You sent forth your wrath and it consumed them" [Exod 15:7]. No one can send forth what is associated with and akin to himself, but something is sent forth that is alien to the one who sends it forth. Thus, when we irritate God by sinning, he sends forth the wrath that he himself does not have.

Restoration

3. After these things, that is, after the turning away, it is said: "Sodom your sister and her daughters will be restored as they were at the beginning" [Ezek 16:55]. I come to the images and figures, and I see that Sodom, having been tortured for so long a time, is restored to its ancient state. But if that which is spoken through a figure happens this way, what will become of him who is truly Sodom? Immediately after the flood, in the tenth generation, Sodom suffered the things that are written in Genesis. For previously it was "like the paradise of God and like the land of Egypt" [Gen 13:10–11]. Nevertheless, to Sodom came about that which even now it is possible to observe in the traces of its region.[8] Consider how many cycles of time have now passed. It is nearly three thousand years, and Sodom is not yet restored, not that Sodom which is recorded as a sign and in an enigma, but that one which is seen clearly in the reckoning of truth. The Hebrews say that Sodom will be restored to the same state in which it was established even earlier, so that it will again be compared with the paradise of God and with the land of Egypt. I do not know if that is so or whether that will happen or not. For subjects of this nature are investigated among those who are very learned. But in order for what is said to happen, three thousand years will be completed for me, and then Sodom, having been tortured for three thousand years, will be restored, that is, my soul, Sodom, a mind full of sins. A great interval of time is appointed between the fall and restoration. Even if you are restored as you were in ancient times, consider what great evils you are working off; consider by what great calamities you are first overwhelmed.

(2) Now what we have said about Sodom, you should also understand about Samaria. For she too is not yet restored, but from that time when the ten tribes were ejected from Judea, Samaria also endured captivity and received a name without having her own inhabitants. But even she will be restored as she was at the beginning, when the ten tribes come back. Thus what is written will be accomplished: "The people were led captive to the Assyrians until the present day" [2 Kgs 17:23]. But if that which came first as a sign will be restored after such a great amount of time, when will you be restored, if indeed you will be restored, you who are a Samaritan and a heretical soul, you who have believed in images and holidays that are not true, and in fic-

tions that proceed from the heart of Jeroboam? [2 Kgs 17:22–23]. When will you be restored, O unhappy soul, seeing that your precedent is to be restored after so many long ages?

(3) But if this happens to Sodom and Samaria, which were justified by Jerusalem, what should be said about Jerusalem herself, which justified the evils of the above-mentioned [cities]? "And you will be restored as you were from the beginning; and you and your daughters will be restored, as you were at the beginning" [Ezek 16:55]. He knows what is said: "as you were at the beginning," and as Isaiah says: "And I will establish your judges as previously, and your counselors as at the beginning" [Isa 1:26].

Long Delay

4. "And if Sodom your sister were not a matter of gossip in your mouth in the days of your pride, just as now you are the reproach of the daughters of Syria and of all who are in your circuit of the daughters of foreigners who surround you in a circle, you must bear your impieties and your iniquities" [Ezek 16:56–58]. O the most clement God who makes satisfaction from restoration and says: Bear your impieties and your iniquities! I do not say in vain: You will be restored, but when you work off your impieties and your iniquities, then you will be restored to your original place. Bodily wounds are often inflicted very quickly, but the healing of the wounds involves extreme torments and is not measured according to an equal amount of time that it took to inflict them, but according to the method of the cure.[9] For example, the breaking of a hand or the spraining of a foot takes place in an instant; but what happens in a very short time is hardly cured in three months or longer. In the same way pleasure, luxury and all the other sins cut through the nerves of the soul, and when they seduce the unhappy soul and lead it into vice in an instant, afterwards they earn a long period for penalties and torments.

(2) This is why the Lord says: "And I will do to you as you have done, just as you have spurned these things by transgressing my covenant; and I shall remember" [Ezek 16:59–60]. First he says: "Just as you have done, I shall do to you"; then: "I shall remember my covenant, which I made with you in the days of your infancy" [Ezek 16:60]. For he made a covenant in the days of her infancy. Now we

have said above[10] how he made a covenant with her. "And I will raise up for you an eternal covenant" [Ezek 16:60]. "I kill and I will make alive" [Deut 32:39], he says. The one who now promises these things causes sufferings, and he will again restore; he strikes and his hands will heal [cf. Deut 32:39]. It is also said in Micah: "I will endure the Lord's wrath, because I have sinned against him, until he justifies my cause" [Mic 7:9]. When does he justify my cause? When I endure the Lord's wrath, I who have "despised the riches of his goodness and patience and long-suffering and according to my hardness and impenitent heart I have stored up for myself wrath on the day of wrath and of revelation of the just judgment of God" [Rom 2:4–5].

Unmerited Alliance

5. "And you will be dishonored for having received your elder sisters with the younger ones, and I will give them to you for edification" [Ezek 16:61]. Above he spoke of one sister as Sodom and the other as Samaria [cf. Ezek 16:55]. Now he repeats this and says: your elder sisters, though the elder is Samaria alone and the younger Sodom. But because their daughters are numbered with these, he says that there is one kind for all of them. But as many as are the daughters of Sodom, so many are the daughters of Samaria. "And I will give them to you for edification and not by your covenant; and I will raise up my covenant with you" [Ezek 16:61–62].

(2) Consider the end of the promise: "And you will know that I am the Lord, as you remember and are ashamed"; that is, when you receive [for] your sins and you remember again, then you will be ashamed. "And it will no longer be [possible] for you to open your mouth" [Ezek 16:62–63]. When I receive for my sins and am restored to the covenant made with me, then I understand my evils more fully and I am ashamed. And having become aware of myself, I am punished within my very self. But see what happens to me, so that I am no longer free to open my mouth from the face of dishonor, and see when this happens: "Because he will be propitiated with you" [Ezek 16:63]. I who have sinned much am not even able to open my mouth at that time when he is propitiated with me, nor am I estranged from dishonor when he forgives my wicked deeds. But by feeling my evil

deeds, I am tortured by the perpetual fire [cf. Jude 7] of my conscience.

(3) Therefore, since dishonor and eternal shame [cf. Dan 12:2] are stored up for us if we sin, let us pray to God with all our heart that he may grant to us the ability to strive for the truth unto the end by the effort of our body and soul, so that, even if some time period is appointed that tests our faith—for "as gold is tested in the furnace" [Wis 3:6], so is our faith tested by danger and persecutions—even if persecution breaks out, it may find us prepared. Otherwise, "our house may collapse in the winter," our "building, as though built on sand, may be swept away by the storms" [cf. Matt 7:24–28]. Rather, when the winds of the devil blow, that is, the evil spirits, may our works endure, which have endured unto this day. But this will happen only if they are not secretly undermined. Having been "girded for action" [cf. 1 Pet 1:13], then, may we manifest our love, which we have for God in Christ Jesus, "to whom is the glory and power for ages of ages. Amen" [1 Pet 4:11].

HOMILY 11

The Two Eagles, the Cedar, the Flourishing Vine (Ezekiel 17:1–7)

Exercise

1. In general, bodily exercise strengthens those who exercise. In particular it makes each of the parts more vigorous and it trains the senses of the members for doing or feeling things. For example, if we train the sharpness of our eyes to see, they become sharper at seeing. Ears that hear more frequently can better take in the distinctions of vocal sounds. And one can detect this for the other members as well, which we have illustrated by these few instances. But what good is it to me for beatitude and for eternal life, if my body is strengthened through exercises? What profit is it to me, even if I become very strong in body, even if I advance as one who is vigorous in all the members?

(2) Yet if, on the contrary, I have the senses of my soul trained to perceive what I am striving to learn day and night, this is a benefit to me not only in this life [cf. 1 Tim 4:8], but it likewise accompanies the one departing from the body. That is why the prophet has spoken in parables and riddles, so that our mind would be expanded—or, rather, that it might be gathered into one and see the precise points that have been made—and by withdrawing from the defects of the body, as it comes to understand the truth, it may direct the course of its life according to that same truth.

(3) We have said these things as a preface, since "the Word of God came to Ezekiel saying: 'Son of man, relate a tale and tell a parable to the house of Israel'" [Ezek 17:1–2]. In place of what the

Septuagint translators have recorded as "relate a tale," another translator has rendered "propose a problem," another "bring forward a problem," another "indicate an enigma."[1] Therefore, a problem, an enigma, a parable is what is read. If we ever had need of the illumination of the knowledge of God, now we especially stand in critical need of it, so that by your prayers not so much I as the grace of God within me [cf. 1 Cor 15:10] would be able to discuss the explanation of the problem and enigma and parable.

The First Eagle

2. What then is the "parable of the eagle," which the Holy Spirit has shown in the present text? It does not merely say an eagle, but also that in comparison with other eagles it is "a great eagle" and "of enormous wings" and "with a long spread" and "full of claws," or, as someone has translated: "full of feathers" is written. Not only in these aspects that we have mentioned is it greater than the other eagles, but chiefly in the fact that "it has a design for entering Libanus" [Ezek 17:3]. In fact, when entering there, "it plucked off the choice [branches] of tenderness from the top of a cedar tree." These had been planted "in Libanus." And "it bore them to the land of Canaan, to the city," either "of [male] merchants" or "to a [female] merchant" or "of middlemen[2]," or at least, as the Septuagint[3] has translated it, "walled." And it put what it had taken from the cedar of Libanus, so that it would be planted and grow in "the land of Canaan" [Ezek 17:3–4].

(2) After these things the same eagle took seed outside of itself from the seed of the land whence it had taken the high branches of the cedar, and "it planted it in the fertile field near much water" [cf. Ezek 17:5]. But that very thing that had been taken from the land in Canaan, from what it had plucked off the heights of Libanus—that is, what it had taken in the second place—"became a vine." It was not a strong vine but a weak one, and also small in stature. And the branches of this weak vine were spread out, for it had been taken from Libanus and from a cedar, to such an extent that it had its roots planted under its trunk. And indeed it "became a vine and made shoots and extended its tendrils" [Ezek 17:5–6].[4]

The Second Eagle

(3) And after these things, "another eagle came." It was itself "great, with great wings and with many" either "feathers" or "claws." "And behold, that vine," of which we have just spoken, when the second eagle came, it "deviated from its covenant with it." "Spurning that covenant" that it had previously made with the tree in which the vine had been spread out, it made shoots and put forth its tendrils more widely. And "it embraced the second eagle" and transferred its roots from the first to the second. Then "it sent forth branches toward the second eagle, that it might water it with the growth of her planting in a good field and by much water" [Ezek 17:7–8]. And indeed this same vine was watered and was transferred "to the second eagle, that it would produce growth and bear fruit, that it would become a great vine" [Ezek 17:8]. This is why the command is given to the prophet that he should say that "the vine, transgressing the covenant" that it made with the first eagle and establishing one with the second "is not directed nor do the roots of its tenderness flourish" [Ezek 17:9]. Instead, on account of its transgression, its fruit "putrifies and everything that arose from it withers, and no longer does it have a mighty arm and many people. But it is torn up from the roots and, even though it is watered, nevertheless it does not persevere and is not directed toward abundance. And at once, when a burning wind hits it, it withers, and with the growth of its planting it is dried up" [Ezek 17:9–10].

Explanation

(4) The setting forth of this story demands that, by means of certain additional words, we narrate more plainly what has been said rather obscurely. And if such great effort is involved in order to make what has been said comprehensible, what need is there to speak of the great obscurity of the "problem"[5] itself? What is the first eagle? What is Libanus? What is the cedar? What is the top of the cedar? What is the second eagle? What is the transfer of the vine from the first to the second? If we ever needed God's help—but always in the interpretation of the Scriptures we need his Holy Spirit—now is really the time when he must supply help to us and disclose the meaning of what he himself has said.

(5) Just as in the Gospels our Savior interprets certain parables himself, so also now the prophet, in the second prophecy that has been read, "indicates"[6] in what follows that the first eagle is Nebuchadnezzar, the king of Babylon, who entered Libanus, that is, Jerusalem, and he "took from the tops of the cedar," that is, "the king of Jerusalem and his princes[7]," and "he bore them to the land of Canaan," namely, to Babylon [cf. Ezek 17:12, 4]. For he took the sons of Israel and planted them in the captivity, and from the royal seed and from the race of princes he established them in the same land. But after this and after the royal offspring, another multitude was also captured by him and became a vine that was not as strong as it had been, when it was in God's vineyard and in the holy land, where the sacrifices of God are celebrated. But the weak vine was transferred to Babylon. When these things were done this way, a war broke out between Pharaoh king of Egypt and Nebuchadnezzar king of Babylon. Therefore, the people, who along with their kings and with the offspring of nobles had been afflicted by the Assyrians, transferred themselves to the second great eagle with great wings, that is, to Pharaoh, when the occasion was found to throw off the yoke of Nebuchadnezzar and be liberated from his control.

(6) Then, with the course of events running on in this way, since God had handed them over not to Pharaoh but to Nebuchadnezzar, and they were not enduring his judgment and had shattered the yoke of Nebuchadnezzar from their necks and had transferred over to Pharaoh, the wrath of God broke out against them, and the opposite of what they had thought came about. For the one who is condemned by God must not flee his sentence of judgment or wish to change the will of the judge. Instead one must endure it very patiently until God himself liberates the one he has condemned. For this reason, since the people had transferred themselves to Pharaoh, God's aid abandons them, and they suffer worse things than had previously been carried out by Nebuchadnezzar. We have given this explanation of the parable according to the letter and according to what is written.

(7) There follows a harder interpretation that is difficult to understand with reference to the true Nebuchadnezzar and the true Pharaoh and to these words that have been said first about the eagles. But the reason we have first given this explanation summarily and superficially before the introduction of the following reading is so that even the present passage would be understood more easily. And yet, the fuller

exposition should be reserved for its own place, when the following parable is likewise explained in very great depth according to allegory.

Objection

3. But now let us add a few things and, as it were, pave the road with the material of the future interpretation, from the things that the grace of God gives us, realizing that we will explain it more fully later. First of all, one should consider why indeed Nebuchadnezzar and Pharaoh are called eagles. Perhaps the person who does not read the Scriptures leisurely and superficially is asking: If Nebuchadnezzar is the great eagle with great wings, and Pharaoh here is another great eagle similarly with enormous wings, and in the law the eagle is recorded among the unclean animals [cf. Lev 11:13], why does even the just man who has become rich "prepare eagle's wings for himself, so that he is able to return to the house of his ruler" [Prov 23:4–5]? Why, too, is there a promise in Isaiah the prophet that says: "The just will receive wings like an eagle's, they will run and will not grow weary, they will walk and will not be thirsty" [Isa 40:31]? For if the eagle is unclean, one does not need to take up wings like an eagle, when we become just, nor is it necessary for us to prepare eagle's wings for ourselves when wealth has increased for us.

Response

(2) One should first respond to this by saying that some of the designations of animals in the Scripture are recorded to be of two kinds, that is, evil and good. For example, the lion is understood for both its good and its evil aspects. Its good side is seen here: "Judah, the whelp of a lion; from the sprout, my son, you have ascended; lying down you have slept like a lion and like the whelp of a lion; who will rouse him?" [Gen 49:9]. But the lion's bad side is described thus: "Our adversary the devil prowls around like a roaring lion seeking to devour; we must resist him, strong in the faith" [1 Pet 5:8–9]. But the evil one, in his desire to trip us up, "plots in secret, like a lion in its cave; he plots in order to seize the poor man" [Ps 10:9]. Therefore, just as one can be called a lion both for its good aspect and for its evil

side, it is not unfitting for the eagle likewise to be understood in both respects. And, as I surmise, the just man is not an eagle but "like an eagle"; for he emulates the eagle. And just as "the airy serpent" [Num 21:8] was a type of the Savior—for he was not truly a serpent, but he emulated the serpent, since the Lord said: "As Moses lifted up the serpent in the desert, so must the Son of man be lifted up" [John 3:14]—in the same manner also the just man is not an eagle so much as he is like an eagle. For it is advantageous for him to aspire to become like the eagle. According to this understanding, in another passage as well the just man receives the command not to become a serpent but to be "as wise as a serpent" [Matt 10:16], that is to say, he is not to be captured by the cleverness of the true serpent.

(3) Now if the Word of God, as it diligently examines the Scriptures, and the Spirit, of whom it is written: "The Spirit searches all things, even the depths of God" [1 Cor 2:10] comes into someone's soul, he will show very plainly from the Scriptures that both the eagle and the lion are recorded on the side of the clean animals. "The cherubim have the face of a man and the face of a lion on the right of four parts and the face of a calf and the face of an eagle on the left of four parts" [Ezek 10:14; 1:10]. And these things that are seen in the cherubim, that is, the eagle and the lion, are clean; for nothing unclean is on the chariot of God. And just as you who believe from the Gentiles have become clean, and it is said of all the things that were shown to Peter hanging down from heaven: "what God has cleansed, you should not call common" [Acts 10:15, 11, 28],[8] so the lion and the eagle that appeared in the cherubim have been cleansed. And indeed, even what is proclaimed for the future coming of Christ recognizes that the lion is clean, and the eagle is clean, which are declared unclean [Lev 11:13]. For it says: "the wolf and the lambs will feed together" [Isa 11:6]. Now a wolf that feeds harmlessly with sheep no longer needs to be watched. It is not concerning that kind of wolf that it is said to me: "Beware of those who come to you in sheep's clothing, but inside they are ravenous wolves" [Matt 7:15]. He has said: "but inside they are ravenous wolves"; for there are others that are not ravenous, when "the wolves and the lambs will feed together, and the calf and the bull and the lion will equally feed" [Isa 11:6]. But since in the Christian faith[9] the fellowship of natures has become so diverse among themselves, a lion will no longer be unclean, but he will forget his fierceness. Indeed, all the animals that are called unclean in the law of God will receive the purity of their ancient condition.[10]

(4) Now this has been done in part even now, and it will be completed at the second coming. Therefore the mystery that has been shown in the cherubim anticipates the truth of the matter. And the reason the faces of a lion and an eagle are related with the other faces is so that what appeared in the cherubim might be seen to a greater extent in us, who feed together with the calf and the bull and the lion. For none of these things that are predicted in Isaiah coheres with itself, nor is it promised that it will be connected together. But in the cherubim each animal is related to another: "the face of the calf to the face of the lion," and "the face of the man to the face of the eagle" [Ezek 1:10]. Therefore you should not be greatly amazed when Pharaoh and, prior to him, Nebuchadnezzar are declared to be eagles. For it says that "the just take up wings like eagles" [Isa 40:31], and the man who becomes rich in the portion of God "prepares eagle's wings for himself" [Prov 23:4–5] for flying.

Nebuchadnezzar

4. But let me return to the subject. Something is indicated about Nebuchadnezzar in particular. It says that he was "a great eagle" and "with great wings" and "with a very long spread" [Ezek 17:3]. So much so was this the case that he dared to say: "I will act in strength, and in the wisdom of understanding I will remove the boundaries of nations and will consume their strength. And I will shake the inhabited cities, and I will seize with my hand all the orb of lands as a nest, and I will remove them as broken eggs" [Isa 10:13–14]. Behold, this is the reach of his wings. Nor does this suffice for him, but he is "full of claws and many feathers" and he "has a design for entering into Libanus," that he might "pluck the top of its cedar" [Ezek 17:3]. As long as those who were living in Libanus did not sin—that is, as long as those who were in Jerusalem were not detected in their evils—that great eagle did not receive authority to enter into Libanus, nor did he lay claim to the choice [branches] of the cedar for himself, the royal seed, and the offspring of princes [cf. Ezek 17:3, 13]. For there are those who are "of his tenderness," who at one time were not of a hard heart. Yet he seized them, because they sinned against the Lord. He was that great eagle. And he transferred the rest of the top of the whole tree to Canaan. For the land of the Babylonians is figuratively called the land of the

accursed Canaan, of whom Noah says: "Cursed is the child of Canaan, he will be a servant to his brothers" [Gen 9:25]. He also put what he had taken from the cedar in the city of [male] merchants, or "of a [female] merchant" or "of middlemen" or at least "walled."[11] And he took for himself from the seed of the land, not only from the higher ones but also from the lesser ones, and from the people of the Jews.

(2) "And he gave it for a fertile field; he established it to be cared for near much water, and it sprang up and became a weak vine" [Ezek 17:5–6]. The people of God were truly weak in Babylon. That is why they were unable to sing the Lord's song, saying: "How shall we sing the Lord's song in a strange land?" [Ps 137:4]. In fact, what had been planted in Babylon could not fail to be weak. How could that which had begun to be a Babylonian vine preserve its original strength? For it had produced no fruit in the holy land, and therefore when it was transferred by the eagle and came to the land of Canaan, it became a weak vine and small in stature. As long as it was in the holy land, it was a huge vine; but when it was transferred to the boundaries of sinners [cf. Isa 10:13], it became small and weak. And you, therefore, the vine who is listening to me, if you want to be great, do not leave the boundaries of the church. Remain in the holy land, Jerusalem. For if on account of sins you fall into worse things, you will be transferred to another land and you will be a small vine and your branches will fall and your roots will be dried up. This will go on to the point that afterward you will desire to rest on another eagle, as now it is said: "with great wings and very many claws" [Ezek 17:7]. It is good that one who is condemned remains under the sentence of condemnation, as long as the one who condemned him liberates him. Let us not willingly run to Pharaoh. For if we run to him, we act against the God who said: "I am the Lord your God who led you out of the land of Egypt, from the house of slavery" [Exod 20:2]. For it is not so much of our own accord that we have hastened to Nebuchadnezzar, as that we have been condemned and dragged off by force to him.

Pharaoh

5. Then follows: "And there came another great eagle with great wings and many claws, and behold, that vine embraced it" [Ezek 17:7], that is, the second eagle. It often happens that we are trans-

ferred from one hostile power to another. For God had commanded the people of the Israelites to submit their necks to the yoke of Nebuchadnezzar, as we read in Jeremiah [cf. Jer 34:2–3], to such an extent that he threatened the one who turned away from his servitude. When we expounded Jeremiah,[12] we tried to explain the things that the grace of the Lord granted to us, in answer to your prayers, or at least what we perceived one way or another. But the people were unwilling to do what had been commanded. Instead they "stretched out their branches to Pharaoh" [Ezek 17:7]. She was established by him in the "growth of his planting, so that she would bear very abundant fruit in the field by much water" [Ezek 17:7–8]. And after having abandoned Egypt, she again longed for Egypt, thinking that she would attain her original abundance. She especially thought that if she were to pass from Nebuchadnezzar to Pharaoh, she would firm up her roots, reduce her stature, and bear fruit. But everything happened contrary to her expectations. For all her fruit putrified and the sprouts that had grown at least a little bit in Babylon withered because of the change of region, to such an extent that it was torn up by the roots. This happened so that she would gain no further strength in her strong arm or by her more numerous people. What kind of mysteries do these things contain, and what is their magnitude? What does each word signify?

Another Jerusalem

(2) If only we have an audience, we can ascend to another Jerusalem and show there how a great eagle made his design and bore away its highest [branches] to this Babylon that we now possess. We can speak of certain more mysterious things concerning Pharaoh. But because we are under time constraints, and perhaps we are rashly promising what we are not able to fulfill, let us return to lesser matters and explain it this way instead, according to the measure of our intellect. That great and true eagle Nebuchadnezzar, that is, the devil,[13] came to this Libanus, that is, to the church,[14] where the sacrifices of God and "the incense of prayers" [Ps 141:2] to God are celebrated, and he seized it. May it be far from our times that he should transfer into Canaan from the top of the cedar, that is, from the rulers and from the royal seed [cf. Ezek 17:12–13]. Let us pray that what has

often taken place not be done. For some have been taken and transferred to Babylon who were rulers in the church, and on account of their sin they were removed from the summit of Libanus.

(3) One should say the following about these things. The great eagle with the great claws that are stretched forth with feathers took from the tops of the cedar and shaved them from Libanus, that is, Jerusalem. It planted them in the land of Canaan. But not only did that eagle lay claim to the top of the cedar, that is, to some of the race of nobles, but also he seizes the seed of the land and transfers it to the land of Canaan, whenever one of the people sins and some of the people of God become entangled in the snares of the devil. This is why day and night both for our own sake and for the sake of our brothers, we must implore the help of God, to prevent anyone from being transferred from Jerusalem to Canaan.[15] Otherwise, having abandoned his sentence of judgment, we may strive after another eagle, against God's will, and greater wrath would come upon us. Then the whole plant would putrify and its fruit together with its roots would wither. For the planting of Jerusalem cannot bear fruit in another land. It does not make branches in foreign borders, but at once with its growth it is withered, if it fails to persevere in the will of God and in his church, that is, in deeds and in words and in the knowledge of the truth of Christ Jesus, "to whom is the glory and power for ages of ages. Amen" [1 Pet 4:11].

HOMILY 12

Interpretation (Ezekiel 17:12–24)

Sweetness or Bitterness

1. The divine word now wants to explain in part the things that I have recalled above about the two great eagles with the great wings and great claws, and indeed the things that the first and second eagle did, as if they are a prophecy, that is, as if these things are figurative. It leaves to us the interpretation of the things that it has left untouched. And first of all, although I have already frequently said it, yet even now I will try to add something that would bestow health to our soul, in view of the fact that it is said to the prophet: "Say to the house that embitters" or "exacerbates"; for he did not add "me" to the "house that exacerbates" or "exasperates." And if we want to see what kind of sin exasperation is, let us hear how sweet are God's words to him who understands, who says: "How sweet are your words to my taste!" [Ps 119:103]. When the faithful take in these naturally sweet things, they are either living well or doing truly the contrary. If they are walking according to the divine standard, the words of God retain the sweetness with which they were first uttered. But I am inclined to think that through the goodness of their life they even increase the sweetness of God's words, by mingling the sweetness of life with the sweet savor of speech.

(2) But if someone sins and "walks perversely" [Lev 26:23], outside of the precepts of God, he takes the most sweet words of God and through the nature of the most bitter sin[1]—for sin is bitter because it banishes the sweetness of the words—turns all the sweetness into a bitter taste. That you may be able to attend more fully to what we are say-

ing, take an example. The plant that is called wormwood is naturally bitter. If you add this plant to honey, it overcomes the honey's sweetness by its bitterness, depending on the quantity and quality of the honey, and it forces what is sweet to be bitter. Sin has the force of this plant. The more I sin, the more bitterness I put into the sweetness of God's words. If the transgressions I commit become great, I convert the entire sweetness of the honey into a bitter savor. And that is why God, who avenges his words when they are trampled upon by sinners [cf. Matt 7:6], has restored the bitterness of punishments and penalties to each one according to the quality of bitterness of one's life and the manner of one's corruption. And indeed, as for us who are saying these things and who have once believed in God, if we sin, we are said to exasperate his words; but the one who has completely fallen away from faith in him and those who have not entered the church, they do not make the words of God bitter. For how can they exasperate the sweetness of words in which they have not yet believed? And therefore the torments that are reserved for us who seem to believe and who sin in that state of belief are different from the penalty that will come to those who did not even have a commencement in the state of belief.

(3) And lest we think that we exasperate merely the word of the Lord if we sin; our sin reaches the point of injuring God himself. For it is written that the one who sins "dishonors God through his transgression of the law" [Rom 2:23].[2] It would have been a small thing if he had said that this person merely "dishonors"; but now he says that through the transgression of the law he "dishonors God." However often we transgress God's law, just so often do we dishonor God. To the extent that we commit greater sins, so much the more do we affect God by greater outrages. The more we sin, the more we dishonor the Father and his Christ, as it is written: "How much more do you think he deserves greater penalties who has trampled upon the Son of God, and has regarded as polluted the blood of the covenant by which he was sanctified, and who has committed outrage against the Spirit of grace" [Heb 10:29]. Therefore, whoever sins exasperates and outrages and dishonors the words of God, which he has received, as well as him who taught them.

HISTORY

Literal

2. "Say now to the exasperating house: do you not know what these things are?"—that is, the things that have been said in the parable of the eagles. "Say: when the king of Babylon comes to Jerusalem and takes its king and his princes" [Ezek 17:12]. As far as pertains to the history of the one prophesying, it has been explained that Nebuchadnezzar came to Jerusalem and led captive Zedekiah the king of Judea and the princes who were with him, and part of the people of the Jews [cf. 2 Kgs 25:7]. Indeed, we have also touched upon the manner in which he planted them in the land of Babylon.

Figurative

(2) But let us not stand on the letter, let us not cleave to the history, but rather you who are advanced in the Scriptures of God also know that "all these things happened to them figuratively, but they were written down for us, upon whom the ends of the ages have arrived" [1 Cor 10:11]. Behold the true Nebuchadnezzar threatens and seeks to capture some of us. And to be sure he first longs, if possible, to lead as captives to himself some of the rulers of the church. But as long as a Hezekiah, a Josiah, or at least a just king reigns among the people, that Nebuchadnezzar cannot lead his prisoners away from Judea or the rulers or the people. But if we who seem to preside in the church sin by giving room to the devil, contrary to the command of Paul, who says: "Do not give room to the devil" [Eph 4:17], in a certain way by our sins that we commit in Jerusalem, we have offered an occasion for Nebuchadnezzar to enter the holy city and lead away whomever he wants. But he who does not sin shuts out Nebuchadnezzar, so that he cannot enter into the land of God.

(3) Therefore let us shut out Nebuchadnezzar with all our strength, so that he will not draw near to the blessed assembly of this church. But let us exclude him by taking the "key of knowledge" [Luke 11:52]. Let us exclude him by a sober manner of life and by good deeds, so that he will not seize the king of Jerusalem and his princes, that he not be able to lead them away to Babylon in the triumph of his captivity. But if the savage enemy succeeds in conquering any of us, he leads him to Babylon, not to the vast territory of some

land but to the soul's Babylòn, that is, to confusion. Frequently we have said that Babylon means confusion.[3] For whoever is overcome by him is led away into confusion of his mind; he is transferred to Babylon. Let us look to our daily life. If at some time we see that a soul is confounded by sin, vice, grief, wrath, desires, or greed, let us know that that is one that the devil is leading off to Babylon. But if in the ruling part of the heart, tranquility, serenity, and peace are bearing fruit, let us know that Jerusalem is living in it; for the "vision of peace"[4] is within.

Covenants

3. "And he leads them to himself in Babylon, and he takes from the seed of the kingdom and he makes a covenant with him" [Ezek 17:12–13]. All of us who have received the word of God are the royal seed; for we are even called a "chosen nation" and a "royal priesthood, a holy nation, a people of acquisition" [1 Pet 2:9]. If one of us, then, who are constituted in the order of royal seed is led off as a captive by the devil through his own sin, it is hardly doubtful that from the royal race he is led off to Babylon and makes a covenant with Nebuchadnezzar. For he has now spurned the covenant with God. For it is impossible that a man be without a covenant. If you have a covenant with God in you, it is not possible for Nebuchadnezzar to make a covenant with you. Moreover, if you have rejected God's covenant through the transgression of his commandments, you have taken up a covenant with Nebuchadnezzar. For it is written: "He makes his covenant with him and leads him into a curse" [Ezek 17:13]. God makes a covenant with us in blessing, but Nebuchadnezzar has established his covenant in cursing. He who has made a pact with Nebuchadnezzar cannot be in blessing.

(2) But someone who is learned in the divine Scriptures says to me: I find in the law of Moses that curses have been appointed against the sinner [Deut 27:13–26]; if, then, by the command of God a curse is appointed against sinners, why conversely should there not also be a certain blessing with the devil, so that some come into blessing with him, others into a curse? To this one who asks such an acute and penetrating question, I will attempt to reply and say that there is both a blessing from Nebuchadnezzar—may God cast it far away from us—

and a curse, of which we should now speak, which comes upon sinners deservedly. What, then, is Nebuchadnezzar's blessing? When someone becomes wealthy and happy in this world and all things flow for him with a prosperous course to such an extent that what is written can be applied to him: "His cow will not miscarry" [Job 21:10].[5] And if he has all the prosperity of the world, Nebuchadnezzar's blessing is upon him. But a curse is on anyone who departs from God and nonetheless, having taken the devil's side, is tormented by wretched penalties. Therefore God wills, as the Scripture now recalls, that Israel's covenant be a curse with Nebuchadnezzar. And therefore, since the king of Jerusalem wanted to spurn the covenant with Nebuchadnezzar and attempted to make a covenant with Pharaoh by "sending his messengers into Egypt," the divine word says: "He is not in the right, he will not be preserved" [Ezek 17:15].

(3) For this reason it is necessary that we bear it patiently when we are handed over to punishment by God. The Apostle handed over a certain man to the devil from the assembly of the church for the destruction of his flesh. And he handed him over "for the destruction of the flesh," not in order to destroy the one handed over, but that he might preserve the spirit of the one handed over. For the Scripture says: "Hand over such a man to Satan for the destruction of his flesh, that his spirit might be saved on the day of the Lord Jesus" [1 Cor 5:5]. Now a sinner is handed over to torments that he might receive penalties in the present, and when he has been tortured for his sins he may attain relief in the future,[6] and it could be said of him: "He received his evils in his own life" [Luke 16:25]. If, then, someone who has been tormented with punishments in accordance with the curse in which God placed sinners chooses instead to flee the penalties and to send to Egypt in order to acquire help from Pharaoh, from whom God liberated his people, "he is not in the right, he will not be saved" [Ezek 17:15]. But if someone patiently endures the curse and punishments of Nebuchadnezzar and completes the time allowed for the torment of his sins, as did that man who according to the Apostle's letters was tormented so that his spirit would be saved on the day of judgment [cf. 1 Cor 5:5], he will attain the very best outcome.

(4) Therefore "he leads him into a curse and he will receive the rulers of his land, that they may become a weak kingdom" [Ezek 17:13–14]. The kingdom becomes weak because it is transferred from the holy land to Babylon. For no one is strong in Babylon, that is, in

the confusion of his mind. A man who is confused cannot be "completely lifted up, so that he keeps my covenant, so that he establishes it and departs from him, so that he sends his messengers to Egypt" [Ezek 17:14–15]. The one who endures torments from Nebuchadnezzar on account of his sins and sends his messengers to Egypt, not bearing the handing over by which God gave him over to the enemy, so that Pharaoh gives him horses and many people, is demanding what is forbidden in another passage. For the Scripture says: "You shall not multiply for yourselves horses" [Deut 17:16]. "He is not in the right, he will not be saved, who does the opposite and violates the covenant" [Ezek 17:15]. The one who had been handed over to a covenant with Nebuchadnezzar should have endured the penalty; but he does not endure it and therefore it is said of him: "He will not be saved."

4. "As I live, says the Lord Adonai, unless in the place of the king who appointed him, who spurned my curse and transgressed my covenant" [Ezek 17:16]. There is one who dishonors the curse of God, and there is another who honors it. Doubtless in the present passage it is about the former that God complains, that is, the one who has dishonored his own curse. For when someone has been handed over to penalties to be chastised and he does not endure what is commanded, he dishonors the curse of God; but if he endures with all meekness and blessing and thanksgiving to God, he honors his curse and when he has honored his curse, it is necessary that likewise he would attain to his blessing. "And he transgressed my covenant, he will die with him in the midst of Babylon; and he will make war with Pharaoh not with great force, nor with a great multitude" [Ezek 17:16–17]. It is not possible for him who has transgressed and dishonored God's curse to give help to Pharaoh, but he will die in the midst of Babylon for his transgression.

Promise

5. Then he goes on to narrate what sinners are going to suffer. And after these things he relates some more favorable things, saying: "I will take from the choice [branches] of the cedar and I will remove from the summit of their heart and I will plant him on the highest mountain" [Ezek 17:22]. After the curses that we spoke about above, at the end of the words a promise is declared of blessedness and of a very sweet offer. For those who needed the penalties had already

endured torments for their sins. But when I ponder the meaning within myself and diligently examine the sense of this passage, I am convinced that it is a prophecy of the apostles. For they are "from the choice [branches] of the cedar," from the summit, from the top, which God gave for the flourishing of the world, when he cleansed their hearts and planted them on the highest mountain, our Lord Jesus Christ. "And I will hang it on the high mountain of Israel, and I will plant, and it will produce a shoot and will bear fruit" [Ezek 17:23]. They produced shoots, they bore fruit. "And it will become a great cedar" [Ezek 17:23]. Consider the sublime greatness of the church of Christ, that you may understand that the following words came about in accordance with the promise of God: "And it will become a great cedar, and every bird will rest under it, and every flying thing will rest under its shade" [Ezek 17:23; cf. Mark 4:32]. Take up for yourself the wings [cf. Isa 40:31] of the word of God and you will be able to rest under this tree that is planted on the highest mountain.

(2) "And it will rest and its branches will be restored" [Ezek 17:23]. Notice how the prophecy finishes on a good note. For it continues: "And all the trees of the field will know that I am the Lord, who humbles the high tree" [Ezek 17:24]. The high tree is the people of the Jews who were humbled for their wicked deeds and suffered punishments. For they dared to lay hands on our Lord Jesus Christ. "And I raised up the low tree" [Ezek 17:24]. You were the low tree, the tree that was cast down, the tree rooted in the ground, but God raised you up. "And I wither the green tree" [Ezek 17:24]. The green tree is the people of circumcision who at one time were sprouting and flourishing, but now have wasted away with utter dryness. For where now is there among them a word full of life? Where is there a choir of virtues? "And I will make the dry tree flourish again" [Ezek 17:24]. You were a dry tree and the coming of Christ made you flourish again. "I the Lord have spoken and I will do it" [Ezek 17:24]. This has been said that we might flourish again, that we might be able to bear fruit, that we might become a sprouting tree and not a dry one, that the axe that is proclaimed in the Gospel will never be laid at our roots [cf. Matt 3:10]. Therefore, let us pray more fervently to Jesus Christ our Lord together with his Father, "to whom is the glory and power for ages of ages. Amen" [1 Pet 4:11].

HOMILY 13

The Prince of Tyre, Pharaoh (Ezekiel 28:12–23)

THE PRINCE OF TYRE

1. The bishops have commanded me to discuss the words about the prince of Tyre.[1] I am to speak of his praises and faults. I have also been asked once again to say some things about Pharaoh king of Egypt.

(2) Well, the prince of Tyre is the object of a complaint. One must not think that this refers to a man. For if we simply follow the letter, there was no man who "was created in the midst of the cherubim" and who was "in the paradise of God" [Ezek 28:13–14]. And there was no man who was "raised." And since there was no one, as we have said, who was "in the paradise of delights," now it is said, "the prince of Tyre was born and raised in the paradise of delights" [Ezek 28:13–14]. Who is this prince of Tyre? Let us seek an opportunity for understanding this by consulting Daniel and say that they are not physical[2] princes for which we are now searching. After consulting Daniel, let us seek for a referent in the Apostle; then let us again call upon the testimonies of the prophets. In addition to all these passages, that passage too in Deuteronomy must be added which Moses refuses to pass over in silence.

DANIEL

(3) Come now, let us go over the references, beginning with Daniel. He says: "Your prince Michael" [Dan 10:21], and again: "the prince" of

Israel, and in what follows: "Michael was helping the prince of the kingdom" [Dan 10:13] of the Gentiles. To these things the Apostle adds: "But glory and honor and peace to everyone who works good, to the Jew first and to the Greek" [Rom 2:10]. Now the help given by the prince of the Israelites to the prince of the kingdom of the Greeks [cf. Dan 10:20] has perhaps already been accomplished. For at the coming of my Lord Jesus Christ, the prince of Israel helped the prince of the kingdom of the Greeks, with the result that the Gentiles attained to salvation and were saved by believing. And so in this manner there is said to be a prince of the Persians, just as Michael is the prince of the Israelites, and there is another prince of the Greeks. They are not men,[3] then, nor are they named according to the [actual] designations of the places over which they hold command.[4]

The Apostle

(4) This is also why the apostle speaks as if he is not dealing with men: "For we speak wisdom among the perfect, but a wisdom not of this age nor of the princes of this age, who are being destroyed, but we speak God's wisdom hidden in a mystery, which God predestined before the ages for our glory, which none of the princes of this age knew; for if they had known, they would never have crucified the Lord of glory" [1 Cor 2:6–8].

Prophecy

(5) Prophecy also testifies that the princes of this age crucified the Savior and Lord, when it says: "The kings of the earth stood up and the princes came together into one place against the Lord, and against his Christ" [Ps 2:2]. This is also why in another place in the Psalms it is written: "I have said: You are all gods and sons of the Most High; but you will die as men, and as one of the princes you will fall" [Ps 82:6–7]. In that passage it is absolutely certain that the words are not about any physical prince. If, then, there is a prince of the kingdom of the Persians, if there is a prince of the Israelites, Michael, it is

consistent as well that there is a prince of Tyre, and it is about these princes that the prophetic words are now being spoken.

Moses

(6) But since we also promised a testimony from Moses,[5] listen to what follows: "When the Most High divided the nations, when he dispersed the sons of Adam, he appointed the boundaries of the nations according to the number of the angels of God"—or, what is better, "according to the number of the sons of Israel"—"and his people Jacob became the Lord's portion" [Deut 32:8–9]. To one prince went the portion of Tyre, to another Babylon, to others the other nations, and so in this manner the princes possessed all the boundaries of the nations. But if someone who reads in the Scriptures thinks that it has been said as though about men, let the spiritual man understand more deeply and be judged by no one [cf. 1 Cor 2:15]. For certain things are recognized about Nebuchadnezzar king of the Assyrians [cf. Jdt 1:1], which do not agree with his person. For he said: "I will act in strength and in the wisdom of understanding I will remove the boundaries of the nations, and I will shake the inhabited cities, and I will seize the whole orb of the lands" [Isa 10:13–14]; and "I will ascend above the stars of heaven and the clouds," etc.; and "I will be like the Most High" [Isa 14:13–14]. This applies to Nebuchadnezzar.

Which Prince of Tyre?

(7) The same thing applies to the prince of Tyre and to Pharaoh.[6] For the true physical Pharaoh was not so disturbed by furies as to say: "The rivers are mine and I made them" [Ezek 29:3]. Now this was read earlier in the prophecy that is against Pharaoh. Nor was that prince, that is, the physical Pharaoh, ever called a dragon, who said: "Behold, I am against Pharaoh, the dragon who sits in the midst of the rivers of Egypt, who says: 'The rivers are mine, and I made them'" [Ezek 29:3]. But this should be reserved for its proper place. The reason we have now taken it up is to make more clear through the knowledge of the Scriptures what seemed hidden. Our battle [cf. Eph 6:12]

is against those princes. And the blessed apostles who were sent to preach endured plots, when they were leading men away from those who had taken possession of the boundaries of the nations. For example, it could be said: When the apostles entered Tyre [cf. Acts 11:19], the prince of Tyre persecuted them; when they went up to Antioch [cf. Acts 11:19], the prince of the kingdom of Syria fought against them; he was the one who was waging war against them, and not all those who were thought to be the ones (like Judas the traitor) [cf. Luke 6:16].

(8) For just as Judas should not be thought to be the principal one who betrayed the Savior, so also for the apostles and all who suffered persecution, there was another prince of their persecutions. For it is written of Judas: "And after the morsel Satan entered into him" [John 13:27]. For "our battle is not against flesh and blood" [Eph 6:12]. It is true that those who persecute us seem to be of flesh and blood, but let us not hate them. Rather let us love them, even should they wish to remain hostile to us. Let us pity them, for they have a demon, they suffer from madness. It is not so much they who persecute us who are against us, as those who have filled their hearts. But let us ask for the Lord's help, that the attempts of such a great adversary would be powerless, as they fight against the human soul. And let us say: "If the Lord were not in us, in him, when men rose up against us, perhaps they would have devoured us alive" [Ps 124:1–3].

(9) Well, then, there is a prince of Tyre, but the prophecy is not teaching us about Hiram [cf. 1 Kgs 7:13]—for that is the name written in the third book of Kingdoms—nor does it concern another prince of Tyre, or any man at all. These words are not teaching us human things, but certain divine, ineffable, and mysterious things under the personae of human beings. Pharaoh is a man; but I am instructed to understand some other Pharaoh. And Nabal of Carmel [cf. 1 Sam 25:2–3] is a man, and Hiram is a man, but I am being taught something else under their image. Who is sufficiently qualified to rise above physical things? Who is able from these visible things to contemplate what is invisible? And who can understand each one of these things according to the will of God?

LAMENTATION

2. Let us learn, then, who this prince is, so that by recognizing the lamentation, we might also avoid what is now being said about it. "The prince of Tyre is being lamented" [Ezek 28:11]. Notice how the good God mourns even for those who have denied him! And this comes from the affection of love. For no one mourns for one whom he hates; and the one who is lamented is lamented as one who is dead, to be sure, but he is loved, as if he is still being sought for, as if there is still the desire for him to be alive. And when Jerusalem is lamented, it is written: "And it came about after Israel was taken captive, and Jerusalem was made desolate, Jeremiah sat weeping and lamenting this lamentation over Jerusalem, and he said: 'How is the city that was overflowing with people sitting alone? She has become as a widow, she that had been multiplied among the nations, a princess among the provinces has become a tributary'" [Lam 1:1 LXX]. Even Nebuchadnezzar is lamented.[7] Where are the heresies? Where are those who say that these men were created for destruction?[8] They accuse the Creator, so that they may free themselves up to make charges. "Take up this lamentation over the king of Babylon, and you will say: How has the extortioner ceased, how has the taskmaster rested?" [Isa 14:4]. These things are said against the king of Babylon: "How has Lucifer fallen from heaven, who was rising in the morning? He is crushed to the earth" [Isa 14:12]. And the one "fell from heaven" and the other was "a seal of the likeness, a crown of beauty, raised in the paradise of delights" [Ezek 28:12–13].

FALL OR DESCENT, ASCENT

(2) Behold, they are both said to have fallen from heaven, not to have descended. But my Lord "descended from heaven," and he who descended, "he is the Son of man" [John 3:13]. But not so Satan; for he did not descend from heaven, nor would any evil have befallen him if he had descended. Listen to what Jesus says: "I saw Satan *falling* like lightning from heaven" [Luke 10:18], not *descending*. But not only did the Savior "descend from heaven," but daily a multitude descend and ascend upon the Son of man. For "you will see heaven opened and the angels of God ascending and descending upon the Son of man" [John

1:52]. And you, await your ascent. Only rise up from your fall and hear: "Arise, Jerusalem" [Isa 51:17], from your fall. Hope that you will ascend into heaven, and beware lest it be said to you as well: "Will not the one who falls rise again? Or will not the one who has turned away be converted?" [Jer 8:4]. Woe to those who are "converted by an evil conversion," says the Lord [cf. Jer 8:5]. So then, he too is one of those who have fallen, and the prince is lamented by a man, when the prince ought to weep for a man. Ezekiel is a man and a son of man [cf. Ezek 2:1]; but the Nebuchadnezzar who is lamented is the king of Babylon [Ezek 29:18]. You too take up your lamentation over the king of Babylon and say: "How has the extortioner rested?" [Isa 14:4] etc.

(3) Consider unto what great hope you have been called, O man, you who, surrounded by flesh, say: "Did you not pour me out like milk, but you curdled me in the likeness of cheese? You clothed me with skin and flesh, you knit me together with bones and nerves" [Job 10:10–11]. You, then, who were describing your own fate, behold you are lamenting, and that one who was not clothed in flesh is lamented by you; for you were called unto that hope from which he fell. "By the sin of Israel salvation for the Gentiles has entered by stealth" [Rom 11:11].

(4) I will dare to say something even more mystical: in place of the angels who fell, you are to ascend, and the mystery that was once entrusted to them will be entrusted to you, of whom it is said: "How has Lucifer fallen, who was rising in the morning" [Isa 14:12]. But you have become "the light of the world" [Matt 5:14], you in his place have become Lucifer; one of the stars that fell from heaven was Lucifer, and you, if only you are of the seed of Abraham, will be reckoned among the stars of heaven. For "God led Abraham outside and said to him: Look, so shall your seed be" [Gen 15:5].[9] But this will be at that time when "the stars will fall like leaves from heaven" [Matt 24:29; cf. Isa 34:4], and there will be "one glory of the sun, and another glory of the moon, another glory of the stars; for star differs from star in brightness; so also the resurrection of the dead" [1 Cor 15:41–42]. But "do not boast against those branches" who fell through unbelief and "were broken off" [Rom 11:18–19]; you, since "you stand by faith" [Rom 11:20], will also ascend by faith. And through the fact that you lament the prince of Tyre and deplore with the lamentation that we have introduced above, be instructed, lest perchance having been found in these good things, which the prince of Tyre had, even you may begin to fall, if you become

a little boastful [cf. Rom 11:18–19], and if you do not "guard your heart with all watchfulness" [Prov 4:23].

Seal and Image

(5) For consider what he says to the prince of Tyre: "You are a seal of the likeness" [Ezek 28:12]. I want to know why it was that he is declared to be like a seal of the likeness. When you make progress, you have received a seal, since God is truly the Father of the one whom he has sealed [cf. 2 Cor 1:22] and sent. And that is why those who always believe are sealed by the Lord. But it has already passed into a common proverb to say: Such and such has not received the seal, such and such has the seal. Who has the seal? The one whom God has sealed. I will dare to say that by that seal he was sealed who "baptizes in the Holy Spirit and fire" [Luke 3:16], he who bestows "the image of the heavenly" [1 Cor 15:49], who forms you for higher things, so that you no longer "bear the image of the earthly" [1 Cor 15:49]. Beware, O man, lest when you leave this world you be impressed by the seal of the devil; for he has a seal: "Just as we bore the image of the earthly" [1 Cor 15:49]. How or when? Or who has sealed us with this sign, so that we have borne the image of the earthly? "The devil goes around" [1 Pet 5:8] and observes all things, wanting also to seal those who have been subjected to him. But after examining them he seals the hearts of each and he impresses into them the figure of the earthly through sin, through vice, so that they bear the image of the earthly.

(6) Listen to what Jesus answers when he is asked about "the image and inscription of Caesar" [Mark 12:16; Luke 20:24; Matt 17:24]. "He who has ears to hear, let him hear" [Matt 11:15]. For since he did not have that image that was being requested, neither he himself nor his disciple, he shows where the image that is sought can be found: "Go," he says, "to the sea and cast in a hook, and take the first fish that comes up. Open its mouth, and when you find a coin, take it and give it for me and you" [Matt 17:27].[10] Neither do I have this image and superscription nor do you, if only "you are truly my disciple" [John 8:31], if only "the gates of hell do not prevail against you" [Matt 16:18]. Therefore Jesus gives in one manner for himself, by taking that image from the sea, which had been shut up in the fish that

is similar to these fish of which it has been read today, which "cleave to the scales of the dragon who sits upon the rivers of Egypt" [Ezek 29:4, 3]. For truly fish of that sort cleave there. And how many fish are there today whose king is he who rules in the waters? For it is written of the invisible dragon that "he is a king of all that is in the waters" [Job 41:25]. But you are not in the waters, but on that land that is promised to you.

(7) And these things have been said that we might show more carefully what is the seal of the likeness. How blessed was he at that time when he was a seal of likeness! You are still lacking it, that you should become the likeness of the seal, and you are far from a gift of this sort. Indeed God has said: "Let us make man in our image and likeness" [Gen 1:26], but you have not yet attained the likeness. For God made man, in the image of God he made him [cf. Gen 1:27]; but where is the likeness? "When he appears, we shall be like him, for we will see him as he is" [1 John 3:2]. This is how I understand both what is said by the prophet: "God, who is like you?" [Ps 71:19] as well as the following: "Who do you think is the faithful and wise steward?" [Luke 12:42] as well as this: "For if he appears, we will be like him" [1 John 3:2]. Who is the one who will be likened to him? There are very few who have received the likeness, as the apostles did.

Beauty

(8) "Let us make man in our image and likeness" [Gen 1:26]. So then, he who is now being lamented was a seal and was full of wisdom. Even you will lament him, if you become an Ezekiel. But I do not know if you will also be filled with wisdom; meanwhile he who is lamented was full of wisdom, and he was a "crown of beauty" [Ezek 28:12]. Consider what sort he was who was a crown of beauty. Not simply beauty or glory was in him, but a crown of glory. Do not seek this beauty outside of yourself, but around the region of your soul, where the seat of thought and the intellectual faculty exist, where there is true beauty. But if you want to seek beauty where there is flesh and blood, where there is tissue and veins, where there is bodily matter, you will not be able to find it; for true beauty is found in the Savior, and it is apportioned out to the souls of each by him in such a way according to his generosity and mercy. "Gird your sword around your

thigh, most powerful one, in your form and beauty" [Ps 45:3]. Therefore there is a beauty in the principal faculty of our heart and in the soul. But that the beauty of that sort also pertains to the human soul, let the prophet teach you when he says: "Listen, daughter, and see and incline your ear, and forget the people, and the house of your father, because the king has desired your beauty" [Ps 45:10–11]. The king refers to the bridegroom. Who has a beautiful soul like this, who possesses such great beauty, who is so estranged from all filth that it could be said to him: "The king has desired your beauty" [Ps 45:11]?

(9) And you indeed are still seeking that beauty and you are striving to please, but that one fell into disgrace from the beauty that he had. And just as we often see happening to bodies, when an attractive woman with a beautiful face loses her beauty because of sickness, and through old age loses the brightness of her face, in the same manner also the soul, which was beautiful, loses its beauty through weakness, and because of old age it becomes ugly. For when it receives "the old man with his deeds" [Col 3:9], it loses its original beauty by old age.

(10) Jesus came to transfer us from the old man and from the marks of old age; for wrinkles are a sign of old age, as the apostle says: "that he might present to himself a glorious church without blemish or wrinkle or anything of that sort, but that it would be holy and spotless" [Eph 5:27]. It is possible, then, to pass from old age and wrinkles to youth; and what is wondrous in this is that while the body progresses from youth to old age, the soul, if it comes to perfection, is transformed from old age to youth.[11] And that is why: "even if our outer man is being corrupted, but the inner man is being renewed from day to day" [2 Cor 4:16]. It was necessary that you recognize the beauty that the king desires; it was necessary that you know him who at one time was a crown of beauty; and you, when you have attained this glory, beware lest you fall [cf. 1 Cor 10:12], since indeed even that one who fell was a seal of the likeness, full of wisdom, and a crown of beauty.

Paradise of Delights

(11) "You committed iniquity among the delights of the paradise of your God" [Ezek 28:13, 15]. He does not simply say "in paradise," but "in the paradise of delights."[12] My question is whether there are different types of paradise and, though someone may have been

in the paradise of God, yet he may not have been in the paradise of delights, as, for example, that thief, when in the first hour he entered into paradise with Jesus [cf. Luke 23:39, 43]. Suppose I ask you: Do you think he entered into paradise or not? No doubt you would respond that he entered it. Then, if I again ask you: What then, when he entered paradise, was he immediately excluded from the place of delights? Perhaps you would say: Since he entered in the first hour, he did not come into the paradise of God's delights. But if you now see him taking from the "tree of life" [Rev 2:7], and from all the trees that God has not forbidden, so that you see him feeding from every tree of paradise and eating food from all that were not prohibited at the time, and I would ask you, Do you think that he came not only into paradise but even into the paradise of God's delights? what else would you respond but that he was in the paradise of delights?[13] You who seem to lament are hastening to this blessedness. But he who is lamented was once in the delights of God.

Precious Stones

3. "He was covered with every good stone, the sardius and carbuncle, the sapphire and beryl and hyacinth and jasper" [Ezek 28:13] and the remaining twelve stones. The exposition of this passage is difficult and surpasses our strength and nature. For who can explain the nature of each stone and describe either its color or force, so that thus he would be able to find out why these stones were taken up? But although we are not the sort who can understand everything, let us see a few things about how he was covered with these twelve stones.

(2) If someone applies himself to the divine literature—frequently we exhort young people to do this, but as far as I can see, the only result is that we have wasted our time; for we have not succeeded in inducing any of them to study the Bible[14]—and he seeks for these twelve stones and the others in the Scriptures, he will also find them named in the Apocalypse in the same manner and order. That which is first there is also recorded as the first here; the one that is second is second, the third is third , the fourth is fourth, and so on to the twelfth stone, the order is preserved [Rev 21:10–21]. Why then are these stones named in the Apocalypse and where are they located? Surely they are on the "gates of the heavenly Jerusalem" [cf. Rev

21:21; Heb 12:22]. And there it is said that the first gate is topaz, the second is emerald, the third is carbuncle, the fourth is sapphire, and so on in this manner each of the stones is distributed on each of the gates [cf. Rev 21:19–21]. If you understand the gates of Jerusalem and the gates of the daughter of Zion, where it is necessary for you to sing to God—for it says: "I will sing all your praises in the gates of the daughter of Zion" [Ps 9:14]—if you turn your mind to how someone is covered with twelve stones and has entered Jerusalem and has entered through different gates, you will observe twelve virgins.

(3) In the book *The Shepherd*, in which the angel teaches penitence, the twelve virgins have their own names, faith, continence, etc.[15] For you can read it if you want. Then, when the tower is being built, when you take up the powers of the virgins, you will equally receive what is said about the gates; for each virtue is an ornament for you. And thus in this way "upon the foundation of Christ they build" not only "gold and silver" but also "precious stones"; but it is prohibited to build with "wood, hay and straw" [1 Cor 3:10–11]. Therefore this twelfth stone is inside.

SIDON

4. It is still commanded to us[16] to speak about Tyre, Sidon, and Pharaoh. Time restraints have not permitted us to fill in what we began to explain above, and what we wanted to explain in a line-by-line fashion[17] has been only briefly touched upon. The threat is directed against Sidon, which is translated "hunters."[18] "Our soul was snatched like a sparrow from the snare of the hunters" [Ps 124:7]. If you read the Hebrew, you have: "from the snare of the Sidonians." Therefore the Sidonians are hunters, and the threat that comes against them comes on account of you, since they want to capture you and they diligently watch to see how they might snatch you beginners away from the faith, how they might remove from the church the hearers of the Scriptures, how they may transfer you from the boundaries of Judea to the boundaries of Sidon. But you: "guard your heart with all watchfulness" [Prov 4:23], and learn that the threat against the hunters comes for your sake.

PHARAOH

(2) The homily already made brief mention of Pharaoh, affirming that he is "the dragon sitting in the midst of the rivers and saying: 'The rivers are mine, and I made them'" [Ezek 29:3]. I know the differences of the rivers and I know the rivers in which the dragon sits. Those who had been taken captive from Israel wept by those rivers, unable to sing a song about Zion, according to what is written in the Psalms: "By the rivers of Babylon, we sat there and we wept" [Ps 137:1]. And I know another river, whose force makes glad the city of God, according to the voice of the Psalmist who says: "The force of the river makes glad the city of God" [Ps 46:4]. Do you want to hear who is this river whose force makes glad the city of God? Jesus Christ our Lord is the river whose force makes glad the church, the city of God. It is he who says through Isaiah: "Behold, I turn away unto you as a river of peace" [Isa 66:12]. I know that certain rivers have been promised that flow from this river. For "everyone who drinks from this water will thirst again; but he who drinks from the water that I give will not thirst forever, but there will be a river in him, a fountain of water welling up to eternal life" [John 4:13–14; and: "rivers will come forth from his belly" [John 7:38].[19] So then, you have holy rivers from which the dragon is far removed. For just as "three things are impossible for me to understand, the way of a serpent on a rock" [Prov 30:18–19]—"but the rock was Christ" [1 Cor 10:4] and where Jesus is there is no way for the serpent—so I am not able to find the traces of the dragon in these rivers. But there is a river that the dragon has made; for the dragon says (and God threatens both the dragon and the rivers in which the dragon is): "The rivers are mine, and I made them" [Ezek 29:3]. Listen to the heretic as he preaches with all craftiness and innate genius that Jesus Christ has not yet come [cf. 1 John 4:2]. These are the rivers in which the dragon lives,[20] and he made them, and the dragon says: "The rivers are mine and I made them." Therefore pay diligent attention when "you drink water," lest perhaps you drink from that river in which the dragon sits. But "drink from the living water" and from that river in which is the Word of God, in which is our Lord Jesus Christ, "to whom is the glory and power for ages of ages. Amen" [1 Pet 4:11].

HOMILY 14

The Closed Gate (Ezekiel 44:1–3)[1]

WHICH GATE?

1. "And the Lord said to him: 'This gate will be closed, it will not be opened, and no one will pass through it, because the Lord God of Israel will pass through it and will go forth, and it will be closed'" [Ezek 44:2]. Ezekiel the son of man describes in detail very many gates of the temple. And to those "who have ears to hear" [Matt 11:15], he now again explains what he had described about each of the gates. He speaks of the "outer gate of the sanctuary which faces the east, and it is always closed" [Ezek 44:1]. "And the Lord said to him: 'This gate will be closed, it will not be opened, and no one will pass through it, because the Lord God of Israel will enter through it and he will go forth, and it will be closed'" [Ezek 44:2]. And he adds another reason why the gate is closed, not only because the Lord God will pass through it, but also because "the leader will sit in it to eat bread before the Lord along the way of Eloam," which is translated vestibule of the gate. "And he will enter along its way and he will go forth" [Ezek 44:3]. The Lord God, the creator of the universe, goes in and out through any gate that is made of sensible matter and that is always closed. And because of him who "founded heaven and earth" [Gen 1:1], of him who enters and goes forth, the gate will never be opened.

Another Explanation

2. But there is another account of the "outer gate" and the words "along the way of the sanctuary" [Ezek 44:1]. What, then, is the other account of the gate that remained closed? The leader mentioned above sits there so that no one sees him eating bread in the presence of the Lord. Does not the one who reads these things carefully somehow hear the Scripture saying: "Arise, you who sleep" [Eph 5:14]? Is he not incited "to rise from the dead" [Eph 5:14] and to seek the things that are closed? [cf. Matt 7:7]. I will boldly say that everything that is more mysterious is closed, and what is more manifest is opened and is not closed. When we open things that are closed, we speak these things, but the Gospels testify: "Woe to you, scribes and Pharisees, hypocrites, and woe to you teachers of the law, for you have removed the key of knowledge and you yourselves have not entered and you prohibit those who are entering!" [Luke 11:52].

(2) There is then a key of knowledge for opening things that are closed, and there are very many who neither enter themselves nor permit those who want to enter. And in another passage the meaning of the Scriptures is said to be a "sealed book": "And the words of this book will be like the words of a sealed book, which if they shall give to a man who does not know letters, saying to him: 'Read,' he will say: 'I do not know letters,' and they will give it to a man who knows letters, saying to him: 'Read,' and he will say: 'I cannot read it, for it is sealed'" [Isa 29:11–12]. But the Apocalypse of John contains more manifestly the intention of this reference when it records: "An angel went around saying: Who is worthy to open the seals and to loose these things and to read what is written? And no one was found, neither in heaven nor on earth nor under the earth, who could open the seals and read what had been written in the book. But I wept, and someone came to me and said to me: 'Do not weep. Behold, the lion from the tribe of Judah has conquered, the root and offspring of David, to open the book and to loose its seals'" [Rev 5:2–5]. And he who was from the tribe of Judah opened it, and he made known what had been written.

(3) As long as my Lord had not come, the law was closed, the prophetic words were closed, the reading of the Old Testament was veiled, and "until this day when Moses is read, a veil lies over the hearts of the Jews" [2 Cor 3:14–15]. But there are some who love the veil and hate those who give an interpretation of the veil. But we "are converted

to the Lord," so that when the veil is removed, we may say: "But we all with unveiled faces that behold the glory of the Lord are being transformed into the same image from glory to glory" [2 Cor 3:16, 18].

The Closed Gate

(4) But there is a gate, one only, and one that is closed, through which "no one passes." For there are certain things unknown to the whole creation and known only to one; for whatever the Son knows [cf. Matt 11:27] he has not disclosed to this world. The creature does not take in what God takes in, and, to come to lesser things, the signs do not take in knowledge equally. There was more [knowledge] in Paul than in Timothy, since he was a "vessel of election" [Acts 9:15]. And again Timothy, who was truly "a large vessel in the house" [cf. 2 Tim 2:21], takes in what I cannot take in. And there is perhaps someone who takes in even less than I. There are some things that only Christ takes in; and that is why "the door[2] of the temple of God is closed" [Ezek 44:2].

(5) What is this, I ask? It is the "outer" gate that discloses things beyond this world, incorporeal things, and things that are, so to speak, immaterial. For not in vain is it recorded that the outer gate is always closed. What is this "outer" gate? That of the sanctuary. Why is it closed? Because the Lord God of Israel alone enters and leaves through it. Why does he leave? That he might be known. By whom? By the "leader." Who is this leader at the closed gate? It is the Savior who eats bread, who closes the gate with the Father, who feeds on spiritual food, saying "my food is to do the will of him who sent me and to perfect his work" [John 4:34]. And so, the door is closed, that no one may see the great priest eating bread in the holy of holies.

The Priests

3. But to prove the things that we have said, the one who reads Leviticus can recognize the priestly mystery, "when the veil has been removed from his heart" [2 Cor 3:16]. For there it is related about sacrifices and foods, which only the priests eat. There are certain

priestly foods that the priest does not eat in his house, nor with his sons, even though they may be priests, nor with his wife, even though he is validly married to her. Rather, he eats them in the holy place and there he eats food in the holy of holies [Lev 6:26].

The Savior

(2) Just as the priest does not eat food in his own house or in any other place but in the holy of holies, so my Savior alone eats bread, since no one is able to eat with him. But there is a certain place in which, when he eats, he draws me [cf. John 12:32] to eat with him.[3] "For behold," he says, "I stand and knock; if anyone opens to me, I will enter to him and will dine with him and he with me" [Rev 3:20]. From which it is evident that even another can "dine with him." On the other hand, there is a food that he alone eats. For his nature surpasses the universal condition and is separated from all. It makes him eat "daily bread" [Matt 6:11] from the nature of the Father.

Each of Us

(3) Each of us asks for "daily bread" [cf. Matt 6:11], and while asking for "daily bread" does not receive the same bread nor the measure of the same, but always in pure prayers and with a pure conscience, in deeds of justice, we eat daily bread. But if someone is less pure, he eats daily bread in another manner. But may the Lord, who is the "judge of all" [Heb 12:23] give us "living bread" [John 6:51], that having been fed and strengthened by it, we may be able to make the journey to heaven, glorifying God Almighty through Christ Jesus, "to whom is the glory and power for ages of ages. Amen" [1 Pet 4:11].

NOTES

General Introduction

1. See Bertrand de Margerie, *An Introduction to the History of Exegesis*, vol. 1, *The Greek Fathers* (Petersham: Saint Bede's Publications, 1993), 115–16. The Canons against Origen listed in H. Denzinger, rev. A. Schönmetzer, *Enchiridion symbolorum, definitionum et declarationum de rebus fidei et morum* (*DS* 13th ed., 203–211), which are taken from the *Book against Origen of the Emperor Justinian*, 543, identify the following errors among others: the doctrine of the preexistence of human souls including Christ's soul; of the spherical shape of resurrection bodies; of the animate nature of the sun, moon, and stars; of the future recrucifixion of Christ on behalf of demons; the assertion that the punishment of the demons and impious men is temporary. It is not possible to discuss in detail the matter of Origen's orthodoxy in this brief introduction.

2. See J. P. Sweeney, "Modern and Ancient Controversies over the Virgin Birth of Jesus," *Bibliotheca Sacra* 160.638 (April–June 2003): 142–58. On p. 158, Sweeney writes: "Celsus probably would have found it amusing to learn that some later scholars who claim to be Christian would one day repeat arguments similar to his own!"

3. Origen's longest surviving exegetical work is his *Commentary on the Epistle to the Romans*, FOTC 103, 104 (Washington, DC: Catholic University of America Press, 2001, 2002). For a study of the legacy of this work in the West, see Thomas P. Scheck, *Origen and the History of Justification: The Legacy of Origen's Commentary on Romans* (Notre Dame, IN: University of Notre Dame Press, 2008).

4. See Jerome, *Commentary on Matthew*, trans. Thomas P. Scheck, FOTC 117 (Washington, DC: Catholic University of America Press, 2008); see also Ronald E. Heine, *The Commentaries of Origen and Jerome on St. Paul's Epistle to the Ephesians* (Oxford: Oxford University Press, 2002).

5. Henri de Lubac, *Medieval Exegesis: The Four Senses of Scripture*, vol. 1, trans. M. Sebanc (Grand Rapids: Eerdmans, 1998), 159.

6. See Jean Leclercq, *The Love of Learning and the Desire for God* (New York: Fordham University Press, 1961), 102.

7. Henri de Lubac, *Theology in History* (San Francisco: Ignatius Press, 1996), 66, takes up the question of why Pico della Mirandola (1463–1494) was so bent on saving Origen by writing his *Apology for Origen* in 1486. He concludes: "What undoubtedly seduced the young thinker was the spiritual impulse he had received from it [Origen's thought]. In him was renewed that kind of miracle that is ascertained down through the centuries: between his soul and the soul of the great Alexandrian, a spark had flashed." For a summary of Pico's arguments, see Scheck, *Origen and the History of Justification*, 159–61.

8. Hans Urs von Balthasar, in: *Origen: An Exhortation to Martyrdom, Prayer and Selected Works*, trans. R. A. Greer (New York: Paulist, 1979), xii.

9. Jean Scherer, *Entretien d'Origène avec Héraclide: Introduction, texte, traduction et notes*, SC 67 (Paris: Cerf, 1969), 13–14 n. 3; Pierre Nautin, *Origène: sa vie et son oeuvre* (Paris: Beauchesne, 1977), 389–409.

10. Joseph Wilson Trigg, "Origen: Homily 1 on Ezekiel," in *Ascetic Behavior in Greco-Roman Antiquity*, ed. V. L. Wimbush (Minneapolis: Fortress, 1990), 45.

11. Marcel Borret, Homélies sur Ézéchiel, SC 352 (Paris: Cerf, 1989), 15.

12. See ibid., 16, 19. For a chronological study of Jerome's life, see J. N. D. Kelly, *Jerome: His Life, Writings, and Controversies* (New York: Harper & Row, 1975).

13. See Pope Benedict XV, encyclical letter *Spiritus Paraclitus*, on St. Jerome, September 15, 1920 (*Acta Apostolicae Sedis* 12:385–420); Pope Pius XII, encyclical letter *Divino afflante Spiritu*, September 30, 1943.

14. Francis X. Murphy, "Saint Jerome," *New Catholic Encyclopedia*, 2nd ed., 7:759.

15. Jerome, *Hebrew Names*, preface (*Liber Interpretationis Hebraicorum Nominum*, ed. P. La Garde, CCSL 72 [Turnhout: Brepols, 1959], 59.26); translation of Origen's Homilies on Ezekiel (PL 25:583D).

16. Jerome, *Vir. ill.* 54.8.

17. Jerome, *Ep.* 33.4 to Paula.

18. Preface to Murphy's translation of Origen's *Two Homilies on the Song of Songs* (PL 23:1117A).

19. The reader is referred to the discussion in my introduction to *St. Jerome's Commentary on Matthew*, FOTC 117 (Washington, DC: Catholic University of America Press, 2008). See also Francis X. Murphy, *Rufinus of Aquileia (345–411): His Life and Works* (Washington, DC: Catholic University of America Press, 1945).

20. See PL 27:35A. Vincentius appears to have attached himself to Jerome at Constantinople and remained with him till around 400. See Jerome, *Against John of Jerusalem* 41; *Apol.* 3.22; *Ep.* 88.

21. See *Origen: Homilies on Jeremiah, Homily on 1 Kings 28*, trans. J. C. Smith, FOTC 97 (Washington, DC: Catholic University of America Press, 1998).

22. See Murphy, *Rufinus of Aquileia*. I have provided a chart showing the length in Migne of Rufinus's translations of Origen in *Origen and the History of Justification*, 1–2.

23. RSV: "as a warning."

24. RSV: "for our instruction."

25. See Karen Jo Torjesen, *Hermeneutical Procedure and Theological Method in Origen's Exegesis* (Berlin: Walter de Gruyter, 1986).

26. De Lubac, *Medieval Exegesis*, 1:150.

27. John A. McGuckin, ed., *The Westminster Handbook to Origen* (Louisville: Westminster John Knox, 2004), 10–11.

28. Richard N. Longenecker, *Biblical Exegesis in the Apostolic Period* (Grand Rapids: Eerdmans, 1999), 198.

29. See L. G. Patterson, *Methodius of Olympus: Divine Sovereignty, Human Freedom, and Life in Christ* (Washington, DC: Catholic University of America Press, 1997).

30. See Scheck, *Origen and the History of Justification*, 173–204.

31. R. P. C. Hanson, *Allegory and Event* (Richmond: John Knox, 1959).

32. Henri Crouzel, *Origen*, trans. A. S. Worrall (Edinburgh: T&T Clark, 1989), 63.

33. These are identified and discussed by de Margerie, *Introduction to the History of Exegesis*, 1:107–12.

34. J. T. Lienhard, "Origen and the Crisis of the Old Testament in the Early Church," *Pro Ecclesia* 9, no. 3 (2000): 362.

35. The fountainhead of this modern tendency, if it is not Luther, seems to be Friedrich Schleiermacher, who, like Marcion before him and Adolf Harnack afterward, wanted a religion of one Testament. In his *In der Glaubenslehre* (1821/22), 12.2, 61, he remarks that "Christianity cannot in any wise be regarded as a remodeling or a renewal and continuation of Judaism," but must be regarded as a distinct religion superseding the faith of the Old Testament. He goes on to conclude that "the Old Testament appears simply a superfluous authority for dogmatics." Classical Protestant liberalism and more recent transcendental theologies that are now flowering in Roman Catholic circles are eager to distance themselves from the history of God's revelation. For a critique of this tendency, see Matthew Levering, *Christ's Fulfillment of Torah and Temple: Salvation according to Thomas Aquinas* (Notre Dame, IN: University of Notre Dame Press, 2002); and Aidan Nichols, *Lovely like Jerusalem: The Fulfillment of the Old Testament in Christ and the Church* (San Francisco: Ignatius Press, 2007), 77–85.

36. Jean Daniélou, *Origen*, trans. W. Mitchell (London/New York: Sheed & Ward, 1955), 8.

37. This term is derived from the Greek verb δ*okéw*, "to seem or appear." Docetists believed that Jesus only *seemed* to be a real human being but was not truly so.

38. See D. Farkasfalvy, "Theology of Scripture in St. Irenaeus," *Revue Bénédictine* 78 (1968): 318–33.

39. Crouzel, *Origen*, 153–54.

40. For a recent attempt to understand Marcion sympathetically, see Harry Gamble, "Marcion and the 'canon,'" in *The Cambridge History of Christianity*, vol. 1, *Origins to Constantine*, ed. M. Mitchell and F. Young (Cambridge: Cambridge University Press, 2006), 195–212.

41. See J. I. Packer and O. R. Johnston, *Martin Luther, The Bondage of the Will: The Masterwork of the Great Reformer* (Old Tappan, NJ: Fleming H. Revell, 1957), 40–65.

42. See Scheck, *Origen and the History of Justification*, chap. 6.

43. Martin Luther, *Bondage of the Will* in *Luther and Erasmus: Free Will and Salvation*, ed. E. Gordon Rupp, trans. Philip S. Watson, LCC (Louisville: Westminster John Knox, 1995), 224.

44. See Desiderius Erasmus, *Controversies: Hyperaspistes 1 & 2*, trans. Clarence H. Miller, Collected Works of Erasmus 76, 77 (Toronto: University of Toronto Press, 1999, 2000).

45. See D. J. Halperin, "Origen, Ezekiel's Merkabah, and the Ascension of Moses," *Church History* 50 (1981): 262.

46. Joseph Wilson Trigg claims that in Origen's thought, "God had no wrath that needed to be propitiated" and that Origen "found the traditional understanding of hell utterly abhorrent" (*Origen: The Bible and Philosophy in the Third-Century Church* [Atlanta: John Knox, 1983), 101, 115. These assessments seem excessive, since they project modern views onto Origen. In reality, it is scarcely probable that Origen could find a "traditional understanding" of church dogma "utterly abhorrent." Rather, abhorrence is a sentiment that describes Origen's feeling for heresy.

47. See: J. Scarborough, "Hades," in McGuckin, *Westminster Handbook to Origen*, 120.

48. See Thomas Aquinas, *De Malo* 16.5; *De Ver.* 24.10; *Summa Theologiae* I, 64.2.

49. Augustine, *De haeresibus* chap. 43, in *The 'De haeresibus' of St. Augustine*, trans. L. G. Müller, Patristic Studies 90, ed. R. Deferrari (Washington, DC: 1956). Caroline P. Bammel describes Augustine's general attitude displayed here as "marked by cautious restraint and avoidance of personal polemics; his interest is directed to the teachings in question rather than to the individual" ("Augustine, Origen, and the Exegesis of St. Paul," *Augustinianum* 32 [1992]: 346).

50. For example, Bammel writes: "The teachings of Origen which Augustine denounces in his later works are in fact a travesty of Origen constructed by anti-Origenists. Augustine would not have found them in this form in the exegetical works available to him in Latin translation, nor even unambiguously expressed as 'teachings' in Rufinus' translation of *De principiis*. Such

denunciations no doubt partly have the function of a safeguard enabling the denouncer to retain the useful insights of Origen and continue reading him without risking being accused as an Origenist" ("Augustine, Origen," 346 n. 26).

51. Daniélou, *Origen*, 289.

52. Cited in Michael Figura, "The Suffering of God in Patristic Theology," *Communio* 30, no. 3 (2003): 367.

53. De Lubac, *Medieval Exegesis*, 1:241.

54. Thomas G. Weinandy, "Origen and the Suffering of God" in Studia Patristica 36: Papers Presented at the Thirteenth International Conference on Patristic Studies Held in Oxford, 1999 (Leuven: Peeters, 2001), 459–60.

55. For a full study of these themes in Origen and his theological predecessors, see Figura, "Suffering of God."

56. J. S. O'Leary, citing Origen, *Commentary on the Epistle to the Romans* 3.3–5, in "Grace," in McGuckin, *Westminster Handbook to Origen*, 116.

57. J. S. O'Leary, "Melanchthon against Origen on Justification," http://josephsoleary.typepad.com/my_weblog/2007/07/melanchthon-aga.html.

58. On the latter theme, see Chris VanLandingham, *Judgment and Justification in Early Judaism and the Apostle Paul* (Peabody, MA: Hendrickson, 2006), chap. 3. For a full discussion, see Scheck, *Origen and the History of Justification*, 23–29, 195–204.

59. VanLandingham, *Judgment and Justification*, 253.

60. See ibid., chap. 4.

61. Verfaillie specifies the following points in common: an original fall, but not a total corruption of humanity, the necessity and efficaciousness of Christ's redemptive work, the application of Christ's redemption through the indivisible cooperation of God and the human being, the effective sanctification of the soul through grace, and the meritorious value of the soul's actions in view of glory. "Such are the doctrines opposed by the Church to the Reformation. Yet they are all already found clearly in Origen" (C. Verfaillie, *La doctrine de la justification dans Origène d'après son commentaire de l'Épître aux Romains* [thèse de la Faculté de théologie catholique de l'Université de Strasbourg; Strasbourg, 1926]), 119.

62. See Scheck, *Origen and the History of Justification*, 191–98.

63. Daniélou, *Origen*, 8.

64. Crouzel, *Origen*, 52, 136; cf. Daniélou, *Origen*, 7.

65. See Verfaillie, *La doctrine de la justification*, 63–67.

66. Origen's views seem strikingly similar to those of St. John Chrysostom, who comments on Romans 1:11. "But when you hear of grace, think not that the reward of resolve on our part is thereby cast aside; for he speaks of grace, not to disparage the labor of resolve on our part, but to undermine the haughtiness of an insolent spirit. Do not thou then, because that Paul

hath called this a gift of grace, grow supine. For he knows how, in his great candor, to call even well doings, graces; because even in these we need much influence from above." NPNF 11:345. See Christopher Hall, "John Chrysostom," in *Reading Romans through the Centuries: From the Early Church to Karl Barth*, ed. J. P. Greenman and T. Larsen (Grand Rapids: Brazos, 2005), 39–57, esp. 47ff.

67. See O'Leary, "Grace."

68. See Origen, *Commentary on Romans* 5.1.21; 5.5.4; 5.9.4; 5.9.11; 7.18.3.

PREFACE OF JEROME

1. On Jerome's dedicatee, see the introduction.

2. Rufinus of Aquileia seems to imitate this passage in *Princ. praef.* 1.3, where he speaks of "making Origen a Latin and giving him to Roman ears."

3. Cf. 1 Sam 9:9: "He who is now called a prophet was formerly called a seer." Jerome is playing on the name of Didymus the Blind (313–398), with whom he studied in Alexandria for about thirty days and whose work *On the Holy Spirit* he translated. Despite blindness incurred from a childhood disease, Didymus became an authority in biblical interpretation and was venerated as the leading Christian scholar of his era in Alexandria. See Richard A. Layton, *Didymus the Blind and His Circle in Late-Antique Alexandria* (Urbana: University of Illinois Press, 2004).

4. "The Apostle" refers to Paul; cf. 1 Tim 2:7; 2 Tim 1:11. Origen adds the title "teacher of the church" in *Hom. in Ex.* 5.1.

5. Jerome also speaks of being tormented by pain in his eyes at the very end of *Ep.* 18 to Damasus (Charles Christopher Mierow, *Letters of St. Jerome*, vol. 1, ACW 33 [New York: Paulist Press, 1962], 96).

6. That is, Origen.

7. In *In Ep. ad Gal., prol.*, Jerome gives the same division of Origen's works in inverse order: *volumina, tractatus, et excerpta.* See also his *In Is., prol.*

8. *Excerpta* (*Scholia*). These are advanced commentary notes that Origen wrote on the Books of Exodus, Leviticus, Isaiah, Psalms 1–15, Ecclesiastes, and the Gospel of John. Rufinus included some of Origen's *Scholia* on the Book of Numbers in his Latin translation of Origen's homilies on Numbers. None of the *Scholia* has survived intact or complete, though several fragments exist in the catenae (the "chains" of patristic commentary notes that were collected in antiquity).

9. Lit., "volumes" or "books." These were designed by Origen as a more systematic and scientific analysis of specific books of Scripture. Extant in large measure are those on John, Romans, Song of Songs, and Matthew. Fragments of others survive.

10. Rufinus imitates this passage in the *Praef.* to his translation of Origen's *Commentary on Romans.*

Homily 1

1. Cf. Origen, *Com. in Rom.* 10.21.
2. *Pietas.*
3. Lit., "leader of the wine."
4. This is probably directed against heretical groups such as the Marcionites. See *Cels.* 4.11.6; 4.72; *Hom. in Lk.* 22; *Princ.* 2.4.4; *Com. in Rom.* 1.16, 18.
5. Cf. *Com. in Rom.* 6.9.12; 10.21.
6. Lit., "sang."
7. Cf. *Hom. in Ps.* 38 1.9.
8. Lit., "loved."
9. Lit., "adulterers."
10. For the theme that God punishes the sinning sons of Christ as a sign of his mercy, in order to make them mend their ways, see 1.3.4–5; *Hom. in Jer.* 50.2.5; *Cat. in Ps.* 118(119); *Cat. in Ex.* 20.5–6; *Com. in Mt.* 16.21.
11. Cf. *Com. in Mt. fr.* 73; Clement *Protr.* 11.114.3; *Strom.* 7.14.86.5.
12. Cf. *Hom. in Lv.* 16.7.
13. Cf. *Sel. in Ezek.* 1.26.
14. Cf. *Hom. in Jer.* 11.5; *Com. in Mt.* 15.23; *Hom. in Lv.* 3.5.
15. Cf. *Hom. in Ex.* 6.3.
16. Cf. *Hom. in Jer.* 16.5–6; 20.3; *Princ.* 2.10.4; *Com. in Jn.* 13.23; *Cels.* 4.13; 5.15.
17. This is a philosophical expression. See Minucius Felix, *Octavius* 35.3; Tertullian, *Apol.* 48.94; Clement, *Paed.* 3.8.44.2; *Strom.* 7.34; *Eclog. Proph.* 25.4.
18. This is a key text cited by Origen in his *Com. in Rom.* 2.4.4; 2.4.8; 2.7.3; 2.8.4; 5.2.13; 7.18.5.
19. Cf. 12.2.3. Vision of peace (*visio pacis,* ἡ ὅρασις τῆς εἰρήνης) was a common etymology of Jerusalem. Cf. Philo *De somn.* 2.250; Clement *Strom.* 1.5.29.4. It is an important one in Origen's exegesis. Cf. 12.2; *Com. in Jn. fr.* 80; *Hom. in Jer.* 9.2; 13.2; *Com. in Rom.* 3.5; 10.14; *Cat. in Ps.* 75(76); 100(101); 119(120); 121(122); *Hom. in Jos.* 21.2; *Com. in Cant.* 2.1.28, 36.
20. Cf. *Hom. in Jer.* 1.3; 19.14; *fr.* 48.
21. Cf. *Hom. in Jer., Lat.* 2.1.10; *Hom. in Jos.* 15.3.
22. See F. Ledegang, *Mysterium Ecclesiae: Images of the Church and Its Members in Origen* (Leuven: Peeters, 2001), 472: "Origen places the heavenly Jerusalem also within a protological framework and identifies it with the Paradise out of which man was driven. In the Jewish rabbinical and apocalyp-

tic literature Jerusalem occurs as a pre-existent city and there is also a connection with Paradise." Cf. *Hom. in Jos.* 6.4; *Hom. in Lk.* 34.3; *fr.* 71; *Com. in Mt.* 16.9.

23. Cf. *Hom. in Nm.* 9.1; 14.2.

24. Cf. *De orat.* 29.13; *Princ.* 1.1–24; *Philoc.* 27.

25. Cf. *Sel. in Ezek.* 1.1.

26. See Ezek 2:1, 3, 8; 3:1, 4, 17, et passim.

27. This is directed against the docetism of the Valentinians and the Marcionites. See *Hom. in Lk.* 17.4: "The Marcionites completely deny that he was born of a woman."

28. *Passiones.*

29. *Scandalum.*

30. *Fides.*

31. The allusion here is to 1 Cor 10:6, 11; Rom 15:4, where Paul says that *everything* in the Old Testament was written for the benefit of Christians, to warn and instruct them. For Origen, Paul's words were programmatic and determined the church's hermeneutical method.

32. Cf. Jerome, *In Ezek.* 1.3.

33. Cf. *Sel. in Ezek.* 1.1.

34. Cf. *Hom. in Nm.* 23.2.

35. Cf. Hermas *Sim.* 8.2.1–3.

36. *Interpolare.* The same word is used to describe Marcion's work in tampering with the Scriptures in *Com. in Rom.*, *Praef. Ruf.* 10.43.2.

37. Lit., "there."

38. Zebulon is apparently a symbol of the devil.

39. Cf. *Sel. in Ezek.* 1.1.

40. Cf. *Com. in Cant.* 3.5.5.

41. *Instrumenta.* Cf. *Hom. in Lv.* 13.4.

42. This is directed against Marcion and other heterodox authors.

43. *Iuxta abusionem.* The linguistic distinction of Greek rhetoric is presupposed here. A thing is named, properly or improperly, with the same expression. In Greek καταχρηστικῶς is contrasted with κυρίως.

44. *Veteri Testamento.*

45. Origen's point seems to be that the Old Testament (LXX) version of Ps 82:6 increases the scope of the promise by adding the word "all." In contrast, when Jesus quotes this text in John 10:34, he drops the word "all." Thus, the Old Testament cannot be disparaged in the way the Marcionites want.

46. On "land of the Chaldeans," see *Sel. in Ezek.* 1.3; *Hom. in Jer. Lat.* 1(3).4-5; *Princ.* 3.3.2; *Philoc.* 21–27.

47. Or "wind" (*spiritus*).

48. Jean Daniélou *Origen* (trans. W. Mitchell [London/New York: Sheed & Ward, 1955], 25) comments on this passage: "Origen here seems to be alluding to his theory that there are certain higher truths which are to be commu-

nicated only to those who have made some progress in Christianity. The quotation needs balancing with this other statement: 'It may be that I shall offend some people if I discuss this question, but even if I do, I must obey the Lord's command rather than seek the favor of men' (*Hom. in Nm.* 20.4)."

49. Aelia (Capitolina) is the name given to the city of Jerusalem by Hadrian after the Bar Kokhba Revolt of AD 132.

50. Cf. *Hom. in Lv.* 7.5; *Com. in Mt.* 10.12, 13.

51. Cf. *Hom. in Jdg.* 8.5.

52. Cf. *Hom. in Jer. fr.* 31; *Hom. in Jdg.* 8.5; *Com. in Mt. ser.* 51.

53. Cf. *Sel. in Ezek.* 1.4; Jerome *In Ezek.* 1.4.

54. A symbol of the devil; see above on 1.7.

55. For this frequent reproach of the heretics, see *Cels.* 2.24; *Hom. in Jer.* 1.16, 18; *Hom. in Lk.* 16.4; *Com. in Mt.* 15.11. For Origen's interpretation, see *Cels.* 4.1, 6–29; *Hom. in Jos.* 13.3–4.

56. Cf. *Hom. in Ps.* 36(37) 1.3; *Com. in Jn.* 28.24(19).215; *Hom. in Jer. fr.* 62; *Hom. in Nm.* 23.8.

57. Cf. *Hom. in Lv.* 16.2; *Com. in Mt. ser.* 111.

58. Or: "favorable"; cf. Prov 27:16.

59. Cf. *Hom. in Nm.* 1.3; *Cels.* 6.23.

60. Cf. *Cat. in Ezek.* (PG 13:680).

61. Cf. *Com. in Rom.* 3.8.5; *Hom. in Nm.* 5.3; 10.3; *Com. in Cant.* 2.

62. Cf. Philo *De vita Mos.* 2.97.

63. Cf. *Cels.* 5.44.

64. Origen's doctrine of the tripartite soul is based on 1 Thess 5:23, but has been influenced by Plato *Rep.* 436a-b; *Tim.* 69c ff. For an excellent discussion of this theme in Paul, Origen, and subsequent Christian thought, see. Henri de Lubac, *Theology in History*, trans. A. E. Nash (San Francisco: Ignatius Press, 1996), 117–200. For a study of Jerome's adaptation of this view, see D. Kries, "Origen, Plato, and Conscience (Synderesis) in Jerome's Ezekiel Commentary," *Traditio* 57 (2002): 67–83.

65. *Nutus.*

Homily 2

1. Cf. *Sel. in Ezek.* 13.2.

2. For the identification of the Church as the true Israel, see Gal 6:16; *Hom. in Gn.* 16.6; *Hom. in Ex.* 1.2; *Com. in Rom.* 7.14; 8.11; *Hom. in Nm.* 16.9; 17.4; 28.2; *Cat. in Ps.* 123(124).1; *Hom. in Jos.* 26.3; *Com. in Mt.* 17.32; Justin *Dial.* 135.3; Clement *Strom.* 6.14.108.1.

3. Cf. *Hom. in Lv.* 4.3.

4. Cf. *Sel. in Ezek.* 13.2

5. Henri Crouzel (*Origen*, trans. A. S. Worrall [Edinburgh: T&T Clark, 1989], 75) cites this passage as evidence to show that Origen had not the slightest sympathy with the principle of the authority of private judgment in scriptural interpretation that arose at the time of the Reformation. Origen here begs his hearers to judge, according to the Scripture and the sense of God which is in the Christian people, whether he is orthodox—a "churchman," or a heretic, a true or false prophet.

6. This is directed against the Valentinian heretics. Cf. *Com. in Mt. ser.* 38.

7. *Ecclesiasticus.* Cf. *Hom. in Lk.* 16.6.

8. Cf. *Hom. in Lv.* 3.8.

9. Cf. *Com. in Mt.* 14.22 under Matt 15:33; *Com. in Jn.* 32.17.215.

10. Cf. Homily 10.1.2.

11. Cf. *Sel. in Ezek.* 13.3.

12. Cf. *Hom. in Nm.* 17.3.

13. Cf. Philo *Quod Deus immut* 39.

14. Cf. *Sel. in Ezek.* 13.4.

15. Cf. *Com. in Cant.* 4.3.8.

16. Origen consulted various Greek versions of the Old Testament in addition to the LXX.

17. Cf. Clement *Strom.* 1.19.95.7.

18. Lit., "in the firmament." Cf. Gen 1.6–8.

19. Cf. F. Ledegang, *Mysterium Ecclesiae: Images of the Church and Its Members in Origen* (Leuven: Peeters, 2001), 471 n. 982.

20. Cf. *Sel. in Ezek.* 13.5.

21. Cf. Homily 2.2.3 above.

22. *Scriptura*; or: "writing," "roll."

23. Cf. *Sel. in Ezek.* 13.9.

HOMILY 3

1. Or: "against" (*super*, Gk. επί).

2. This refers to the literal sense.

3. Origen was the first to use the designation God-man, θεάνθρωπος, which was to remain in the terminology of Christian theology. See Johannes Quasten, *Patrology*, 3 vols. (Westminster, MD: Newman, 1950–60), 2:80.

4. Lit., "head of his flesh."

5. Cf. *Hom. in Ex.* 10.3.

6. For other uses of "daughters" in a negative sense, see *Hom. in Nm.* 11.7; 22.1.

7. Cf. *Com. in Rom.* 2.13.29–30.

8. Basilides was a Gnostic theologian of the second century who taught in Alexandria. Cf. *Com. in Mt. ser.* 38; *Com. in Rom.* 2.13. Irenaeus *Adv. Haer.* 3.18.5 speaks of heretics who pour contempt upon the martyrs, but he does not identify them as followers of Basilides.

9. Origen shows awareness of his responsibility to edify the church by preaching in *Hom. in Ex.* 2.4; *Hom. in Nm.* 14.1; 19.4; 27.9; *Com. in Rom.* 10.35, 37.

10. In the vocabulary of the early church, *presbyteros* (elder) referred to ordained priests.

11. Cf. *Princ.* 2.10.4; *Com. in Rom.* 2.6.2; 5.1.40.

12. "*Homo, homo*" (LXX: ἄνθρωπος, ἄνθρωπος) corresponds to the Hebrew idiom *'îš 'îš*, according to which the repetition of single words is used to express a distributive sense ("every man"). See *Gesenius' Hebrew Grammar*, ed. E. Kautzsch, 2nd ed. by A. E. Cowley (Oxford: Clarendon Press, 1988) §123c. Origen follows the Jewish interpretative tradition in seeing a mystical meaning in the unusual construction. Philo (*Gig* 33) said that the repeated word was a sign that God means not the man who is compounded of soul and body but the man whose life is one of virtue.

13. For a list of passages in Origen where he uses horses as the image of passions and of people who allow themselves to be governed by them, see F. Ledegang, *Mysterium Ecclesiae: Images of the Church and Its Members in Origen* (Leuven: Peeters, 2001), 577 n. 477.

14. Cf. *Cat. in Ezek.* 14.4; *Hom. in Nm.* 24.2; Philo *Gig.* 33.

15. For a list of other passages where Origen speaks of the church as the people of God, see Ledegang, *Mysterium Ecclesiae*, 399 n. 366.

16. See note on 3.8.1 above.

Homily 4

1. Or: "sinner (female)."

2. Or: "land," et infra.

3. Apart from this text, Noah is mentioned in Gen 5–10; Isa 54:9; and 1 Chr 1:4. He serves Ezekiel's purpose very well as one whose personal justice brought no benefits to his contemporaries. Job is the model of justice known from the biblical book that bears his name. The mention of Daniel here, however, creates difficulties for modern interpreters, but not for Origen. Modern scholars ask: How could Daniel, Ezekiel's younger contemporary, earn the right to stand alongside Noah and Job? Moreover, why does Ezekiel spell his name Danel (in the Hebrew)? Because of these problems, many modern commentators wish to identify the referent with a Danel mentioned in twelfth-century BC Ugaritic tablets, a legendary pagan king and hero, renowned for his jus-

tice, wisdom, and piety. Yet the biblical Daniel's fame is attested elsewhere in 1 Macc 2:60. Moreover, it is hard to imagine that Ezekiel's audience would accept the association of a pagan worshiper of foreign gods alongside the biblical Noah and Job. Daniel I. Block (*The Book of Ezekiel*, 2 vols., New International Commentary on the Old Testament [Grand Rapids: Eerdmans, 1997, 1998], 1:449) observes: "If the Daniel of the book by this name was indeed a historical figure, it is inconceivable that Ezekiel's audience would not have been familiar with him, and it might even be surprising if Ezekiel had never mentioned him." See also John Day, "The Daniel of Ugarit and Ezekiel and the Hero of the Book of Daniel," *Vetus Testamentum* 30 (1980): 174–84.

4. Origen seems to be using satire here. He asks his audience to concentrate on the biblical passage the way they do at the theater!

5. For a list of other passages where Origen discusses the earth as a sinner, who "shows the image of the earthly," see F. Ledegang, *Mysterium Ecclesiae: Images of the Church and Its Members in Origen* (Leuven: Peeters, 2001), 521 n. 48.

6. In *Hom. in Jgs.* 7.1, Origen himself adopts what he here calls a facile interpretation.

7. Jerome uses the masculine *peccator* as predicate of the feminine *terra.* The feminine *peccatrix* occurs in the lemma. A similar construction is used and discussed in *Com. in Rom.* 6.8.11 (FOTC 104:35 n. 200).

8. Or: "earth."

9. Brittany was a Roman province in northwest France, southwest of modern Normandy.

10. Mauretania, a Roman province in western North Africa, stretched from the Ampsaga to the Atlantic and embraced the western half of the Atlas range.

11. Cf. *Hom. in Ex.* 1.4.

12. Origen cites the Hebrew reading this time. Usually he prefers the LXX, which reads "angels of God."

13. Matt 13:3–7, 18–23; cf. Luke 8:15; *Ad Mart.* 49; *Cat. in Ezek.* 14.13; *Cat. in Prov.* 3.19; *Hom. in Nm.* 23.8.

14. For this use of "earth" as a neutral indication of the heart or the soul, see also *Cat. in Ezek.* 14.13; *Cat. in Prov.* 3.19; *Hom. in Lv.* 5.3; 16.5–6.

15. Origen believed that just as natural goods are administered under the supervision of angels, so the evil angels, or demons, are the causes of famine, plague, and sickness. Cf. *Cels.* 1.31; 8.31; *Hom. in Jos.* 23.3. In holding these views, Origen stands in the tradition of Tatian and the Pseudo-Clementine *Homilies.* See Jean Daniélou, *Gospel Message and Hellenistic Culture,* trans. John Austin Baker (Philadelphia: Westminster, 1973), 435–36.

16. Cf. Homily 4.1.2 above.

17. F. Ledegang (*Mysterium Ecclesiae,* 372 n. 137) thinks that Carl Heinrich Eduard Lommatzsch's decision to read "Sem" for "Seth" is correct

(*Origenes Opera*, 25 vols. [Berlin, 1831–48]). Interchange of the two names occurs more often in the manuscripts. See Justin *Dial.* 139.2.

18. Cf. *Com. in Jn.* 20.10.

19. Cf. Homily 4.8.4 below.

20. Cf. *Com. in Mt.* 15.5; Jerome *Adv. Jov.* 1.25; *Com. in Dn.* 1:3. For a discussion of Origen's interpretation here and below at 4.8.2 and its connection to the rabbinic tradition, see Jay Braverman, *Jerome's Commentary on Daniel: A Study of Comparative Jewish and Christian Interpretations of the Hebrew Bible*, Catholic Biblical Quarterly Monograph Series 7 (Washington, DC: Catholic Biblical Association of America, 1978), 57–62.

21. Cf. *Com. in Mt.* 16.17.

22. Lit., "God's first name."

23. This is a rare glimpse of Origen's family life. According to Eusebius *HE* 6.1, Origen's father, Leonides, was martyred in Alexandria under Emperor Severus in the beginning of the third century.

24. Cf. *Hom. in Ex.* 11.4. Braverman (*Jerome's Commentary on Daniel*, 59–62) discusses rabbinic parallels to Origen's interpretation. He shows that Origen followed the rabbinic tradition but filled in the outlines with his own extended explanations suitable for didactic homilies. But even in his expansions, Origen made use of other Jewish traditions.

25. Cf. Justin *Dial* 19.4: "the beginning of another race."

26. Cf. Matt 7:24–27, where Jesus compares the final judgment with Noah's flood. Origen's thought may have been influenced by Philo *De Abrahamo* 10.

Homily 5

1. Cf. Homily 4.2.1.

2. Cf. Homily 4.7.2.

3. Lit., "iron."

4. Following the Sources Chrétiennes editors, who follow W. A. Baehrens, I take it that *Neque enim* controls both clauses.

5. The Gnostic heretics believed that the Creator was only just and punished the wicked out of vindictiveness. Cf. Origen *Peri Archon* 4.2.1.

6. The sequence would seem to require here "double-edged sword," but the text repeats "death."

7. Cf. *Hom. in Ex.* 8.4.

8. Lycurgus was the (possibly legendary) founder of the constitution and military regime of Sparta, first mentioned by Herodotus and given a *Life* by Plutarch.

9. Cf. *Hom. in Gn.* 16.5; *Hom. in Nm.* 2.1; 9.1; 22.4; *Hom. in Jer.* 11.3; *Hom. in Lv.* 6.4; *Cels.* 8.75; *De Or.* 28.3.

10. Cf. Homily 4.8.1.

11. F. Ledegang (*Mysterium Ecclesiae: Images of the Church and Its Members in Origen* [Leuven: Peeters, 2001], 539 n. 193) observes that Origen's remark on the uselessness of the wood of the vine is wrong. "It is firm and durable. In actual practice it was little used in historical times."

12. *Mappa* refers to a cloth or napkin thrown down in the circus as a signal for the races to begin. Cf. Juvenal 11.191; Suetonius *Nero* 22.2; A. Otto, *Die Sprichwörter und sprichwörtlichen Redensarten der Römer* (1890; repr., Hildesheim: Olms, 1962), 1059. Origen's use of this proverb is a little puzzling, but Erasmus of Rotterdam (*Adages* III vii 81 [Collected Works of Erasmus 35:270]) seems correct when he suggests that Origen has adapted the proverb to mean that God will cover our infamies by placing a napkin over them. Erasmus also noticed that Tertullian used the same expression in *Against the Valentinians* 36 (CSEL 47:210).

13. Ledegang (*Mysterium Ecclesiae,* 272) calls this passage "a splendid description of what Origen exactly understands by edification."

Homily 6

1. Jerome was particularly inspired by this homily in his own *In Ezek.* 4.

2. Lit., "of the Sodomites."

3. This passage seems to be directed against the claims of the Montanists, who believed that in prophetic inspiration the Holy Spirit suspends the consciousness and freedom of the prophet and puts him or her in a trance, a state of sacred derangement. The prophet or prophetess is used as a passive instrument to utter the words of the Spirit, as a lyre is plucked by the plectrum. This conception of inspiration was debated in Greek philosophy (cf. Plato's *Ion*) and had some support in the writings of the Jewish theologian Philo. In spite of Origen's admiration for Philo, Origen holds, on the contrary, that the prophet collaborates freely with the Spirit who inspires him. Wills are never compelled, except in the case of demonic possession. See Henri Crouzel, *Origen,* trans A. S. Worrall (Edinburgh: T&T Clark, 1989), 72; E. Nardoni, "Origen's Concept of Biblical Inspiration," *Second Century* 4 (1984): 9–23.

4. Lit., "feet."

5. Cf. *Com. in Rom.* 4.2.

6. RSV: Rephaim.

7. Cf. *Hom. in Jer.* 9.4; *De Or.* 22.4; *Cat. in Ex.* 20.5–6; *Cat. in Ps.* 101 (102).21; *Hom. in Lk. fr.* 67.

8. Origen (or Jerome) is explaining the reading of the Hebrew. The LXX does not have this phrase.

9. Or: "navel."

10. *Umbilicus* (umbilical cord).

11. Origen seems to be alluding to a commentary or homily that he has written on Job.

12. Jean Daniélou (*Origen,* trans. W. Mitchell [London/New York: Sheed & Ward, 1955], 54ff.) describes Origen's theology of the sacrament of baptism in these terms: "He always stresses the importance of receiving the sacraments in the right frame of mind. He even goes so far as to say that no one who comes for Baptism *peccans* [sinning] can obtain the remission of sins. And with reference to the symbolism of Baptism, he writes: 'You must first die to sin if you would be buried with Christ" [*Com. in Rom.* 5.8]....But while stressing the importance of the right dispositions for receiving the sacrament, he also teaches that the sacrament produces its effect by its own inherent virtue."

13. F. Ledegang (*Mysterium Ecclesiae: Images of the Church and Its Members in Origen* [Leuven: Peeters, 2001], 645) references the following texts as sources and parallels: Plutarch *Quaest. Conv.* 5.10.3; Varro *De re rustica* 2.4.10; Cicero *De nat. deor.* 2.64; Philo *De spec. leg.* 1.289.

14. Cf. Clement *Paed.* 1.8.74.4.

15. Cf. *Hom. in Jer.* 18.6; *Princ.* 2.4.4.

16. *Impassibilis.*

17. Henri de Lubac (*Histoire et Esprit: L'intelligence de l'Écriture d'après Origène* [Paris: Aubier, 1950], 241) considered this passage of Origen to be "no doubt one of his most beautiful pages, both his most human and his most Christian." Cf. Michael Figura, "The Suffering of God in Patristic Theology," *Communio* 30, no. 3 (2003): 366–85; and most importantly, Thomas G. Weinandy, "Origen and the Suffering of God," in *Studia Patristica 36: Papers Presented at the Thirteenth International Conference on Patristic Studies Held in Oxford, 1999* (Leuven: Peeters, 2001), 456–60.

18. That is, baptism.

19. Cf. *Hom. in Lv.* 15.2; 11.2; 2.4.

20. Cf. *Com. in Cant. Prol.* 1.4–6.

21. Christ means "one anointed with oil."

22. Cf. *Sel. in Ezek.* 16.10; *Hom. in Lv.* 4.6; 6.6; *Hom. in Ex.* 13.3.

23. Cf. *Hom. in Gn.* 8.7; *Hom. in 1 Sm.* 1.6.

24. Lit., "hands."

25. Lit., "earring."

26. Cf. *Hom. in Ex.* 13.2.

27. Origen believed that each vice proceeds from a particular demon. He attributed this doctrine to the *Testaments of the Twelve Patriarchs.* Cf. *Hom. in Jos.* 15.5–6. There is a prince-demon for each of these vices, who appoints his

underlings to attack each individual. For Origen's demonology, see Jean Daniélou, *Gospel Message and Hellenistic Culture,* trans. John Austin Baker (Philadelphia: Westminster, 1973), 434–41.

28. Lit., "fabricated discipline" (*fictam disciplinam*).

Homily 7

1. For the same example, see *Hom. in Jer.* 4.5.
2. Cf. Homily 6.11.2.
3. Cf. *Hom. in Nm.* 21.2; *Dial. c. Heracl.* 15.17–23.
4. Cf. Num 4:7; 7:13; 8:2–3; 3:31; Exod 25:10, 31; 37:1, 17.
5. Cf. *Princ.* 1 *praef.* 2.
6. Cf. *Com. in Mt. ser.* 33.
7. Cf. *Com. in Mt. ser.* 9ff.
8. Cf. *Sel. in Ezek.* 16.18; *Hom. in Lv.* 13.5.
9. Cf. *Sel. in Ezek. Cat.*
10. Cf. *Hom. in Lv.* 5.6; 13.3–4.
11. Origen often speaks of the heart and soul as a house from which the evil powers must be expelled and in which God, the Father, the Son, and the Holy Spirit wish to dwell. Cf. *De Or.* 23.4; *Hom. in Gn.* 1.17; 13.3; *Hom. in Ex.* 8.4; *Com. in Rom.* 2.1; 6.13; *Cat. in Ezek.* 8.9; *Hom. in Jgs.* 2.5; *Hom. in Lk.* 21.5-7; *fr.* 72; *Cat. in Cant.* 5.2; *Com. in Cant.* 3.14; *Hom. in Cant.* 2.7; *Com. in Mt. ser.* 29; 59, 60, 79; *Com. in Mt. fr.* 279.
12. Cf. *Hom. in Ex.* 5.5; *Cat. in Ezek.* 16.26.
13. Cf. *Hom. in Nm.* 19.3.
14. The LXX and Hebrew read "Chaldea" here.

Homily 8

1. Cf. *Hom. in Ex.* 8.5.
2. Cf. Tertullian *Adv. Marc.* 4.5.
3. Cf. *Hom. in Nm.* 20.2; *Hom. in Gn.* 10.2; *Hom. in Lv.* 2.9.

Homily 9

1. The pronouns are plural, whereas formerly they were singular.
2. The first "your" is singular, the second plural.

3. Or: "multitude," or "plurality."

4. Cf. F. Ledegang, *Mysterium Ecclesiae: Images of the Church and Its Members in Origen* (Leuven: Peeters, 2001), 118 n. 606: "Unity in Origen is related to God and discord to sin." Cf. *Com. in Jn.* 5.5; *De Or.* 21.2; *Hom. in Lk. fr.* 78; *Hom. in Lv.* 5.12; *Hom. in 1 Sm.* 1.4; *Com. in Hos.* = *Philoc.* 8.2–3; *Com. in Mt. fr.* 375–76. On this scriptural and traditional theme, see Henri de Lubac, *Catholicism* (San Francisco: Ignatius, 1988), 77–81.

5. Or: "plurality."

6. Here I have signified the singular pronoun with "thy" and the plural with "your."

7. Cf. *Hom. in Nm.* 12.4.

8. Cf. *Hom. in Ex.* 11.6.

9. Lit., "synagogue."

10. Cf. Clement *Strom.* 1.18.89.2.

11. For other passages where the church is compared with the moon, see *Com. in Jn.* 1.25(24).163; 6.55(37).287; *Hom. in Gn.* 1.5; 7.8–9, 20–21; *Hom. in Nm.* 23.5.

12. He means in the daily liturgies.

13. This is a noteworthy occurrence of *eucharistia.*

Homily 10

1. Lit., "work of confusion" (*opus confusionis*).

2. The comparison of apostasy to a shipwreck is found in Paul, 1 Tim 1:19. The image is also found in Plato *Phaedo* 85d; Seneca *Benef.* 3.9.2; Cicero *Of.* 3.23.89. Among Christian writers, see Tertullian, *Paen.* 4.2; Jerome, *In Is.* 2.3.9; *In Ezek.* 5.16.52.

3. Cf. *Hom. in Ex.* 3.3.

4. Of "evil persons."

5. For other passages on the restoration of fallen clerics, see *Hom. in Jos.* 7.6; *Hom. in Lv.* 15.2; *Cels.* 3.51; *Com. in Mt.* 13.24; 14.22. For discussion of these texts, see Hermann Josef Vogt, *Das Kirchenverständnis des Origenes* (Cologne: Böhlau, 1974), 48–49, 139, 255.

6. Cf. Homily 9.1.

7. Cf. *Com. in Rom.* 3.2.

8. Cf. *Hom. in Gn.* 5.1.

9. Cf. Homily 5.1 above, and *Hom. in Jer.* 12.3; *Lat.* 2.6; *Hom. in Nm.* 8.1.

10. Cf. Hom 1.3.3.

Homily 11

1. These are apparently the Greek versions of Aquila, Symmachus, and Theodotion that Origen compiled in his *Hexapla.* Notice that Origen does not reject the alternate versions.

2. *Translatorum,* "one who carries or hands over, a transferor." In late Latin, "a translator."

3. Lit., "the seventy."

4. For *arbusta vitis,* see Pliny *Nat. hist.* 17.207.

5. Cf. Homily 11.1.3 above.

6. Cf. Homily 11.1.3 above.

7. I have translated *princeps* as "prince" when it refers to the Israelite rulers taken captive by Nebuchadnezzar, and "ruler" when it refers to leaders of the church.

8. Cf. *De Or.* 27.12; *Hom. in Ex.* 4.6; *Com. in Rom.* 5.1; 10.3; *Hom. in Lv.* 7.4.

9. Lit., "in the faith of Christ."

10. In *Cels.* 4.92–93, Origen developed the idea that demons are associated with certain animals, based on the observation that Moses declared unclean precisely those animals that were used by the Egyptians for divination. In Gnosticism demons were associated with animals, but also in the Jewish tradition (*Letter of Aristeas* 128; *Epistle of Barnabas* 10), the unclean animals of the OT law symbolize demons. See Jean Daniélou, *Gospel Message and Hellenistic Culture,* trans. John Austin Baker (Philadelphia: Westminster, 1973), 437.

11. See Homily 11.2.1 above.

12. Cf. *Hom. in Jer.* 1.3; 19.41.

13. Cf. *Hom. in Jer.* 1.3; 19.14; *Hom. in Nm.* 11.4.

14. Cf. *Hom. in Jos.* 2.4.

15. Cf. Clement *Strom.* 3.1.2.4–5.

Homily 12

1. Cf. *Hom. in Nm.* 12.2.

2. This passage is nearly reminiscent of St. Anselm, *Cur Deus Homo,* in which the thesis is argued that human sin offended God's honor.

3. Cf. *Hom. in Jer. Lat.* 2.5–6; *Hom. in Jer. fr.* 26; *Hom. in Jos.* 15.3; *Cels.* 7.22, 24.

4. See note above on Homily 1.3.6.

5. Lit., "make an abortion."

6. Cf. *Hom. in Lv.* 14.4.

Homily 13

1. Origen refers to the bishop in the context of delivering a homily in *Hom. in 1 Sm.* 5.1. cf. *Hom. in Nm.* 15.1.

2. Lit., "bodily."

3. Cf. *Princ.* 1.5.4.

4. In Origen's angelology, the diversity of nations is not something evil in itself but is a secondary divine dispensation that resulted from the sin of Babel (cf. *Cels.* 5.30). God entrusted each nation to its own presiding good angel, but each nation also has its own evil angel (cf. *Hom. in Lk.* 12). Before Christ came, the good angels were powerless and the evil angels controlled the nations and incited them to make war on one another. See Jean Daniélou, *Gospel Message and Hellenistic Culture,* trans. John Austin Baker (Philadelphia: Westminster, 1973), 436.

5. Cf. Homily 13.1.2 above; *Hom. in Lk.* 35.6; *Princ.* 1.5.2; *Cels.* 5.25.9; *Hom. in Nm.* 11.4–5.

6. Cf. *Hom. in Jgs.* 3.1.

7. Cf. Homily 1.3; *Princ.* 1.5.4–5; *Cels.* 6.66.32–35; *Philoc.* 26.7.35; *Hom. in Nm.* 11.4; *Hom. in Jos.* 1.6.

8. This refers to the Gnostic heretics Valentinus, Basilides, Marcion, and Manichaeus, who taught that salvation is based on one's ingrained nature.

9. Cf. Rom 4:18, 24. For parallel passages (listed in F. Ledegang, *Mysterium Ecclesiae: Images of the Church and Its Members in Origen* [Leuven: Peeters, 2001], 631 n. 853), see *Hom. in Lv.* 5.2; *Com. in Rom.* 4.6; *Com. in Cant.* 3.13.22; Irenaeus *Dem.* 35; *Adv. Haer.* 4.7. The combination of Gen 15.5; Matt 5:14; and Phil 2:15 is found also in Irenaeus *Adv. Haer.* 4.7.3; 8.1.4–18.

10. Cf. *Com. in Mt.* 13.10.

11. Cf. *Hom. in Ex.* 8.6.

12. Cf. *Hom. in 1 Sm.* 5.9; *Princ.* 2.3.7; 2.11.6.

13. Origen typifies the paradise of delights as *beatitudo.* It is the final goal of supreme perfection and bliss. Cf. *Hom. in Nm.* 12.3; *Com. in Cant.* 1.4.

14. Lit., "sacred volumes." Ledegang (*Mysterium Ecclesiae,* 367) observes: "Although Origen stimulates the personal use of the Bible, nonetheless in saying these words he will especially have thought of the assembly of the church, where the Scriptures are explained. In that sense the church is 'paradisus deliciarum.'"

15. Cf. Hermas *Sim.* 9.92. For other citations of Hermas in Origen, see *Princ.* 1.3.5; 2.1.5; 3.2.4; *Sel. in Ps. Hom. 1 in Ps. 37*; *Hom. in Nm.* 8.1; *Com. in Mt.* 14.21; *Com. in Mt. ser.* 53; *Com. in Rom.* 10.31.

16. Cf. Homily 13.1.1 above.

17. *Commenti more,* "in the manner of a commentary."

18. Cf. *Hom. in Jos.* 14.2.

19. Ledegang (*Mysterium Ecclesiae,* 488 n. 1136) notes that John 4:14 in combination with John 7:38 is cited in *Com. in Cant.* 3.14.25.

20. Cf. Clement *Strom.* 1.19.96.3–4.

HOMILY 14

1. Ezek 44:1–3 became important in later church tradition when it was applied to the doctrine of *Virginitas in Partu* of the Virgin Mary (i.e., the preservation of Mary's virginity during the birth of Jesus). In the *De institutione virginum,* St. Ambrose introduced this mystery by identifying Mary as the "closed gate" through which Christ entered this world, when he was brought forth in the virginal birth and the manner of his birth did not break the seals of virginity. While supporting the doctrine of Mary's perpetual virginity, Origen, in the present passage, does not interpret the passage of Mary. See Luigi Gambero, S.M., *Mary and the Fathers of the Church: The Blessed Virgin Mary in Patristic Thought,* trans. Thomas Buffer (San Francisco: Ignatius, 1999).

2. *Ianua.* Up to this point, Jerome had used *porta.*

3. Cf. *De Or.* 27.11.

BIBLIOGRAPHY

Texts and Translations

Jerome

Archer, G. trans. *Jerome's Commentary on Daniel.* Grand Rapids: Baker, 1958.

Origen/Origène/Origenes

Baehrens, W. A. *Origenes Werke VIII: Homiliae in Regn., Ez., et al.* GCS 33. Leipzig: Berlin-Brandenburgische Akademie der Wissenschaften, 1925.

Balthasar, Hans Urs von, ed. *Origen: Spirit and Fire. A Thematic Anthology of His Writings.* Translated by Robert J. Daly. Washington, DC: Catholic University of America Press, 1984.

Borret, Marcel. *Homélies sur Ézéchiel.* SC 352. Paris: Cerf, 1989.

Scheck, Thomas P. *Origen: Commentary on the Epistle to the Romans.* 2 vols. FOTC 103, 104. Washington, DC: Catholic University of America Press, 2001–2.

Tollinton, R. B. *Selections from the Commentaries and Homilies of Origen.* London: SPCK, 1929.

Trigg, Joseph Wilson. "Origen: Homily 1 on Ezekiel." In *Ascetic Behavior in Greco-Roman Antiquity,* edited by V. L. Wimbush, 45–65. Minneapolis: Fortress, 1990.

Secondary Works

Block, Daniel I. *The Book of Ezekiel.* 2 vols. New International Commentary on the Old Testament. Grand Rapids: Eerdmans, 1997, 1998.

Braverman, Jay. *Jerome's Commentary on Daniel: A Study of Comparative Jewish and Christian Interpretations of the Hebrew Bible.* Catholic Biblical Quarterly Monograph Series 7. Washington, DC: Catholic Biblical Association of America, 1978.

Christman, Angela Gale Russell. *What Did Ezekiel See? Christian Exegesis of Ezekiel's Vision of the Chariot from Irenaeus to Gregory the Great* (Leiden: Brill, 2005).

Crouzel, Henri. "The Literature on Origen 1970–1988." *Theological Studies* 49 (1988): 499–516.

———. *Origen.* Translated by A. S. Worrall. Edinburgh: T&T Clark, 1989.

Daniélou, Jean. *Gospel Message and Hellenistic Culture.* Translated by John Austin Baker. Philadelphia: Westminster, 1973.

———. *Origen.* Translated by W. Mitchell. London/New York: Sheed & Ward, 1955.

———. *The Theology of Jewish Christianity.* Translated by John Austin Baker. London: Darton, Longman & Todd, 1964.

Eyzaguirre, S. F. "'Passio Caritatis' according to Origen in *Ezechielem Homiliae* VI in the Light of Dt 1,31." *Vigiliae Christianae* 60 (2006): 135–47.

Figura, Michael. "The Suffering of God in Patristic Theology." *Communio* 30, no. 3 (2003): 366–85.

Halperin, D. J. "Origen, Ezekiel's Merkabah, and the Ascension of Moses." *Church History* 50 (1981): 261–75.

Kelly, J. N. D. *Jerome: His Life, Writings, and Controversies.* New York: Harper & Row, 1975.

Ledegang, F. *Mysterium Ecclesiae: Images of the Church and its Members in Origen.* Leuven: Peeters, 2001.

Lienhard, J. T. "Origen and the Crisis of the Old Testament in the Early Church." *Pro Ecclesia* 9, no. 3 (2000): 355–66.

Lubac, Henri de. *Histoire et Esprit: L'intelligence de l'Écriture d'après Origène.* Paris: Aubier, 1950. Eng. trans. *History and Spirit: The Understanding of Scripture according to Origen.* Translated by Anne Englund Nash. San Francisco: Ignatius Press, 2007.

———. *Medieval Exegesis: The Four Senses of Scripture.* Translated by M. Sebanc (vol. 1) and E. M. Macierowski (vol. 2). 2 vols. Grand Rapids: Eerdmans, 1998, 2000. French original, *Exégèse médiévale: Les quatre sens de l'écriture.* 3 vols. Paris: Aubier, 1959.

———. *Theology in History*: Part One, *The Light of Christ;* Part Two, *Disputed Questions and Resistance to Nazism.* Translated by Anne Englund Nash. San Francisco: Ignatius Press, 1996.

Margerie, Bertrand de. *An Introduction to the History of Exegesis.* Volume 1, *The Greek Fathers.* Petersham: Saint Bede's Publications, 1993.

McGuckin, John A., ed. *The Westminster Handbook to Origen.* Louisville: Westminster John Knox, 2004.

Nautin, P. *Origène: sa vie et son oeuvre.* Paris: Beauchesne, 1977.

Scheck, Thomas P. *Origen and the History of Justification: The Legacy of Origen's Commentary on Romans.* Notre Dame, IN: University of Notre Dame Press, 2008.

Steinmann, Jean. *Saint Jerome and His Times.* Translated by R. Matthews. Notre Dame, IN: Fides, 1959.

Trigg, Joseph Wilson. *Origen: The Bible and Philosophy in the Third-Century Church.* Atlanta: John Knox, 1983.

VanLandingham, Chris. *Judgment and Justification in Early Judaism and the Apostle Paul.* Peabody, MA: Hendrickson, 2006.

Verfaillie, C. *La doctrine de la justification dans Origène d'après son commentaire de l'Épître aux Romains.* Thèse de la Faculté de théologie catholique de l'Université de Strasbourg. Strasbourg, 1926.

Vogt, Hermann Josef. *Das Kirchenverständnis des Origenes.* Cologne: Böhlau, 1974.

Weinandy, Thomas G. "Origen and the Suffering of God." In *Studia Patristica 36: Papers Presented at the Thirteenth International Conference on Patristic Studies Held in Oxford, 1999*, 456–60. Leuven: Peeters, 2001.

SCRIPTURE INDEX

Jerome's Preface (pref) is referenced by section number; Origen's Homilies are referenced by homily number, section, and paragraph (separated by ".").

Old Testament

Genesis

Gen 1:1 14.1.1
Gen 1:6–8 2.4.2
Gen 1:26 7.6.1; 13.2.7; 13.2.8
Gen 1:27 13.2.7
Gen 2:7 4.1.6
Gen 2:8 1.3.7
Gen 2:15 1.3.8
Gen 3:1–2 1.3.7
Gen 3:14 1.3.7
Gen 3:17 4.1.5
Gen 3:19 4.1.3
Gen 3:22 1.9.1
Gen 3:24 5.1.1
Gen 4:9 4.1.5
Gen 4:11 4.1.5
Gen 4:25 4.4.3
Gen 5—10 4.1.1
Gen 5:31 4.4.3
Gen 6:11 4.1.7
Gen 7—8 1.2.4
Gen 9:25 11.4.1
Gen 13:10 9.4.1
Gen 13.10–11 10.3.1
Gen 15:5 13.2.4
Gen 15:15 6.3.2
Gen 15:20–21 6.3.1
Gen 18:20—19:28 1.2.4
Gen 20:18 4.1.2
Gen 32:28 4.4.1
Gen 35:4 1.12.3
Gen 37:3 6.9.1
Gen 39:1ff. 1.1.2
Gen 39:6–12 9.3.3
Gen 41:1ff. 1.1.2
Gen 41:25ff. 1.1.2
Gen 45:5, 7 1.1.2
Gen 49:3–12 4.4.1
Gen 49:9 11.3.2
Gen 49:27 4.4.2

Exodus

Exod 12:2 1.4.4
Exod 12:37 1.2.4
Exod 15:7 5.2.2; 10.2.4
Exod 20:2 11.4.2
Exod 20:13 7.10.1
Exod 23:26 4.1.2
Exod 25:1ff. 7.10.4
Exod 25:10 7.2.1
Exod 25:31 7.2.1
Exod 35:1ff. 7.10.4
Exod 37:1 7.2.1
Exod 37:17 7.2.1

Leviticus

Lev 6:26	14.3.1
Lev 11:13	11.3.1; 11.3.3
Lev 17:8	3.8.1
Lev 23:40	1.5.2
Lev 25:4	4.1.4
Lev 26:23	12.1.2
Lev 26:40	3.8.2
Lev 26:43	4.1.4

Numbers

Num 2:3	1.14.1
Num 2:18	1.14.1
Num 2:25	1.14.1
Num 3:31	7.2.1
Num 4:7	7.2.1
Num 7:13	7.2.1
Num 8:2–3	7.2.1
Num 14:7	2.5.4
Num 21:8	11.3.2
Num 23:5	6.1.1
Num 23:16	6.1.1
Num 23:23	2.5.2
Num 28:16	1.4.4

Deuteronomy

Deut 1:31	6.6.3
Deut 5:31	2.4.2
Deut 8:11–14	9.5.3
Deut 17:16	12.3.4
Deut 27:13–26	12.3.2
Deut 32:1	4.1.4
Deut 32:8	1.7.1
Deut 32:8–9	13.1.6
Deut 32:15	9.5.3
Deut 32:39	10.4.2
Deut 33:6	4.4.2

Judges

Judg 2:5	1.3.7
Judg 15:4–5	2.4.1

Ruth

Ruth 3:7	6.8.6
Ruth 3:9	6.8.6

1 Samuel

1 Sam 2:25	5.4.2
1 Sam 9:9	pref 1; 2.3.4
1 Sam 21:4–5	9.5.5
1 Sam 25:2–3	13.1.9

2 Samuel

2 Sam 11:2–27	9.5.5

1 Kings

1 Kgs 4:29	9.3.3
1 Kgs 4:29–34	1.2.2
1 Kgs 7:13	13.1.9
1 Kgs 12:16	9.1.4
1 Kgs 12:28	9.1.4

2 Kings

2 Kgs 2:23–24	4.7.2
2 Kgs 2:24	4.7.2
2 Kgs 17:22–23	10.3.2
2 Kgs 17:23	10.3.2
2 Kgs 17:25	4.7.2
2 Kgs 25:7	12.2.1

1 Chronicles

1 Chr 1:4	4.1.1

2 Chronicles

2 Chr 34:2	9.2.5
2 Chr 35:18	9.2.5

Ezra

Ezr 7:1–10	1.3.6

Judith

Jdt 1:1	13.1.6

1 Maccabees
1 Macc 2:60 4.1.1
1 Macc 2:66 9.3.3

2 Maccabees
2 Macc 15:10 9.3.3

Job
Job 1:2 4.8.5
Job 1:3 4.8.5
Job 1:6 1.3.7
Job 1:21 4.4.3
Job 2:7 4.8.5
Job 2:12 4.8.5
Job 10:10–11 13.2.3
Job 21:10 12.3.2
Job 38:1 4.8.5
Job 40:5 4.4.3
Job 40:10 4.4.3
Job 40:16 6.4.2
Job 41:25 13.2.6
Job 42:12–13 4.8.5

Psalms
Ps 1:1 9.3.1
Ps 2:2 13.1.5
Ps 2:7 6.3.2
Ps 6:1 1.2.3; 2.5.4
Ps 7:9 5.1.4; 10.1.2
Ps 9:14 13.3.2
Ps 10:9 11.3.2
Ps 17:1–3 9.5.5
Ps 22:22 9.1.3
Ps 27:3 4.8.1
Ps 30:9 1.5.1
Ps 31:19 1.3.5
Ps 34:8 4.8.1
Ps 36:8 3.3.1
Ps 37:4 3.3.1
Ps 40:2 2.4.2
Ps 43:20, 26 1.3.7
Ps 45:3 13.2.8
Ps 45:10–11 13.2.8
Ps 45:11 13.2.8
Ps 46:4 13.4.2
Ps 47:8–9 1.7.1
Ps 49:12 3.8.1
Ps 51:4 9.3.4
Ps 62:1 1.15.1
Ps 63:1–2 7.8.1
Ps 69:28 2.5.4
Ps 71:19 13.2.7
Ps 72:2 2.5.4
Ps 73:1–2 2.4.2
Ps 73:8 1.7.2
Ps 74:19 4.7.2
Ps 80:1 1.15.1
Ps 80:5 1.2.2
Ps 80:8 5.5.1
Ps 82:6 1.9.1
Ps 82:6–7 13.1.5
Ps 82:7 1.9.1
Ps 83:7 1.3.7
Ps 103:8 6.6.3
Ps 104:32 4.1.3
Ps 118:8–9 4.8.1
Ps 119:18 2.3.4
Ps 119:103 12.1.1
Ps 124:1–3 13.1.8
Ps 124:7 13.4.1
Ps 132:11 1.3.2
Ps 137:1 13.4.2
Ps 137:1–3 1.5.2
Ps 137:4 11.4.2
Ps 141:2 11.5.2
Ps 143:2 9.3.3
Ps 146:3 4.8.1
Ps 148:4 1.15.1

Proverbs
Prov 3:11–12 1.2.2; 2.5.4
Prov 4:23 8.3.3; 13.2.4; 13.4.1
Prov 5:3 8.2.3
Prov 9:15 8.2.4

Prov 17:25 4.1.6
Prov 23:4–5 11.3.1; 11.3.4
Prov 27:1 6.10.3
Prov 27:16 1.14.1
Prov 30:8–9 9.5.3
Prov 30:18–19 13.4.2

Ecclesiastes
Eccl 12:11 1.4.3

Wisdom
Wis 1:13 1.3.8
Wis 1:14 5.1.4
Wis 3:6 1.13.1; 10.5.3
Wis 6:5–6 10.2.3
Wis 7:2 1.4.2

Sirach
Sir 1:2–3 4.2.1
Sir 3:18 9.2.3
Sir 7:6 5.4.1
Sir 10:9 9.2.2
Sir 13:2 5.4.1
Sir 15:14–17 1.11.4
Sir 16:21 4.2.1
Sir 20:11 10.1.5
Sir 43:20 1.14.1

Isaiah
Isa 1:1 2.3.4
Isa 1:2 4.1.4; 4.1.5
Isa 1:10–11 6.1.1
Isa 1:26 10.3.3
Isa 5:6 1.12.4
Isa 5:7 5.5.1
Isa 5:18 7.9.1
Isa 7:14 1.4.2
Isa 10:7 1.3.4
Isa 10:13 11.4.2
Isa 10:13–14 9.2.2; 11.4.1
Isa 10:16 1.3.4
Isa 11:6 11.3.3
Isa 14:4 13.2.1; 13.2.2
Isa 14:12 1.3.7; 1.3.8; 13.2.1; 13.2.4
Isa 14:13–14 13.1.6
Isa 24:5 4.1.3; 4.1.6
Isa 24:14 4.1.6
Isa 29:11–12 14.2.2
Isa 34:4 13.2.4
Isa 39:7 4.8.4
Isa 40:31 11.3.1; 11.3.4; 12.5.1
Isa 44:4 1.5.2
Isa 47:14–15 1.3.4
Isa 49:9 1.3.9
Isa 50:11 3.7.2
Isa 51:17 13.2.2
Isa 54:9 4.1.1
Isa 61:1–2 1.3.9
Isa 66:12 13.4.2

Jeremiah
Jer 1:9–10 1.12.2
Jer 1:10 1.12.3
Jer 1:13 1.14.1
Jer 2:21 5.5.1
Jer 5:8 3.8.1
Jer 6:16 8.2.2
Jer 8:4 13.2.2
Jer 8:5 13.2.2
Jer 17:5 4.8.1
Jer 22:29–30 4.1.4
Jer 24:1 1.1.1
Jer 25:11 4.1.4
Jer 34:2–3 11.5.1

Lamentations
Lam 1:1 13.2.1

Ezekiel
Ezek 1:1 1.3.1; 1.4.1; 1.4.3; 1.4.4; 1.5.1; 1.5.2; 1.6.1; 1.7.1; 1.8.1; 1.10.3
Ezek 1:2 1.8.1
Ezek 1:2–3 1.10.3
Ezek 1:3 1.4.3; 1.9.1; 1.10.1; 1.10.2

Ezek 1:4 1.11.1; 1.12.1; 1.12.4; 1.13.1; 1.14.1; 1.16.1
Ezek 1:5 1.3.1; 1.11.1; 1.16.1
Ezek 1:5ff. 1.11.1
Ezek 1:5–7 1.15.1
Ezek 1:10 1.16.1; 11.3.3; 11.3.4
Ezek 1:12 1.16.1
Ezek 1:13 1.11.1
Ezek 1:16 1.3.1; 1.16.2
Ezek 1:27 1.3.2
Ezek 2:1 1.3.1; 1.4.1; 13.2.2
Ezek 2:3 1.4.1
Ezek 2:8 1.4.1
Ezek 3:1 1.4.1
Ezek 3:4 1.4.1
Ezek 3:17 1.4.1
Ezek 3:20 3.8.3
Ezek 10:9 1.16.1
Ezek 10:14 11.3.3
Ezek 13:1–2 2.2.1; 3.1.1
Ezek 13:2 2.2.2; 2.3.1
Ezek 13:2–3 2.3.3
Ezek 13:3 2.3.4
Ezek 13:4 2.4.1
Ezek 13:4–5 2.4.2; 2.5.1
Ezek 13:5–6 2.5.1
Ezek 13:6 2.5.2
Ezek 13:6–7 2.5.2
Ezek 13:7–8 2.5.2
Ezek 13:8–9 2.5.4
Ezek 13:9 2.5.4
Ezek 13:17 3.1.1; 3.1.2; 3.2.1
Ezek 13:18 3.2.1; 3.3.1; 3.3.2; 3.4.1
Ezek 13:20 3.4.1
Ezek 13:21 3.5.1
Ezek 13:21–22 3.5.1
Ezek 13:22 3.6.1
Ezek 13:23 3.6.1
Ezek 14:1 3.7.1
Ezek 14:1–3 3.7.1
Ezek 14:3 3.7.1; 3.7.2; 3.8.1
Ezek 14:4 3.8.1
Ezek 14:5 3.8.2
Ezek 14:6 3.8.2
Ezek 14:7 3.8.3
Ezek 14:7–8 3.8.3
Ezek 14:8 3.8.3
Ezek 14:12–13 4.1.1; 4.1.8
Ezek 14:13 4.1.2; 4.1.7; 4.2.1; 4.3.1; 4.7.2
Ezek 14:13–14 4.4.1; 4.7.1; 4.7.2
Ezek 14:14 4.5.1; 4.5.2; 4.6.1; 4.7.1; 4.8.1
Ezek 14:15 4.1.1; 4.7.2; 4.8.1
Ezek 14:16 4.1.1; 4.8.1
Ezek 14:18 4.1.1; 4.5.1; 4.8.1
Ezek 14:19–20 4.1.1
Ezek 14:21 4.1.1; 5.3.1; 5.4.1
Ezek 15:4 5.5.2
Ezek 16:2 6.1.2
Ezek 16:2–3 6.2.1
Ezek 16:3 6.3.1; 9.1.1; 9.1.2
Ezek 16:4 6.4.1; 6.4.2; 6.4.3; 6.5.1; 6.6.1; 6.6.2; 6.8.3
Ezek 16:5 6.6.2; 6.7.1
Ezek 16:6 6.7.2; 6.8.1
Ezek 16:6–7 6.8.1
Ezek 16:7 6.8.1; 6.8.2; 6.8.3; 6.8.4
Ezek 16:7–8 6.8.4
Ezek 16:8 6.8.3; 6.8.5; 6.8.6
Ezek 16:8–9 6.9.1; 7.5.2
Ezek 16:9 6.9.1
Ezek 16:10 6.9.1; 6.10.1
Ezek 16:11 6.10.1
Ezek 16:12 6.10.1
Ezek 16:13 6.10.1; 6.10.2
Ezek 16:14 6.10.2; 6.11.1
Ezek 16:15 6.11.1
Ezek 16:15–16 6.11.1
Ezek 16:15–25 6.1.2
Ezek 16:16 7.1.2; 7.6.1
Ezek 16:17 7.1.2; 7.2.1
Ezek 16:18 7.3.1; 7.3.4; 7.4.1
Ezek 16:19 7.4.2
Ezek 16:19–20 7.5.1
Ezek 16:20–21 7.5.1

Ezek 16:22 7.5.2
Ezek 16:23–24 7.6.1
Ezek 16:25 7.7.1; 7.7.2
Ezek 16:26 7.8.1
Ezek 16:27 7.8.1
Ezek 16:27–28 7.8.2
Ezek 16:28 7.9.1
Ezek 16:29 7.9.1
Ezek 16:30 7.10.4; 8.1.1; 8.1.2; 8.1.3
Ezek 16:31 8.1.3; 8.2.3; 8.3.1
Ezek 16:31–33 8.1.1
Ezek 16:33 8.3.2
Ezek 16:45 9.1.1; 9.1.2
Ezek 16:45–46 9.1.3
Ezek 16:46 9.1.6
Ezek 16:47 9.1.6
Ezek 16:49 9.2.1; 9.4.1; 9.4.3; 9.5.1
Ezek 16:50 9.5.1
Ezek 16:51 9.1.6; 9.2.4; 9.3.1
Ezek 16:51–52 9.3.1
Ezek 16:52 10.1.1; 10.1.2; 10.1.4; 10.2.1
Ezek 16:52–53 10.2.2
Ezek 16:53–54 10.2.3
Ezek 16:54 10.2.3
Ezek 16:55 1.2.4; 10.3.1; 10.3.3; 10.5.1
Ezek 16:56–58 10.4.1
Ezek 16:59–60 10.4.2
Ezek 16:60 10.4.2
Ezek 16:61 10.5.1
Ezek 16:61–62 10.5.1
Ezek 16:62–63 10.5.2
Ezek 16:63 10.5.2
Ezek 17:1–2 11.1.3
Ezek 17:3 11.2.1; 11.4.1
Ezek 17:3–4 11.2.1
Ezek 17:4 11.2.5
Ezek 17:5 11.2.2
Ezek 17:5–6 11.2.2; 11.4.2
Ezek 17:7 11.4.2; 11.5.1
Ezek 17:7–8 11.2–3; 11.5.1
Ezek 17:8 11.2.3
Ezek 17:9 11.2.3
Ezek 17:9–10 11.2.3
Ezek 17:12 11.2.5; 12.2.1
Ezek 17:12–13 11.5.2; 12.3.1
Ezek 17:13 11.4.1; 12.3.1
Ezek 17:13–14 12.3.4
Ezek 17:14–15 12.3.4
Ezek 17:15 12.3.2; 12.3.3; 12.3.4
Ezek 17:16 12.4.1
Ezek 17:16–17 12.4.1
Ezek 17:22 12.5.1
Ezek 17:23 12.5.1; 12.5.2
Ezek 17:24 12.5.2
Ezek 18:20 4.8.1
Ezek 18:22 4.8.1
Ezek 18:24 4.8.1; 8.3.3
Ezek 22:18 1.13.1
Ezek 22:19–23 1.13.1
Ezek 28:11 13.2.1
Ezek 28:12 1.3.7; 13.2.5; 13.2.8
Ezek 28:12–13 13.2.1
Ezek 28:13 1.3.7; 13.2.11; 13.3.1
Ezek 28:13–14 13.1.2
Ezek 28:15 1.3.7; 13.2.11
Ezek 29:3 13.1.7; 13.2.6; 13.4.2
Ezek 29:4 13.2.6
Ezek 29:18 13.2.2
Ezek 43 1.14.1
Ezek 44:1 14.1.1; 14.2.1
Ezek 44:1–3 14.1.1
Ezek 44:2 14.1.1; 14.2.4
Ezek 44:3 14.1.1

Daniel
Dan 1:3 4.5.1; 4.8.4
Dan 1:6 1.2.1; 4.5.1
Dan 1:19 1.2.1
Dan 7:10 2.3.1
Dan 9:2 1.2.1; 4.1.4
Dan 9:2–4 4.8.4
Dan 9:4–19 4.8.4

Dan 10:13 13.1.3
Dan 10:20 13.1.3
Dan 10:21 13.1.3
Dan 12:2 4.8.3; 10.1.5; 10.5.3
Dan 12:3 9.3.4
Dan 13:52 6.3.2
Dan 13:56 6.3.1

Hosea
Hos 7:12 1.2.3
Hos 12:10 1.7.2
Hos 14:10 9.5.1

Amos
Amos 3:12 4.7.2
Amos 6:1 9.1.5
Amos 7:12–13 2.3.4

Jonah
Jonah 1:4–7 6.2.1
Jonah 1:15 6.2.1
Jonah 2:1 6.2.1
Jonah 3:2, 5 6.2.1

Micah
Mic 7:1 1.5.1
Mic 7:2 1.5.1
Mic 7:9 10.4.2

Nahum
Nah 1:9 1.2.4

Haggai
Hag 1:1 1.2.1

Zechariah
Zech 1:1 1.2.1

Malachi
Mal 4:2 1.2.4; 9.3.3

New Testament

Matthew
Matt 1:23 1.4.2
Matt 3:7 3.8.1
Matt 3:10 12.5.2
Matt 3:13 1.4.1
Matt 3:16 1.6.1
Matt 4:11 1.7.1
Matt 5:8 3.7.1
Matt 5:13 6.6.1
Matt 5:14 13.2.4
Matt 5:16 9.3.3
Matt 5:45 1.2.4
Matt 6:11 14.3.2; 14.3.3
Matt 6:17 6.10.2
Matt 6:23 9.3.3
Matt 7:2 7.7.2
Matt 7:6 1.11.3; 12.1.2
Matt 7:7 14.2.1
Matt 7:11 8.1.2
Matt 7:13 8.2.4
Matt 7:15 11.3.3
Matt 7:24–27 4.8.3
Matt 7:24–28 10.5.3
Matt 9:2 6.3.2
Matt 9:30 1.3.9
Matt 10:15 1.2.4
Matt 10:16 11.3.2
Matt 10:34 5.1.2
Matt 11:15 13.2.6; 14.1.1
Matt 11:27 14.2.4
Matt 12:37 2.3.1
Matt 13:3–7, 18–23 4.1.8
Matt 13:46 8.2.2
Matt 13:47 1.11.3
Matt 13:48 1.11.3
Matt 16:18 13.2.6
Matt 16:24 3.4.2
Matt 17:5 1.12.4
Matt 17:24 13.2.6
Matt 17:27 13.2.6

Matt 18:10 1.7.1
Matt 18:12–14 4.6.1
Matt 22:11 3.8.4
Matt 22:11–13 6.9.1
Matt 22:14 6.9.1
Matt 22:32 7.4.1
Matt 23:2–3 7.3.3
Matt 24:24 3.5.2
Matt 24:29 13.2.4
Matt 24:35 4.1.7
Matt 28:19 7.4.1

Mark
Mark 4:32 12.5.1
Mark 12:16 13.2.6
Mark 13:22 3.3.2

Luke
Luke 1:78 10.1.5
Luke 1:79 1.3.9
Luke 2:7 6.6.2
Luke 2:12 6.6.2
Luke 2:13 1.7.1
Luke 3:8 6.7.1
Luke 3:16 13.2.5
Luke 3:17 1.11.4
Luke 3:21 1.4.1
Luke 3:23 1.4.1
Luke 4:18 1.3.9
Luke 6:16 13.1.7
Luke 8:15 4.1.8
Luke 8:29 1.3.9
Luke 10:18 1.3.8; 13.2.2
Luke 11:52 12.2.3; 14.2.1
Luke 12:42 13.2.7
Luke 12:49 1.3.3; 5.1.2
Luke 13:32 2.4.1
Luke 15:4–7 4.6.1
Luke 15:7 1.7.2
Luke 16:19 9.4.2
Luke 16:20–21 9.4.3
Luke 16:22 1.2.4
Luke 16:25 1.2.4; 12.3.3
Luke 18:11–14 9.2.3
Luke 18:14 9.4.3
Luke 19:10 4.6.1
Luke 20:24 13.2.6
Luke 23:39 13.2.11
Luke 23:39–43 10.1.3
Luke 23:43 13.2.11

John
John 1:1 1.9.1; 1.10.1
John 1:5 9.3.3
John 1:14 1.7.1
John 1:18 1.10.1
John 1:52 1.7.1; 13.2.2
John 3:5 6.5.1
John 3:13 13.2.2
John 3:14 11.3.2
John 4:13–14 13.4.2
John 4:14 13.4.2
John 4:24 1.12.1
John 4:34 14.2.5
John 5:17 1.3.8
John 5:28–29 4.8.3
John 6:51 14.3.3
John 7:38 13.4.2
John 8:31 13.2.6
John 8:39 4.4.3; 4.8.1; 9.1.3
John 8:41 4.8.1
John 8:44 6.3.2
John 9:39 2.3.4
John 10:30 9.1.2
John 10:34 1.9.1
John 10:35 1.9.1
John 11:43–44 1.3.9
John 12:32 14.3.2
John 13:25 6.4.3
John 13:27 13.1.8
John 13:33 4.5.2
John 14:6 8.2.2
John 15:1 1.5.1
John 15:1–2 5.5.3
John 15:2 5.5.2
John 15:6 5.5.2

John 16:7 1.6.1
John 17:11–12 9.1.2
John 19:23 3.3.3
John 20:17 9.1.3
John 21:11 1.11.3

Acts of the Apostles
Acts 4:32 9.1.2
Acts 8:13 6.5.1
Acts 8:20 6.5.1
Acts 9:15 14.2.4
Acts 10:11 11.3.3
Acts 10:15 11.3.3
Acts 10:28 11.3.3
Acts 11:12 2.2.3
Acts 11:19 13.1.7
Acts 13:9 6.6.1
Acts 21:3 13.1.7

Romans
Rom 2:4 1.3.5; 10.2.1
Rom 2:4–5 10.2.4; 10.4.2
Rom 2:5 10.1.4
Rom 2:8–9 5.2.2
Rom 2:10 13.1.3
Rom 2:15 2.3.2
Rom 2:23 12.1.3
Rom 3:4 9.3.4
Rom 4:18 13.2.4
Rom 4:24 13.2.4
Rom 6:4 2.5.1
Rom 8:13 1.13.1
Rom 8:19 1.7.2
Rom 8:21 4.1.5
Rom 8:22 4.1.5
Rom 11:11 13.2.3
Rom 11:18–19 13.2.4
Rom 11:20 6.3.1; 13.2.4
Rom 11:33 4.2.1
Rom 12:16 6.11.1
Rom 13:9 7.10.2
Rom 13:14 6.8.4
Rom 15:4 1.4.3; 7.8.2
Rom 16:7 4.8.1
Rom 16:13 4.8.1

1 Corinthians
1 Cor 1:10 9.1.2
1 Cor 1:12 9.1.2
1 Cor 1:23 1.4.2
1 Cor 1:24 1.4.3
1 Cor 1:30 2.4.1
1 Cor 2:6–8 13.1.4
1 Cor 2:10 1.16.1; 11.3.3
1 Cor 2:12 2.2.3
1 Cor 2:13 1.2.4; 1.4.3; 6.4.2
1 Cor 2:15 4.7.2; 13.1.6
1 Cor 2:16 2.2.3
1 Cor 3:1 1.3.5
1 Cor 3:2 1.3.3; 7.10.2
1 Cor 3:12 1.13.1; 3.7.2
1 Cor 3:12–15 1.3.3
1 Cor 3:13 1.3.3; 5.2.2
1 Cor 3:17 7.10.1
1 Cor 4:7 9.5.6
1 Cor 4:15 6.3.2
1 Cor 5:1 7.10.3
1 Cor 5:5 3.8.3; 12.3.3
1 Cor 7:1–2 7.10.2
1 Cor 7:40 2.2.3
1 Cor 8:1 9.5.4
1 Cor 8 7.10.2
1 Cor 10:4 13.4.2
1 Cor 10:6 1.4.3
1 Cor 10:11 1.4.3; 7.8.2; 12.2.2
1 Cor 10:12 13.2.10
1 Cor 11:1 4.5.1
1 Cor 11:4 3.1.1; 3.3.2
1 Cor 11:7 3.3.2
1 Cor 12:9–10 2.2.4
1 Cor 12:27 4.6.1
1 Cor 13:9 2.3.4
1 Cor 13:10 2.5.1
1 Cor 13:11 6.8.5
1 Cor 14:15 2.3.3
1 Cor 14:30 6.1.1

1 Cor 15:9 10.2.3
1 Cor 15:10 11.1.3
1 Cor 15:22 1.3.7
1 Cor 15:25 1.15.1
1 Cor 15:26 5.2.1
1 Cor 15:33 8.1.2
1 Cor 15:41–42 9.3.4; 13.2.4
1 Cor 15:49 13.2.5

2 Corinthians
2 Cor 1:22 2.5.1; 13.2.5
2 Cor 3:14–15 14.2.3
2 Cor 3:16 3.1.1; 14.2.3; 14.3.1
2 Cor 3:18 3.1.1; 3.5.1; 14.2.3
2 Cor 4:16 13.2.10
2 Cor 5:9 5.5.3
2 Cor 5:10 1.11.5
2 Cor 5:20 5.2.1
2 Cor 8:3 9.5.1
2 Cor 9:10 4.1.8
2 Cor 11:3 7.6.1
2 Cor 12:7 9.5.4
2 Cor 12:8–9 9.5.4

Galatians
Gal 1:4 1.16.1
Gal 3:7 4.4.3
Gal 4:19 4.5.1
Gal 4:26 5.4.1
Gal 6:1 6.10.3
Gal 6:16 2.2.1
Gal 6:17 4.5.1

Ephesians
Eph 1:21 4.1.4
Eph 2:2 4.1.4
Eph 2:14 1.3.6
Eph 4:4 9.1.2
Eph 4:8 1.6.1
Eph 4:10–12 1.6.1
Eph 4:13 9.1.2
Eph 4:14 3.1.2
Eph 4:15 2.3.1
Eph 4:27 12.2.2
Eph 5:14 14.2.1
Eph 5:27 13.2.10
Eph 6:12 1.3.9; 4.1.4; 7.8.2; 7.9.1; 9.3.3; 13.1.7; 13.1.8
Eph 6:13 2.3.1
Eph 6:14 6.10.1
Eph 6:15 6.9.1

Philippians
Phil 2:10 1.15.1; 1.16.1
Phil 2:12 1.3.8
Phil 2:15 13.2.4
Phil 3:5 4.4.2
Phil 3:6 9.3.3

Colossians
Col 1:15 1.5.1
Col 1:16 4.1.4
Col 3:9 13.2.9
Col 3:12 6.8.4; 7.3.1
Col 3:12–13 6.8.4
Col 4:6 6.6.1

1 Thessalonians
1 Thess 5:23 1.16.1; 7.10.4

1 Timothy
1 Tim 1:9 7.10.1
1 Tim 1:19 10.1.1
1 Tim 2:7 pref 1
1 Tim 3:6 9.2.2
1 Tim 3:16 1.10.1; 6.6.3
1 Tim 4:1 1.7.2
1 Tim 4:2 7.3.2
1 Tim 4:8 11.1.2
1 Tim 5:24–25 2.3.2

2 Timothy
2 Tim 1:11 pref 1

2 Tim 2:20 5.5.2
2 Tim 2:21 14.2.4
2 Tim 3:4 3.5.2
2 Tim 4:3 2.5.1

Titus
Titus 3:5 1.7.2; 6.7.1; 7.4.1

Hebrews
Heb 1:14 1.7.1
Heb 5:12–14 7.10.2; 7.10.3
Heb 6:1 7.10.3
Heb 6:5 5.3.1; 5.4.1
Heb 7:10 1.3.2; 6.4.2
Heb 10:26 5.3.2
Heb 10:28–29 5.3.2
Heb 10:29 5.3.2; 12.3.1
Heb 12:2 1.7.1
Heb 12:5–6 1.2.2
Heb 12:7–8 1.2.2
Heb 12:22 6.3.1; 13.3.2
Heb 12:23 14.3.3
Heb 12:29 1.3.3; 1.12.1

James
Jas 4:6 9.2.2
Jas 5:20 4.8.1

1 Peter
1 Pet 1:13 10.5.3
1 Pet 2:2 6.6.2; 7.10.3
1 Pet 2:9 12.3.1
1 Pet 4:11 1.16.2; 2.5.4; 3.8.4; 4.8.5; 5.5.3; 6.11.2; 7.10.4; 8.3.3; 9.5.6; 10.5.3; 11.5.3; 12.5.2; 13.4.2; 14.3.3
1 Pet 5:8 4.7.2; 6.11.1; 13.2.5
1 Pet 5:8–9 11.3.2

2 Peter
2 Pet 1:4 1.9.1
2 Pet 2:4 1.9.1
2 Pet 2:21 5.3.1

1 John
1 John 2:15 3.5.2
1 John 3:2 13.2.7
1 John 3:8 6.3.2; 9.1.3
1 John 4:2 13.4.2

Jude
Jude 6 4.1.5
Jude 7 10.5.2
Jude 10 2.4.1

Revelation
Rev 1:9 10.1.3
Rev 2:7 13.2.11
Rev 2:23 9.5.2
Rev 3:20 14.3.2
Rev 5:2–5 14.2.2
Rev 5:8 7.4.1
Rev 7:9 4.1.5
Rev 12:7–9 4.1.5
Rev 12:9 6.4.2
Rev 19:8 6.9.1
Rev 21:10–21 13.3.2
Rev 21:19–21 13.3.2
Rev 21:21 13.3.2

GENERAL INDEX

The Translator's Introduction (int) is referenced by page number. An endnote is referenced by page number, "n," and note number. Jerome's Preface (pref) is referenced by section number. Origen's Homilies are referenced by homily number, section, and paragraph (separated by ".").

Aelia, 1.11.3
Alexandria, 1.11.3
Ambrose, 14.1.1
Anselm, 12.1.3
Aquinas, Thomas, int 12
Aristeas, 11.3.3
Aristotle, int 13
Augustine, int 12

Balthasar, 172n8
Bammel, 174n49, 174n50
Bar Kokhba, 1.11.3
Barnabas, Epistle of, 11.3.3
Basilides, int 9, int 19; 3.4.2; 7.4.2; 8.2.3
Benedict XV, pope, 172n13
Bishops, 8.1.3; 13.1.1
Block, 4.1.1
Borret, int 3
Braverman, 4.5.1; 4.8.2
Brittany, 4.1.6

Catechism of the Catholic Church, int 1
Chrysostom, John, 175n66
Church, 1.7.1; 1.11.3–4; 1.12.2; 2.1.1; 2.2.1; 2.2.3; 2.2.4; 2.5.1; 2.5.3; 3.4.2; 3.5.1; 3.6.1; 3.7.1; 4.1.6; 4.4.2; 5.4.1; 6.4.1; 6.7.1; 6.7.2; 6.11.2; 7.3.3–4; 7.5.1–2; 7.10.1; 8.2.3; 9.1.3; 9.1.5; 9.3.3; 10.1.4; 11.4.2; 11.5.2–3; 12.1.2; 12.2.2; 12.2.3; 12.3.3; 12.5.1; 13.2.10; 13.4.1–2
Church, man of the, 2.2.4
Cicero, 6.6.1; 10.1.1
Clement of Alexandria, *Eclog Proph* 25.4: 1.3.3; *Paed* 1.8.74.4: 6.6.3; 3.8.44.2: 1.3.3; *Protr* 11.114.3: 1.2.4; *Strom* 1.5.29.4: 1.3.6; 1.18.89.2: 9.3.3; 1.19.95.7: 2.4.1; 1.19.96.3–4: 13.4.2; 3.1.2.4–5: 11.5.3; 6.14.108.1: 2.2.1; 7.14.86.5: 1.2.4; 7.34: 1.3.3
Clement, Pseudo-, 4.2.1
Constantinople, Second Council of (553), int 2
Cowley, 3.8.1
Crouzel, int 6, int 9, int 18; 2.2.3; 6.1.1
Cyprian, int 18

Daniel, 4.1.1
Daniélou, int 7, int 13, int 17; 1.11.3; 4.2.1; 6.5.1; 6.11.1; 11.3.3; 13.1.3
Day, J., 4.1.1
Denzinger, 171n1
Didymus the Blind, int 23
Docetism, int 8; 1.4.2

Erasmus, int 10; 5.5.3
Eucharistia, 9.5.5
Eusebius, int 1, int 2; 4.8.1

Farkasfalvy, 174n38
Fifth General Council. *See* Constantinople, Second Council of
Figura, 175n52; 6.6.3

Gambero, 14.1.1
Gamble, 174n40
Gesenius, 3.8.1
Gnosticism, int 8
Gregory Nazianzen, int 3
Gregory of Nyssa, int 13

Hadrian, 1.11.3
Hall, 175n66
Halperin, 174n45
Hanson, int 6
Harnack, 173n35
Heracleon, int 7
Heretics (heresy), 1.1.2; 1.3.5; 1.4.2–3; 1.11.2; 1.12.2–3; 2.2.3; 2.2.4; 2.4.1; 2.5.1–4; 3.4.2; 3.5.2; 6.7.2; 6.11.2; 7.3.1–3; 7.4.2; 7.5.1; 7.7.1; 8.1.2; 8.2.2–4; 9.1.2; 9.1.5; 10.2.2; 10.3.2; 13.2.1; 13.4.2
Hermas, *Sim* 8.2.1–3: 1.5.2; 9.92: 13.3.3
Hippolytus, int 8

Inspiration, 6.1.1
Instrumentum, 1.9.1
Irenaeus, int 8, int 9; *Adv Haer* 3.18.5: 3.4.2; 4.7.3: 13.2.4; 8.1.4–18: 13.2.4; Dem 35: 13.2.4

Jerome, int 1–21 passim; pref 1; *Adv Jov* 1.25: 4.5.1; *Com in Dn* 1.3: 4.5.1; Ep 18: pref 1; *In Ep ad Gal*, prol: pref 2; *In Ezek* 1.3: 1.4.4; 1.4: 1.12.1; 5.16.52: 10.1.1; *In Is*, prol: pref 2; 2.3.9: 10.1.1
Johnston, 174n41
Justice (righteousness), 1.2.4; 1.3.8; 1.5.1; 2.4.1; 3.8.3; 4.7.1; 4.8.1; 6.10.1; 7.3.2; 8.1.2; 8.3.3; 9.1.6; 9.2.4–5; 9.3.3; 9.5.5–6; 10.1.1; 14.3.3
Justification (justify), int 15–17; 2.3.1; 2.3.2; 9.2–5; 9.3.1–4; 10.1.2; 10.1.6; 10.2.1–2; 10.3.3; 10.4.2
Justin, int 8; *Dial* 19.4: 4.8.3; 135.3: 2.2.1; 139.2: 4.4.3
Justinian, 171n1
Juvenal, 5.5.3

Kautzsch, 3.8.1
Kries, 1.16.1

Layton, 176n3
Leclercq, 171n6
Ledegang, 1.3.7; 2.5.1; 3.8.1; 3.8.2; 4.1.2; 4.4.3; 5.5.1; 5.5.3; 6.6.1; 9.1.2; 13.2.4; 13.3.2; 13.4.2
Leonides, int 1, int 19; 4.8.1
Levering, 173n35
Lienhard, int 7
Logos, int 2
Longenecker, int 4
Lubac, de, int 2, int 4, int 6, int 14; 1.16.1; 6.6.3; 9.1.2

Luther, int 10, int 15
Lycurgus, 5.3.1

Mappa, 5.5.3
Marcion (Marcionites), int 7–10; 1.1.2; 1.4.2; 1.7.2; 1.9.1; 1.12.3; 2.5.3; 7.3.1; 7.4.2; 8.2.3
Margerie, 171n1
Martyrdom (martyr), int 1, int 18–20; 3.4.2; 4.7.2; 4.8.1
Mary, perpetual virginity of, 14.1.1
Mauretania, 4.1.6
McGuckin, int 4
Melanchthon, int 15
Methodius of Olympus, int 6
Minucius Felix, *Octavius*, 35.3: 1.3.3
Montanism, int 18; 6.1.1
Moors, 4.1.6
Murphy, 173n22

Nardoni, 6.1.1
Nautin, int 2
Nichols, 173n35
Normandy, 4.1.6

O'Leary, int 15

Packer, 174n41
Patterson, 173n29
Pelagianism, int 20
Philo, int 7; 6.1.1; *De Abrahamo* 10: 4.8.3; *De somn* 2.250: 1.3.6; *De spec leg* 1.289: 6.6.1; *De vita Mos* 2.97: 1.15.1; *Gig* 33: 3.8.1; *Quod Deus immut* 39: 2.3.4
Pico della Mirandola, 172n7
Pietas, 1.1.1
Pius XII, pope, 172n13
Plato, int 13; 1.16.1; 6.1.1; 10.1.1
Pliny the Elder, 11.2.2
Plutarch, 6.6.1
Pride (arrogance), 7.1.2; 9.2.1–3; 9.4.1–3; 9.5.4–6; 10.1.2; 10.4.1
Purification, int 11–13

Quasten, 3.3.1

Reformers, German, int 17
Rome, 1.11.3
Rufinus of Aquileia, int 1, int 3, 176n2, 176n8, 177n10

Scarborough, 174n47
Scheck, 171n3, 175n62
Scherer, int 2
Schism, int 17–18; 2.5.1; 9.1.2; 9.1.4; 10.1.4
Schleiermacher, 173n35
Seneca, 10.1.1
Severus, 4.8.1
Suetonius, 5.5.3
Suffering, of God, int 13–15
Sweeney, 171n2

Tatian, 4.2.1
Tertullian, int 8, int 18; *Adv Marc* 4.5: 8.2.3; *Apol* 48.94: 1.3.3; *Against the Valentinians* 36: 5.5.3; *Paen* 4.2: 10.1.1
Testament of the Twelve Patriarchs, 6.11.1
Torjesen, 173n25
Trent, Council of, int 17
Trigg, int 2
Tripartite soul, 1.16.1

Ugaritic, 4.1.1

Valentinus (Valentinian), int 7–10; 1.4.2; 2.2.3; 2.5.3; 3.4.2; 7.3.1; 7.4.2; 8.2.3
VanLandingham, 175n58, 175n59
Varro, 6.6.1
Verfaillie, int 17, 175n65
Vincentius, int 3
Vision of Peace, 1.3.6
Vogt, 10.1.4

Weinandy, int 14–15; 6.6.3

INDEX OF ORIGEN'S WORKS

The Translator's Introduction (int) is referenced by page number. Jerome's Preface (pref) is referenced by section number. Origen's Homilies are referenced by homily number, section, and paragraph (separated by ".").

Against Celsus (Cels)
1.31: 4.2.1
2.24: 1.12.3
3.51: 10.1.4
4.1: 1.12.3
4.6–29: 1.12.3
4.11.6: 1.1.2
4.13: 1.3.3
4.92–93: 11.3.3
5.15: 1.3.3
5.25.9: 13.1.6
5.30: 13.1.3
5.44: 1.15.1
6.23: 1.14.1
6.66.32–35: 13.2.1
7.22: 12.2.3
7.24: 12.2.3
8.31: 4.2.1
8.75: 5.4.1

Cat in Cant
5.2: 7.6.1

Cat in Ex
20.5–6: 1.2.4; 6.3.2

Cat in Ezek
8.9: 7.6.1
PG 13.680: 1.14.1
14.4: 3.8.1
14.13: 4.1.8
16.26: 7.8.1

Cat in Prov
3.19: 4.1.8

Cat in Ps
75(76): 1.3.6
100(101): 1.3.6
101(102).21: 6.3.2
118(119): 1.2.4
119(120): 1.3.6
121(122): 1.3.6
123(124).1: 2.2.1

Commentary on the Canticle (Song of Songs)
Prol 1.4–6: 6.8.5
1.4: 13.2.11
2: 1.15.1
2.1.28, 36: 1.3.6
3.5.5: 1.9.1
3.13.22: 13.2.4
3.14: 7.6.1
3.14.25: 13.4.2
4.3.8: 2.4.1

Commentary on John
1.25(24).163: 9.3.3
5.5: 9.1.2
6.55(37).287: 9.3.3
13.23: 1.3.3
20.10: 4.4.3
28.24(19).215: 1.12.3
32.17.215: 2.2.4

Commentary on John Fragments
80: 1.3.6

Commentary on Matthew
(on Matt 16.13—22.33)
10.12–13: 1.11.3
13.10: 13.2.6
13.24: 10.1.4
14.21: 13.3.3
14.22: 2.2.4; 10.1.4
15.5: 4.5.1
15.11: 1.12.3
15.23: 1.3.2
16.9: 1.3.7
16.17: 4.5.2
16.21: 1.2.4
17.32: 2.2.1

Commentary Series on Matthew
(on Matt 22.24—27.66)
[traditionally called *Homilies*]
9ff.: 7.3.3
29: 7.6.1
33: 7.3.1
38: 2.2.3; 3.4.2
51: 1.11.5
53: 13.3.3
59: 7.6.1
60: 7.6.1
79: 7.6.1
111: 1.12.4

Commentary on Matthew Fragments
73: 1.2.4
279: 7.6.1
375–76: 9.1.2

Commentary on Romans
Praef Ruf: 1.7.2
1.16: 1.1.2
1.18: 1.1.2
2.1: 7.6.1
2.4.4: 1.3.5
2.4.8: 1.3.5
2.6.2: 3.7.2
2.7.3: 1.3.5
2.8.4: 1.3.5
2.13.29–30: 3.4.2
3.2: 10.2.2
3.5: 1.3.6
3.8.5: 1.15.1
4.2: 6.3.1
4.6: 13.2.4
5.1: 11.3.3
5.1.40: 3.7.2
5.2.13: 1.3.5
5.8: 6.5.1
6.8.11: 4.1.3
6.9:12: 1.2.1
6.13: 7.6.1
7.14: 2.2.1
7.18.5: 1.3.5
8.11: 2.2.1
10.3: 11.3.3
10.14: 1.3.6
10.21: 1.1.1; 1.2.1
10.31: 13.3.3
10.35: 3.6.1
10.37: 3.6.1
10.43.2: 1.7.2

Dialogue with Heraclides
15.17–23: 7.1.2

Exhortation to Martyrdom
(Ad Mart)
49: 4.1.8

Homilies on the Canticle (Song of Songs)
2.7: 7.6.1

Homilies on Exodus
1.2: 2.2.1
1.4: 4.1.6
2.4: 3.6.1
3.3: 10.1.2
4.6: 11.3.3
5.1: pref 1
5.5: 7.8.1
6.3: 1.3.3
8.4: 7.6.1
8.5: 8.1.3
8.6: 13.2.10
10.3: 3.3.3
11.4: 4.8.2
11.6: 9.2.3
13.2: 6.10.1
13.3: 6.10.1

Homilies on Genesis
1.5: 9.3.3
1.17: 7.6.1
5.1: 10.3.1
7.8–9: 9.3.3
7.20–21: 9.3.3
8.7: 6.10.1
10.2: 8.3.3
13.3: 7.6.1
16.5: 5.4.1
16.6: 2.2.1

Homilies on Jeremiah
1.3: 1.3.6; 11.5.1; 11.5.2
1.16: 1.12.1
1.18: 1.12.1
2.1.10: 1.3.6
4.5: 7.1.1
[50.]2.5: 1.2.4
9.2: 1.3.6
9.4: 6.3.2
11.3: 5.4.1
11.5: 1.3.2
12.3: 10.4.1
13.2: 1.3.6
16.5–6: 1.3.3
19.14: 1.3.6; 11.5.2
19.41: 11.5.1
20.3: 1.3.3
Lat 1(3).4–5: 1.10.2
Lat 2.5–6: 12.2.3

Homilies on Jeremiah Fragments
26: 12.2.3
31: 1.11.5
48: 1.3.6
62: 1.12.3

Homilies on Joshua
1.6: 13.2.1
2.4: 11.5.2
6.4: 1.3.7
7.6: 10.1.4
13.3–4: 1.12.3
14.2: 13.4.1
15.3: 1.3.6; 12.2.3
15.5–6: 6.11.1
21.2: 1.3.6
23.3: 4.2.1
26.3: 2.2.1

Homilies on Judges
2.5: 7.6.1
3.1: 13.1.7
7.1: 4.1.2
8.5: 1.11.4; 1.11.5

Homilies on Leviticus
2.4: 6.7.1
2.9: 8.3.3
3.5: 1.3.2
3.8: 2.2.4
4.3: 2.2.2
4.6: 6.10.1

5.2: 13.2.4
5.3: 4.1.8
5.6: 7.4.2
6.4: 5.4.1
6.6: 6.10.1
7.4: 11.3.3
7.5: 1.11.3
11.2: 6.7.1
13.3–4: 7.4.2
13.4: 1.9.1
13.5: 7.4.1
14.4: 12.3.3
15.2: 6.7.1; 10.1.4
16.2: 1.12.4
16.5–6: 4.1.8
16.7: 1.2.4

Homilies on Luke
12: 13.1.3
16.4: 1.12.3
16.6: 2.2.4
17.4: 1.4.2
22: 1.1.2
34.3: 1.3.7
35.6: 13.1.6

Homilies on Luke Fragments
67: 6.3.2
71: 1.3.7
72: 7.6.1
78: 9.1.2

Homilies on Numbers
1.3: 1.14.1
2.1: 5.4.1
5.3: 1.15.1
8.1: 10.4.1; 13.3.3
9.1: 1.3.8; 5.4.1
10.3: 1.15.1
11.4: 11.5.2; 13.2.1
11.4–5: 13.1.6
11.7: 3.3.3
12.2: 12.1.2
12.3: 13.2.11
12.4: 9.2.2
14.1: 3.6.1
14.2: 1.3.8
15.1: 13.1.1
16.9: 2.2.1
17.3: 2.3.4
17.4: 2.2.1
19.3: 7.8.2
19.4: 3.6.1
20.2: 8.3.3
20.4: 1.11.3
21.2: 7.1.2
22.1: 3.3.3
22.4: 5.4.1
23.2: 1.5.1
23.5: 9.3.3
23.8: 1.12.3; 4.1.8
24.2: 3.8.1
27.9: 3.6.1
28.2: 2.2.1

Homilies on Psalms 36–38
36(37) 1.3: 1.12.3
38 1.9: 1.2.2

Homily on 1 Sm
1.4: 9.1.2
1.6: 6.10.1
5.1: 13.1.1
5.9: 13.2.11

On First Principles (Princ = Peri Archon)
Praef 1.3: pref 1; 2: 7.2.1
1.1–24: 1.3.8
1.3.5: 13.3.3
1.5.2: 13.1.6
1.5.4: 13.1.3
1.5.4–5: 13.2.1
2.1.5: 13.3.3

2.3.7: 13.2.11
2.4.4: 1.1.2
2.10.4: 1.3.3; 3.7.2
2.11.6: 13.2.11
3.2.4: 13.3.3
3.3.2: 1.10.2
4.2.1: 5.1.3
4.2.4: int 4

On Prayer (De Orat)
21.2: 9.1.2
22.4: 6.3.2
23.4: 7.6.1
27.11: 14.3.2
27.12: 11.3.3
28.3: 5.4.1
29.13: 1.3.8

Philocalia
8.2–3: 9.1.2
21–27: 1.10.2
26.7.35: 13.2.1
27: 1.3.8

Selections on Ezekiel
1.1: 1.4.1; 1.5.1; 1.9.1
1.3: 1.10.2
1.4: 1.12.1
1.26: 1.3.2
13.2: 2.1.1; 2.2.2
13.3: 2.3.3
13.4: 2.4.1
13.5: 2.5.1
13.9: 2.5.4
16.10: 6.10.1
16.18: 7.4.1

Paulist Press is committed to preserving ancient forests and natural resources. We elected to print this title on 30% post consumer recycled paper, processed chlorine free. As a result, for this printing, we have saved:

4 Trees (40' tall and 6-8" diameter)
1 Million BTUs of Total Energy
358 Pounds of Greenhouse Gases
1,722 Gallons of Wastewater
105 Pounds of Solid Waste

Paulist Press made this paper choice because our printer, Thomson-Shore, Inc., is a member of Green Press Initiative, a nonprofit program dedicated to supporting authors, publishers, and suppliers in their efforts to reduce their use of fiber obtained from endangered forests.

For more information, visit www.greenpressinitiative.org

Environmental impact estimates were made using the Environmental Defense Paper Calculator. For more information visit: www.papercalculator.org.